PRO TOOLS® 10

ADVANCED MUSIC PRODUCTION TECHNIQUES

Robert J. Campbell

Course Technology PTR
A part of Cengage Learning

COURSE TECHNOLOGY
CENGAGE Learning®

Australia, Brazil, Japan, Korea, Mexico, Singapore, Spain, United Kingdom, United States

**Pro Tools® 10 Advanced Music
Production Techniques**
Robert J. Campbell

**Publisher and General Manager,
Course Technology PTR:**
Stacy L. Hiquet

Associate Director of Marketing:
Sarah Panella

Manager of Editorial Services:
Heather Talbot

Senior Marketing Manager:
Mark Hughes

Acquisitions Editor:
Orren Merton

Development Editor:
Frank D. Cook

Project Editor:
Kezia Endsley

Technical Reviewers:
Justin Fraser, Frank D. Cook

Copy Editor:
Gene Redding

Interior Layout:
Shawn Morningstar

Cover Designer:
Mike Tanamachi

DVD-ROM Producer:
Brandon Penticuff

Indexer:
Valerie Haynes Perry

Proofreader:
Sue Boshers

For product information and technology assistance, contact us at
Cengage Learning Customer & Sales Support, 1-800-354-9706

For permission to use material from this text or product,
submit all requests online at **cengage.com/permissions**
Further permissions questions can be emailed to
permissionrequest@cengage.com

Pro Tools is a registered trademark of Avid Technology, Inc.
All other trademarks are the property of their respective owners.

All images © Cengage Learning unless otherwise noted.

Library of Congress Control Number: 2011942190

ISBN-13: 978-1-133-72800-9

ISBN-10: 1-133-72800-6

Course Technology, a part of Cengage Learning
20 Channel Center Street
Boston, MA 02210
USA

Cengage Learning is a leading provider of customized learning solutions with office
locations around the globe, including Singapore, the United Kingdom, Australia,
Mexico, Brazil, and Japan. Locate your local office at:
international.cengage.com/region

Cengage Learning products are represented in Canada by Nelson Education, Ltd.

For your lifelong learning solutions, visit **courseptr.com**.

Visit our corporate Web site at **cengage.com**.

**This book includes material that was developed in part by the Avid Technical
Publications department and the Avid Training department.**

Printed in the
United States of America
1 2 3 4 5 6 7 14 13 12

This book is dedicated to aspiring and professional recording engineers, mixers, audio enthusiasts, and anyone else who loves working with music and Pro Tools.

Acknowledgments

The author would like to acknowledge the following individuals from Avid/Digidesign (current and former), who have provided critical assistance, input, information, and material for this book and its many editions over the years—Simon Sherbourne, Tom Dambly, Eric Kuehnl, Tim Mynett, Andy Cook, Mark Altin, Andy Hagerman, Joe Kay, Jim Metzendorf, Bobby Lombardi, Jordan Glasgow, Curt Raymond, Rich Holmes, Scott Church, Jon Connolly, Ozzie Sutherland, Christopher Woodland, Toby Dunn, Shane Ross, Doug Tissier, Pete Richert, Danny Caccavo, Stan Cotey, Gannon Kashiwa, Scott Wood, Tom Graham, Greg Robles, Mark Jeffery, Paul Foeckler, Rachelle McKenzie, Tim Carroll, Wendy Abowd, and Dave Lebolt.

Special Thanks

The exercise materials used in this book are provided courtesy of Oisin O'Malley and the band, Mrnorth (Mr. North). The exercise material comes from the album title song, "Everything." Many thanks to the band for providing the entire session used on the album for this book and course. For more information about Mrnorth, please visit http://www.myspace.com/mrnorthmusic.

Joel Krantz, for co-authoring portions of this book and the *310P Pro Tools 10 Advanced Post Production Techniques* book, as well as providing editorial comment and advice.

Frank Cook, for offering development editorial advice, templates, and always a voice of reason.

Justin Fraser, for offering extremely thorough and useful editorial comments, which really helped to make the book the best that it could be.

Matt Cohen, for helping to prepare chapters and exercise material for this book.

John McGleenan and the rest of the engineering staff at One Union Recording Studios for all their support.

Extra-Special Thanks

To my wife Tina and my sons Ethan, Miles, and Chase for understanding the late nights, crazy schedule, and the absence of any free time while I'll completed this book.

Kudos and extra-special thanks to all Avid Learning Partners and certified instructors, who have tirelessly worked with us to help shape this program and who have generously provided their valuable feedback for our courseware.

About the Author

The courseware for this book was developed by **Robert Campbell**, with contributions from numerous Avid staff and independent contractors. The book is published through an ongoing partnership between Cengage Learning and Avid Technology, Inc.

Rob has a diverse background in the recording industry. Starting as a professional woodwind player in the San Francisco Bay area, Rob completed his B.A. in Jazz Studies as well as an M.A. in Music Performance at San José State University. While completing his master's degree, he worked for a variety of Silicon Valley companies during the boom of the early 1990s, including Hewlett-Packard, Apple Computer, and General Magic. After completing his degrees, Rob wanted to work for a company that combined his computer experience with his musical expertise. Eventually his search led to Digidesign. Rob was hired as a tech support rep in 1993, soon after Pro Tools 2.0 was released to the public.

For 10 years Rob worked his way up in Digidesign, serving in various technical roles. His last role was as Hardware Product Manager of all workstation and interface products. A partial list of products he worked on include Pro Tools|HD (including HD Cards, 192 IO, 96 IO, PRE, SYNC IO), Digi002, the original Mbox, Pro Tools|MIX, 888/24, Digi001, and the AudioMedia III card.

After leaving Digidesign in 2003, Rob founded three different Pro Tools training facilities—Mindlab Learning Center, AudioMe, and Encompass Audio. He served as Chief Instructor at each of the facilities while also teaching Pro Tools courses at San Francisco State University, College of Extended Learning. Rob has continued to consult and author many official Avid courseware titles, including Pro Tools, ICON, and VENUE courses.

Rob currently serves as Director of Operations at One Union Recording Studios in San Francisco, California, as well as Director of Operations at his family's winery, Story Winery in Plymouth, California. Rob continues to consult for Avid as an author, lecturer, and as an Avid Master Instructor for Pro Tools, ICON, and VENUE products. Outside of his daily job duties, Rob enjoys mixing live sound on Avid's VENUE products and spending time with his growing family.

Contents

Lesson 1
Pro Tools HD Hardware Configuration   1

Exercise 1
Pro Tools HD Hardware Configuration   39

Lesson 2
Troubleshooting a Pro Tools System   43

Exercise 2
Troubleshooting a Pro Tools System   77

Lesson 3
Tactile Control of Pro Tools   81

Exercise 3
Tactile Control   103

Lesson 4
Importing and Recording Audio   111

Exercise 4
Importing/Exporting and Session Interchange   145

Lesson 5
Advanced Editing   155

Exercise 5
Advanced Beat Detective   183

Lesson 6
Synchronization   199

Exercise 6
Synchronization   227

Lesson 7
Pro Tools HD/HDX Mixing Concepts   239

Exercise 7
Mixer Experiments   275

Lesson 8
Advanced Mixing Techniques   297

Exercise 8
Advanced Mixing and Routing   349

Lesson 9
Music Delivery
365

Exercise 9
Exporting Multitrack Sessions
381

Appendix A
Pro Tools HD-Series Audio Interface Calibration
389

Appendix B
Exercise Answer Keys   393

Introduction

Welcome to *Pro Tools 10 Advanced Music Production Techniques* and the Avid Learning Series. Whether you are interested in self-study or would like to pursue formal certification through an Avid Learning Partner, this book in the Avid Learning Series provides key information toward attaining the highest level of Avid Pro Tools certification: Expert Certification for Music Production. This book builds on the information provided in the *210M Pro Tools Music Production Techniques* book, providing advanced configuration, troubleshooting, recording, editing, signal routing, and mixing tips, techniques, and workflows for working in professional music production. To complete this course, readers can enroll with an Avid Learning Partner to take the Avid Pro Tools Expert Certification exam for music production (after completing all lower-level certification exams).

The material in this book covers advanced music production techniques and workflow principles you need to complete aspects of an advanced Pro Tools music project, from initial setup and configuration of a Pro Tools HD system, through editing, ending with advanced mixing. After completing and mastering the material in this final book in the Avid Learning Series, you will have essential knowledge required for a career in professional music production using Pro Tools.

Using This Book

This book has been designed to teach you advanced audio post-production workflows and techniques using the Pro Tools HD 10 software. It is divided into the following nine lessons (with accompanying hands-on exercises):

- Lesson 1: Pro Tools HD Hardware Configuration
- Lesson 2: Troubleshooting a Pro Tools System
- Lesson 3: Tactile Control of Pro Tools
- Lesson 4: Importing and Recording Audio
- Lesson 5: Advanced Editing
- Lesson 6: Synchronization
- Lesson 7: Pro Tools HD/HDX Mixing Concepts
- Lesson 8: Advanced Mixing Techniques
- Lesson 9: Music Delivery

There are also two appendixes, one covering audio interface calibration and one that contains the answers to many of the exercises, to complement your knowledge.

Using the DVD

The DVD-ROM included with this book contains media files for the exercises that appear at the end of each lesson.

If you purchased an ebook version of this book, you can download the contents from www.courseptr.com/downloads. Please note that you will be redirected to the Cengage Learning site.

Exercise Media

The *Exercise Media* folder on the DVD provides all the required audio and related media files for the nine exercises in this book. The exercise session files are all saved as Pro Tools template files (.PTXT), so when opening each exercise file, you will be prompted to save the session to an appropriate storage location. The *Completed Exercises* folder provides session files of each completed exercise for reference.

Tip: For best playback results, you should copy all the exercise media files to a
      local hard drive prior to using them.

Prerequisites

This book has been written for use by individual self-learners or students enrolled in the PT310M course at an Avid Learning Partner (ALP). The PT310M course is the fifth course in a series designed to prepare candidates for Pro Tools Expert Certification in Music Production. As such, this book assumes the reader has a thorough understanding of all the concepts covered in the following lower-level courses and books:

- Pro Tools 101: An Introduction to Pro Tools
- Pro Tools 110: Pro Tools Production I
- Pro Tools 201: Pro Tools Production II
- Pro Tools 210M: Pro Tools Music Production Techniques

Tip: Readers who have not completed the lower-level courses or obtained
      equivalent professional experience should seek out an Avid Learning Partner
      and complete the necessary study to ensure their understanding of the
      background material required for this book.

System Requirements

The exercises included in this book require access to a system configuration suitable to run Pro Tools HD 10.*x* software using DSP-accelerated PCIe hardware with an Avid SYNC Peripheral, Avid PRE (or other PRE-compatible microphone preamp), MIDI or USB keyboard, and a single-port (or multi-port) MIDI interface. A multi-track tape machine with (RS-422) 9-pin machine control is also discussed (but not required). To verify the most recent system requirements, visit www.avid.com/US/products/Pro-Tools-Software/support.

Becoming Avid Certified

Avid certification is a tangible, industry-recognized credential that can help you advance your career and provide measurable benefits to your employer. When you're Avid certified, you not only help to accelerate and validate your professional development, but you can also improve your productivity and project success.

Avid offers programs supporting certification in dedicated focus areas, including Media Composer, Sibelius, Pro Tools, Worksurface Operation, and Live Sound.

To become certified in Pro Tools, you must enroll in a program at an Avid Learning Partner, where you can complete additional Pro Tools coursework if needed and take your certification exam. For information about how to locate an Avid Learning Partner, please visit: www.avid.com/training.

Pro Tools Certification

Avid offers three levels of Pro Tools certification:

- Pro Tools User
- Pro Tools Operator
- Pro Tools Expert

The 100-, 200-, and 300-level Pro Tools courses are designed to prepare candidates for each of these certification levels, respectively.

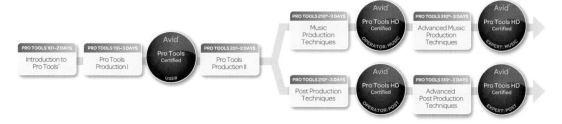

User Certification

User certification prepares individuals to operate a Pro Tools system in an independent production environment.

Courses/books associated with User certification include:

- Pro Tools 101, An Introduction to Pro Tools 10
- Pro Tools 110, Pro Tools Production I

These core courses can be complemented with Pro Tools 130, Pro Tools 10 for Game Audio.

Operator Certification

Operator certification prepares engineers and editors to competently operate a Pro Tools system in a professional environment. Candidates can specialize in music production, post-production, or both.

Courses/books associated with Operator certification include:

- Pro Tools 201, Pro Tools Production II
- Pro Tools 210M, Music Production Techniques
- Pro Tools 210P, Post Production Techniques

Control surface certification options and a live sound certification option are also available at the Operator level.

Expert Certification

The Expert curriculum offers professionals the highest level of proficiency with individual or networked Pro Tools systems operating in a professional, fast-paced environment. Candidates can specialize in music production, post-production, and/or ICON worksurface techniques.

Courses associated with Expert certification include:

- Pro Tools 310M, Advanced Music Production Techniques
- Pro Tools 310P, Advanced Post Production Techniques
- Pro Tools 310I, Advanced ICON Techniques

Pro Tools HD Hardware Configuration

This lesson explains the configuration, features, components, and benefits of Avid's hardware-based DSP accelerated Pro Tools systems—Pro Tools|HDX and Pro Tools|HD. These systems start with the same Pro Tools software covered in the lower-level Pro Tools courses, but add purpose-built PCIe expansion cards and audio interfaces (HD I/O, MADI I/O, and HD OMNI) to meet the needs of professional engineers and producers. By adding dedicated processing power and predictable signal routing, Pro Tools|HDX and Pro Tools|HD provide a reliable and scalable system for any professional audio production environment.

Media Used: None

Duration: 90 minutes

GOALS

- Set up and identify the components and connections in a Pro Tools HD hardware system

- Verify system compatibility

- Configure Avid hardware peripherals

- Optimize and configure the settings for a Pro Tools system

- Understand the need and uses for non-administrator (standard) accounts

- Understand Pro Tools session file interchange

Many options and settings affect the reliability of your hardware-based Pro Tools environment. A properly installed and maintained Pro Tools system will provide many hours of trouble-free operation. This lesson discusses the proper way to install and configure a hardware-based Pro Tools system, helping you to avoid costly downtime and allowing your system to operate at peak efficiency.

Setting Up a Pro Tools HD System

When using a Pro Tools HD system, a variety of hardware configurations and options can be used. This section discusses the supported Pro Tools HD hardware options that are available.

Pro Tools HD/HDX System Basics

As you've learned in earlier courses, Avid offers three types of Pro Tools systems: Pro Tools software systems for personal music and desktop post-production, Pro Tools|HD Native systems for medium budget production and post-production facilities, and Pro Tools|HDX and Pro Tools|HD systems for the ultimate in professional audio production. Pro Tools|HDX and Pro Tools|HD hardware systems are far more powerful than typical host-based systems; however, the systems are also more complex and can include a variety of interconnected components and interfaces.

Pro Tools HD Terminology

Throughout this course book, the term Pro Tools is used to refer to the standard Pro Tools software running on any supported hardware configuration. The term Pro Tools HD refers to Pro Tools HD software running on a supported system. When referring to previous generation Pro Tools HD PCIe hardware (such as HD Core and HD Accel PCIe cards), the phrase Pro Tools|HD hardware is used. When referring to the newest generation of (non-Native) Pro Tools HD PCIe hardware, the phrase Pro Tools|HDX *hardware* is used. Finally, when referring collectively to all Pro Tools HD PCIe hardware (Pro Tools|HD, Pro Tools|HDX, and Pro Tools|HD Native), the phrase *Pro Tools HD PCIe hardware* will be used.

Pro Tools 10 Systems Comparison

Pro Tools software (excluding Pro Tools HD) is sold separately from the hardware, allowing you to run it on a wide range of digital audio hardware platforms including Avid, M-Audio, Core Audio, ASIO, Pro Tools|HD Native, Pro Tools|HD, and Pro Tools|HDX.

Note: Only Pro Tools|HDX, Pro Tools|HD, and Pro Tools|HD Native hardware support
Pro Tools HD software.

Table 1.1 compares the features of the different Pro Tools platforms, allowing you to judge which platform will work best for a given project.

Components of Pro Tools HD PCIe Hardware Systems

In order to achieve greater power and flexibility, Pro Tools|HDX and Pro Tools|HD PCIe hardware require various system and core components. Optional components are available to expand the capabilities of the system as needed.

Basic System Components

Although the various configurations of Pro Tools|HDX and Pro Tools|HD systems have different input and output capacities, track counts, and plug-in and mixer processing, all systems must include the following basic system components: the computer, the Pro Tools software, and one or more storage volumes.

- **Computer**: All Pro Tools systems require a qualified Mac or Windows computer for basic operation. The computer houses the Pro Tools HD PCIe hardware (cards), runs the Pro Tools software, and carries out related host processing tasks, such as running Native (host-based) plug-ins and virtual instruments.

- **Pro Tools Software**: Pro Tools software handles the display, recording, playback, editing, and mixing of audio and MIDI data, controls audio interfaces and synchronization peripherals, manages digital signal processing and software plug-in controls, routes system inputs and outputs, and controls operation of the hard drives.

- **Storage Volumes:** All Pro Tools systems require one or more Avid-compatible storage volumes, in addition to the storage device used to boot your system. (The actual number of volumes required depends on the track count of the system as well as the Disk Cache setting.) Although the Pro Tools software will be installed on the boot or system drive, recording to and playing back from this drive is not recommended. Additional networked or local storage volumes should be connected and dedicated to the recording and playback of audio, MIDI, and Pro Tools session data.

Pro Tools HD PCIe Hardware Components

The Pro Tools HD software is compatible with a number of different Pro Tools HD PCIe cards, which are discussed next.

Table 1.1   Pro Tools 10 Features Comparison Chart

Capabilities	Pro Tools Software	Pro Tools Software with Complete Production Toolkit	Pro Tools HD Software with HD|Native Hardware	Pro Tools HD Software with Pro Tools|HD Hardware	Pro Tools HD Software with Pro Tools|HDX Hardware
Maximum number of voices (at 44.1/48kHz)	96 mono or stereo	256	256	192	256/HDX card (768 maximum)
Total number of voiceable tracks (at 44.1/48kHz)	128	768	768	768	768
Maximum number of Auxiliary Input tracks	128	512	512	512	512
Maximum number of Master Fader tracks	64	64	64	64	64
Total I/O channels	Up to 32	Up to 32	Up to 64	Up to 160	Up to 192
Maximum sample rates	Up to 192kHz	Up to 192kHz	Up to 192kHz	Up to 192kHz	Up to 192kHz
Maximum Automatic Delay Compensation (at 44.1/48kHz)	16,383 samples	16,383 samples	16,383 samples	4095 samples	16,383 samples
Maximum internal mix buses	256	256	256	256	256

■ **Pro Tools|HD Native PCIe Card**: The Pro Tools|HD Native Core card, shown in Figure 1.1, is the main card of a Pro Tools|HD Native hardware system. The Pro Tools|HD Native Core card provides up to 256 tracks of recording or playback, with a maximum of 768 total tracks in a session. The Pro Tools|HD Native Core card also provides 64 channels of I/O to the system, supporting a total of four HD-series audio interfaces. Unlike Pro Tools|HD DSP-based hardware systems, Pro Tools|HD Native hardware systems are not expandable, supporting only a single Pro Tools|HD Native Core card in the system. Also, because the Pro Tools|HD Native card has no built-in DSP processing for plug-ins, it relies entirely on the host for plug-in processing power.

Figure 1.1
Pro Tools|HD Native Core card.

For more information about Pro Tools|HD Native hardware systems, consult the Pro Tools 200-level course books or visit www.avid.com/
On the Web **protools.**

■ **Pro Tools|HDX PCIe Card**: The HDX PCIe card, shown in Figure 1.2, is the newest generation of DSP accelerated Pro Tools hardware, and is the main card of an HDX-based system. You must have at least one HDX PCIe card installed in an Avid-qualified computer or expansion chassis, although you can add more HDX PCIe cards for expanded track counts, expanded I/O, and increased DSP processing power (up to a maximum of three). Each HDX PCIe card installed in the system provides up to 256 simultaneous record/play tracks (at 44.1/48kHz), with up to 768 tracks maximum in a three-card system. The HDX card supports up to 32-bit, 192kHz Pro Tools sessions. In addition, each HDX card provides two DigiLink Mini ports for connecting up to four HD audio interfaces, providing up to 64 channels of I/O per card, with a three-card system supporting a maximum of 192 channels of I/O. Each HDX card includes 18 DSP chips that have double the processing power of previous generation Accel DSP chips, so adding multiple HDX cards to a single system greatly expands the total available DSP processing power of the system. The DSP chips on a Pro Tools|HDX card run new DSP-based AAX plug-ins, which are 32-bit floating-point equivalents of Native plug-ins.

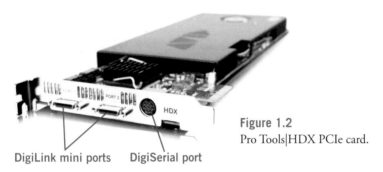

DigiLink mini ports   DigiSerial port

Figure 1.2
Pro Tools|HDX PCIe card.

Caution: You cannot combine Pro Tools|HDX PCIe cards with Pro Tools|HD Core/Accel PCIe cards in the same system. The newer generation HDX PCIe cards can only be combined with other cards of the same type.

- **Pro Tools|HD Core Card**: The previous generation HD Core card is the base card of a Pro Tools|HD DSP accelerated system. The Pro Tools|HD Core card, shown in Figure 1.3, provides up to 96 simultaneous tracks of audio recording or playback (at 44.1/48kHz). The HD Core card also provides 32 channels of I/O to the system, supporting up to two HD-series audio interfaces.

Figure 1.3
Pro Tools|HD PCIe Core card.

Note: A single Pro Tools|HD Core card can be installed in a system with up to six additional HD Accel cards. Pro Tools|HDX PCIe cards are not compatible with any other Pro Tools|HD PCIe cards.

■ **Pro Tools|HD Accel Card:** Previous generation Pro Tools|HD hardware systems with HD Core cards installed can use one or more HD Accel cards to expand the capacity and power of the system. Like HDX PCIe cards, these cards can expand the number of simultaneous record/play tracks (up to 192 tracks maximum at 44.1/48kHz), allow additional I/O (up to 160 channels), and expand the available DSP processing power. Up to six HD Accel cards can be installed in a single Pro Tools|HD hardware system (in addition to the HD Core card), for a total of seven cards in a supported Expansion Chassis. HD Accel cards provide support for DSP-based plug-ins and have more powerful DSP chips than the older generation HD Process cards, although they are not as powerful as the newer generation HDX PCIe cards.

Figure 1.4
HD Accel PCIe card.

Caution: Pro Tools|HD hardware supports only TDM DSP plug-ins, and does not support AAX DSP plug-ins. Likewise, Pro Tools|HDX hardware supports only AAX DSP plug-ins, and does not support TDM DSP plug-ins.

Pro Tools HD Audio Interfaces

As mentioned in the previous section, a Pro Tools HD system's I/O can be expanded with additional HD-series audio interfaces.

■ **HD Audio Interfaces**: All Pro Tools HD hardware systems require at least one rack-mountable HD-series audio interface that handles analog-to-digital (or digital-to-digital) and digital-to-analog conversion of input and output signals. The audio interface allows you to connect Pro Tools to the rest of your studio. The HD-series audio interfaces currently available include the HD I/O (shown in Figure 1.5), HD MADI, and HD OMNI. The HD I/O interface comes in three configurations:

- Eight analog in × eight analog out × eight digital in/out

- 16 analog in × 16 analog out

- 16 digital in × 16 digital out

Figure 1.5
Pro Tools HD I/O interface.

Pro Tools|HD Hardware Future Support

Previous generation HD-series interfaces such as the 192 I/O and 96 I/O continue to be supported in Pro Tools 10 and are still commonly used. In future software releases beyond Pro Tools 10, previous generation Pro Tools|HD hardware will no longer be officially tested or supported by Avid.

Multiple audio interfaces can be added to all Pro Tools HD systems to increase the number of I/O channels available. For example, with a three card HDX system, you can have 12 HD I/Os connected for 192 channels of input/output, or three MADI I/Os for 192 channels of MADI. Pro Tools|HD systems continue to support a maximum of 160 channels of I/O.

Note: On all Pro Tools HD hardware systems, only a single HD OMNI interface can be used, with or without additional HD-series audio interfaces.

For a review of the available Pro Tools HD-series audio interfaces, please consult the Pro Tools 201 course book or visit www.avid.com/

On the Web protocols.

Optional Pro Tools HD Hardware Components

In addition to the Pro Tools HD PCIe hardware components and HD-series audio interface options mentioned in the previous sections, you can also add the following optional hardware components to any HD hardware system.

- **PRE**: The Avid PRE is an eight-channel preamp designed specifically for the Pro Tools HD environment. PRE accepts microphone, line, and direct instrument (DI) level inputs on all eight channels and can be placed anywhere in the studio. Furthermore, the PRE can be remote controlled through MIDI using settings stored and recalled with sessions.

Configuration and usage of the Avid PRE is discussed later in this lesson and in Lesson 4, "Importing and Recording Audio."

■ **SYNC HD**: SYNC HD and the older SYNC I/O are common multi-purpose synchronization peripherals for synchronizing Pro Tools HD hardware systems to a variety of devices. SYNC HD supports both standard definition (SD) and high definition (HD) video reference, making it ideal for Pro Tools HD system installations in modern commercial music and post-production facilities. Although SYNC HD supports all major industry-standard clock sources and timecode formats, the previous generation of SYNC I/O supports only SD reference rates.

Benefits of Pro Tools DSP Accelerated Hardware Systems

Pro Tools HD systems using DSP Accelerated PCIe cards offer a significant performance advantage over both standard Pro Tools software systems and Pro Tools|HD Native systems, including expandability to incorporate up to 192 channels of I/O; optional expansion cards for real-time audio processing on dedicated DSP chips; and incredible low latency control—all of which give Pro Tools HD and HDX hardware the ability to handle the largest music production tasks.

Pro Tools|HDX hardware systems utilize Avid's dedicated DSP hardware and custom FPGA (Field Programmable Gate Array) technology to carry out real-time signal routing, mixing, and processing of multiple audio signals. The FPGA technology of Pro Tools|HDX hardware provides ultra low audio latency and greatly expands the audio throughput and signal routing capabilities of the system.

 Lesson 7, "Pro Tools HD/HDX Mixing Concepts," provides more detailed information about Pro Tools|HD and HDX hardware signal routing and the DSP-based processing power in the Pro Tools HD mixer.

The power of a Pro Tools HD system comes from a combination of Pro Tools HD software and the Pro Tools HD PCIe hardware components. As previously discussed, the capabilities of a Pro Tools|HDX hardware system can be increased by installing additional HDX PCIe cards. Because Pro Tools|HDX hardware systems can utilize the DSP-based processing power on the HDX cards in addition to the Native (host-based) processing power of the computer, they are the most powerful Pro Tools systems ever built.

System Compatibility Information

Ensuring rock solid reliability and stability with your Pro Tools system starts with making sure you are using Avid tested and approved hardware and software. The components of a Pro Tools HD system, such as the computer, hard drives, and a range of hardware and software options, are subject to compatibility requirements, which reflect configurations of Avid products and third-party products that have been tested and qualified by Avid.

For the latest compatibility information, visit the Avid website at www.avid.com or from within the Pro Tools 10 software, choose Help > Avid Knowledge Base. Support information can be found under the Support & Services link on the Avid website. The Avid support section is arranged by Avid product family (for example Pro Tools, Media Composer, Euphonix, and Pinnacle).

Tip: You can access additional help options from within the Pro Tools 10 software by choosing Help > Avid Audio Forums and Help > Customer Assist.

Pro Tools|HD/HDX Hardware Installation

Every Pro Tools Expert should be comfortable installing Pro Tools hardware and software. For Pro Tools operators early in their career, this level of technical skill will open the door to many opportunities. For experienced engineers and mixers, being able to maintain and troubleshoot a system is also essential to keep sessions running smoothly.

To install the hardware for a Pro Tools|HDX system:

1. Install the HDX PCIe cards into your computer before installing Pro Tools software. HDX PCIe cards require power beyond what the PCIe bus can deliver. A custom power cable (included) is used to connect HDX PCIe cards to the optional power connector on the motherboard in your Mac or to a hard drive power source in your PC. For systems with more than one HDX PCIe card, each card will require a connection to the power source utilizing the single power cable.

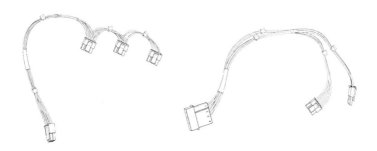

Figure 1.6
HDX PCIe card Mac power cable (left) and PC power cable (right).

2. If you are using multiple HDX cards, the cards must be interconnected using an **HDX TDM** cable. The cable can be installed only one way, so look for the **IN** and **OUT** ports on each card as well as the connector. The OUT cable connector must be connected to the OUT port of the card in the lowest slot number. This is considered the "first" card in the system.

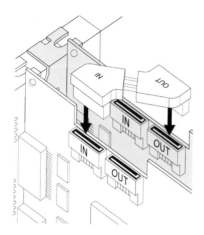

Figure 1.7
Connecting two HDX PCIe cards with an HDX TDM cable.

3. Once the cards are installed, connect the HD-series audio interface(s) using the DigiLink cable(s) included with each HD-series audio interface. Again, the first card in your system must be connected to the first interface in the chain. If you are using multiple audio interfaces, also connect the Loop Sync cables at this point. If you are using a SYNC HD, connect the Loop Sync cables through it as well and connect the SYNC HD to the first HDX card in your system using the DigiSerial cable supplied with the SYNC HD.

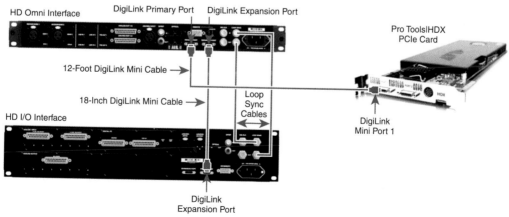

Figure 1.8
Connecting HD-series interfaces with DigiLink and Loop Sync cables.

Tip: Complete step-by-step details on how to install, connect, and configure the components of a Pro Tools HD PCIe hardware system (PCIe cards, software, and audio interfaces) can be found in the Pro Tools|HDX, HD, and HD Native Quick Start Guides.

Configuring Avid Peripherals

When using Pro Tools HD PCIe hardware, a number of optional Avid hardware peripherals can be connected to the system, providing additional features and functionality. These peripherals must be set up and configured properly before you attempt to use them with your system.

PRE

PRE (shown in Figures 1.9 and 1.10) is an eight-channel remote controllable microphone preamplifier designed by Avid. Although PRE is designed to be integrated into Pro Tools systems, it can also be utilized as a standalone mic preamp. PRE and other third-party PRE-compatible microphone preamps are ideally suited to working with Pro Tools, because they can be controlled from within the Pro Tools application and from an Avid worksurface. Additionally, any mic preamp settings are stored with the session and can be recalled with the session.

Tip: Although this section details the connection and configuration of an Avid PRE for use with Pro Tools, other third-party PRE-compatible microphone preamps would be configured in a similar way.

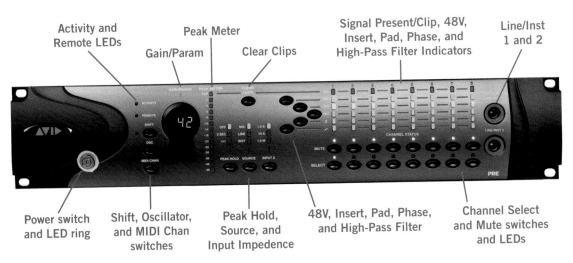

Figure 1.9
PRE front panel.

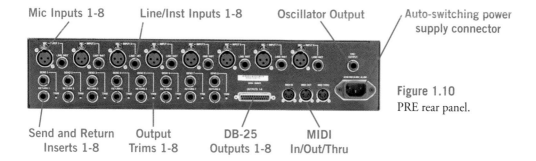

Mic Inputs 1-8   Line/Inst Inputs 1-8   Oscillator Output   Auto-switching power supply connector

Send and Return Inserts 1-8   Output Trims 1-8   DB-25 Outputs 1-8   MIDI In/Out/Thru

Figure 1.10
PRE rear panel.

Connecting to Pro Tools

There are four steps in setting up PRE to be controlled by Pro Tools:

1. Make audio and MIDI connections to PRE.

2. Configure the MIDI settings.

3. Declare **PRE** in the Peripherals dialog box.

4. Map PRE outputs to an audio interface's inputs within the I/O Setup dialog box.

Each step is discussed in more detail in the following sections.

Making Audio Connections

To use PRE as a preamp in a Pro Tools system, the PRE's DB25 audio output must be physically connected to analog inputs on an audio interface (such as an HD I/O) in your Pro Tools system or through a patchbay that is then connected to Pro Tools inputs (see Figure 1.11). The PRE does not have any A/D converters and is an analog-only device.

If the audio interface that the PRE is connected to has more than eight analog inputs (like an HD I/O with an extra analog input card), be sure to note which inputs are being connected to the PRE. Pro Tools uses the input channel association to understand which mic pre channel to control. This routing association between the PRE output and audio interface input is made through the mic-preamps page of the I/O Setup dialog box.

Using PRE with D-Command or D-Control

After connecting a PRE to an HD-series audio interface, the interface outputs are then connected to the main inputs on the XMON interface, allowing control room monitoring using the D Command/D Control.

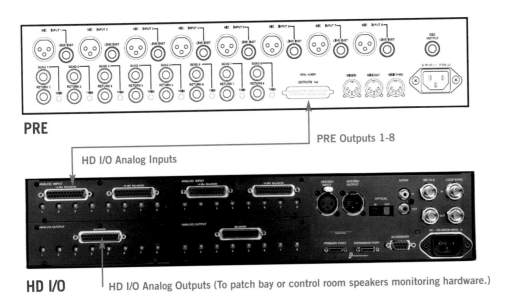

PRE

PRE Outputs 1-8

HD I/O Analog Inputs

HD I/O   HD I/O Analog Outputs (To patch bay or control room speakers monitoring hardware.)

Figure 1.11
Avid PRE outputs connected to an HD I/O interface's inputs.

Tip: PRE control using the Pro Tools software is covered later in this book.

Making MIDI Connections

Remote control commands are sent to PRE over a standard MIDI connection. To facilitate this communication, the Pro Tools computer requires a compatible MIDI interface. When connecting a single Avid PRE, the unit can be connected to any available MIDI In and Out ports on your MIDI Interface.

To connect a PRE to a MIDI interface:

1. Make sure that a MIDI interface is connected and configured.

Tip: Refer to the MIDI interface's reference guide for information on how to connect and configure the interface.

2. Connect a MIDI cable between the **MIDI Out** port on your PRE and a **MIDI In** port on your MIDI interface.

3. Connect a MIDI cable between the **MIDI In** port on your PRE and a **MIDI Out** port on your MIDI interface.

Up to nine PREs can be accessed by Pro Tools. When connecting multiple PREs, each PRE can be connected to a separate MIDI In/Out port on a multi-port MIDI interface. In this configuration, when using separate dedicated MIDI ports for each PRE, MIDI channel number assignments can be the same or different. As an alternative, when only a single MIDI In/Out port is available, multiple PREs can be daisy-chained through a single shared MIDI In/Out port, in which case, each PRE must be assigned a unique MIDI channel number.

To daisy-chain multiple PREs using a single shared MIDI port:

1. Connect a MIDI interface **MIDI OUT** port to the first PRE's **MIDI IN**.

2. Connect the first PRE's **MIDI OUT** to the second PRE's **MIDI IN**. Repeat for each additional PRE that needs to be connected to the system.

3. Connect the last PRE's **MIDI OUT** to a **MIDI IN** port on your MIDI interface.

Configuring MIDI

If you are using multiple PREs, set each unit to a unique MIDI channel number. Keep in mind that if multiple PRE units are set to the same MIDI channel daisy-chained through one single shared MIDI In/Out port, they will not be able to receive messages to change their controls and settings independently. In other words, changing a setting on one unit will change that setting on all units set to the same MIDI channel.

To set a global receive/transmit MIDI channel on PRE:

1. Power on PRE.

2. On the PRE front panel, press **MIDI CHAN**. The LED should be lit; if not, press and release again. The **GAIN/PARAM DISPLAY** will show the current MIDI channel (1–16).

3. Turn the **GAIN/PARAM** control to change the MIDI channel. Turning the **GAIN/PARAM** control will step through MIDI channel numbers. The channel will be set once you stop moving the control; you do not need to press an **ENTER** key to set the channel.

4. Press **MIDI CHAN** to exit MIDI Channel mode.

5. Repeat the previous steps for any additional PREs. Once completed, you must configure the PRE in AMS (Mac) or MSS (Windows).

Next you will launch and configure the MIDI Studio for your PRE.

To configure AMS (Mac) or MSS (Windows) from within Pro Tools:

1. Choose SETUP > MIDI > MIDI STUDIO. AMS or MSS will launch, as appropriate for your system (Mac or Windows, respectively).

2. Add a new device. For convenience, you can choose Digidesign for the Manufacturer and PRE for the Model when specifying the properties for the new device. On a Mac, this will insert a picture of the PRE in the device page. If you have multiple PREs (as shown in Figure 1.12), be sure to give each a unique name so you can distinguish between them later.

3. Create your studio setup.

   - **In AMS (Mac):** Draw cable connections between the device icons so that the AMS graphical display accurately represents your actual MIDI connections.

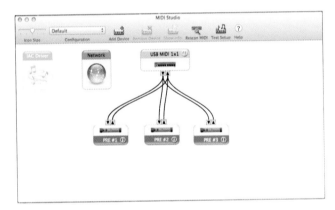

Figure 1.12
Multiple PREs in AMS using a single shared MIDI port.

or

   - **In MSS (Windows):** Select each PRE in turn and choose the port they are connected to (this will be the same for each PRE). Choose which Send and Receive channels the PRE is operating on (this will be different for each PRE). Figure 1.13 shows the MIDI Studio Setup window.

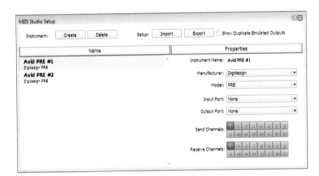

Figure 1.13
Configuring PRE in MIDI Studio Setup.

Declaring PRE for Pro Tools Software

After PRE is configured in AMS/MSS, it needs to be declared in the Pro Tools Peripherals dialog before it can be mapped in the I/O Setup dialog box.

To declare PRE as a peripheral in Pro Tools:

1. Choose SETUP > PERIPHERALS.

2. Click on the MIC PREAMPS tab. The Mic Preamps tab is shown in Figure 1.14.

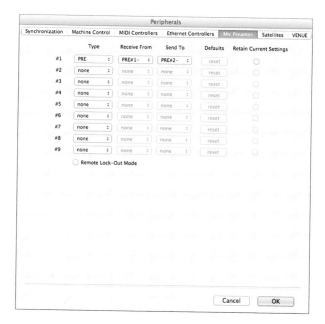

Figure 1.14
Peripherals dialog box:
Mic Preamps tab.

3. Choose PRE from the TYPE pop-up menu.

4. From the RECEIVE FROM pop-up menu, choose PRE's source port and a MIDI channel (derived from the AMS/MSS MIDI setup) to receive data.

5. From the SEND TO pop-up menu, choose a destination port (this will be the same device that you chose in the previous step), and a MIDI channel to transmit data.

6. Repeat Steps 3-5 for any additional PREs.

7. Click OK.

In addition to declaring PRE in the Peripherals dialog box, you can also set the following options:

■ **Reset**: Press RESET to return PRE parameters to their defaults. Resetting takes place immediately; you do not need to press **OK** to reset parameters.

■ **Retain Current Settings**: If this setting is enabled and you open a session, the PRE settings will not be changed. However, if you save the session, any PRE settings that were in the session will now be overwritten with the current settings. Also, if you create a new session with RETAIN CURRENT SETTINGS enabled, the new session will inherit the PRE settings.

■ **Remote Lock-Out Mode**: Select REMOTE LOCK-OUT mode to disable front panel controls from being used to control PRE. Lock-Out mode does not occur until you click **OK** to close the Peripherals dialog box.

Tip: PRE can be taken out of Remote Lock-Out mode by unchecking the Remote Lock-Out Mode box in the Pro Tools Peripherals dialog box or by powering PRE off and then back on.

All front panel settings are stored in the Pro Tools session, but a number of other settings are stored in the Pro Tools system's global preferences. It is important to note which settings these are, as they may change when the session is moved to a different Pro Tools system.

The following settings are stored in the global preferences:

■ Number of PREs declared

■ Lockout state

■ Retain Current Setting state

■ Online/Offline status

■ Output assignments

Mapping PRE Outputs to an Audio Interface in I/O Setup

PRE outputs must manually be mapped to the HD-series interface inputs before their audio and remote controls will be available within Pro Tools.

To map PRE outputs to the HD-series interface's inputs:

1. Choose SETUP > I/O SETUP.

2. Click the MIC PREAMPS tab (shown in Figure 1.15).

3. Click on the box directly under the interface inputs that are connected to the PRE.

4. Repeat for each of the PRE paths that are connected to the Pro Tools system.

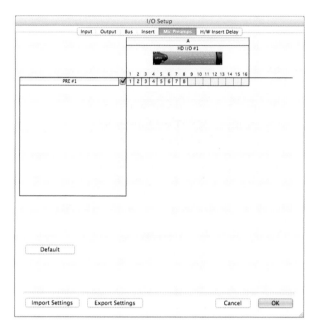

Figure 1.15
I/O Setup: Mic Preamps tab.

Mic preamp paths can be:

- Renamed, for easier identification after changing or renaming audio interfaces.

- Remapped to different input destinations.

- Deactivated (or reactivated) to manage unavailable or unused I/O resources.

Mic preamp paths cannot be:

- Deleted.

- Exported or imported with an I/O setup.

If you have multiple PRE units in the I/O setup, the order in which PRE paths appear follows the order in which they were assigned in the Mic Preamps tab of the Peripherals dialog box.

Using PRE in Standalone Mode

PRE can be used as a standalone mic/line/instrument preamplifier, either without Pro Tools or with Pro Tools when a MIDI connection is not available for remote control. At power up, PRE units in Standalone mode default to the settings they had when last powered down.

Connecting Audio Sources and Adjusting PRE Parameters

Most PRE parameters can be changed using the front panel switches, from the Pro Tools software, or using an approved Avid worksurface. In the following sections, all PRE channel parameters are controlled using the front panel switches.

 Controlling a PRE from the Pro Tools software is covered in Lesson 4.

To edit channel controls:

1. Press the **SELECT** switch for the channel you want to edit. You can select multiple channels for simultaneous editing by holding **SHIFT** while selecting channels.

2. Press a channel control switch to change its current setting. For example, if the 48V LED is off, pressing **48V** will enable phantom power for all the selected channels.

To connect a microphone as an audio source:

1. Press the **CHANNEL SELECT** switch for the mic input you will be using.

2. Change the input source to **MIC**, by pressing **SOURCE** one or more times.

3. Make sure the gain is turned down, especially if the monitors are turned up.

4. Verify that **48V PHANTOM** power is disabled. Press **48V**, so that the LED is off.

5. Plug a microphone directly into the **MIC** input on the back of the PRE. These inputs accept XLR connections.

6. If your microphone requires phantom power, press **48V**.

7. Turn the **GAIN/PARAM** control to raise the gain. Use the **PEAK METER** to determine the proper level.

To connect a line/instrument level audio source:

1. Press the **CHANNEL SELECT** switch for the Line/Inst Input you will be using.

2. Change the **INPUT** source to **LINE** or **INST**, by pressing **SOURCE** one or more times.

3. Plug a line level source (such as a DVD player) or a DI source (such as a guitar) into a Line/Inst Input on the front or back of PRE. These inputs accept balanced/unbalanced TRS connectors.

4. Turn the **GAIN/PARAM** control to raise the gain. Use the **PEAK METER** to determine the proper level.

Tip: If using line inputs with balanced devices, be sure to use balanced cables to maximize performance.

To set the input gain on a channel:

1. If the GAIN/PARAM display currently shows a MIDI channel, press **MIDI**. The display should now show an input gain level.

2. Press the SELECT switch for the channel you want to adjust.

3. Rotate the GAIN/PARAM control to adjust the input gain.

Audio Interface Calibration

The installation and connection of audio interfaces is considered to be part of the basic Pro Tools HD system installation (covered earlier in this lesson). However, included here is a section on how and why to calibrate the input and output levels of your interfaces.

I/O Calibration Example

Pro Tools 201 discussed the importance of selecting the correct input operating levels when connecting analog signals from external devices. For example, the HD I/O's analog inputs (and outputs) can be switched in the Hardware Setup dialog box between +4dBu and –10dBV. However, within these general operating standards, the HD I/O's input and output levels can be trimmed up or down by several decibels. There are three reasons you might do this:

■ To ensure the operating levels are equal on all channels.

■ To match the interface's input and output levels to the optimum working levels and headroom of external equipment.

■ To conform to particular industry or regional standards.

Tip: Only the HD I/O and the previous generation 192 I/O audio interfaces support reference level calibration on both input and output. The HD OMNI interface supports only speaker/monitor output calibration. All other HD-series audio interfaces have fixed calibrations that cannot be altered.

Some Notes About Calibration

Traditionally, the operating levels of different pieces of analog equipment (such as a recorder and mixing desk) are adjusted so that their nominal 0VU levels match.

Ideally, they will have the same amount of headroom, so signals from one device cannot clip the circuitry on the other. The situation is less clear with digital equipment like Pro Tools, which effectively has no headroom in the sense used for analog equipment.

The maximum signal level that Pro Tools can encode is given the designation 0 decibels, Full Scale (dBFS), and there is no headroom above this. Anything louder than 0dBFS is clipped. Trim controls on the HD I/O interface allow you to adjust the voltage that represents the 0dBFS point, allowing you to calibrate the operating levels of Pro Tools with external analog equipment.

In a typical scenario, preamps (or an analog mixer's channel or tape outputs) are connected to the analog inputs of an HD I/O interface. The preamps have a headroom, which is the loudest the signal can get above the 0VU point before clipping occurs. One good approach to calibration is to trim the HD I/O's inputs so that the maximum output level of the preamp matches the 0 dBFS point in Pro Tools. This means that the preamp can never clip Pro Tools. If the preamp had a headroom of +18dB above 0 VU, this would mean creating a pseudo-headroom of 18dB in Pro Tools. To do this you would trim the HD I/O inputs so that a signal at 0 VU on the preamp/desk channel aligns with −18dBFS in Pro Tools.

This approach is the safest. You should then work to the operating levels of the preamp and not worry if your signals appear low in Pro Tools. It is more important to have the safety net of headroom in real-life recording scenarios and not overdrive your preamps.

Tip: Being able to build headroom into your recording signal path is one of the main advantages of working at a high bit depth (such as 24-bit). Bear in mind that if your input signal peaks at −10dBFS, you are still using 134dB of the available 144dB dynamic range of a 24-bit file!

However, in some situations you may decide to use a smaller amount of headroom on your HD I/O interfaces. If you are working in an environment with very predictable signal levels with controlled peaks, you may decide to reduce the artificial headroom and record hotter into Pro Tools. Another situation is if you need to run your preamps at lower levels because they are noisy or distort easily on peaks over 0 VU.

The most common industry standards for calibration are 0VU (referenced to either +4dBu nominal or +6dBu peak) calibrated to −18dBFS, −20dBFS, or −22dBFS. After choosing a calibration reference level, you will need to calibrate the analog inputs and outputs of your audio interfaces. After calibration is complete, you can choose analog input or output reference levels of either +4dBU or −10dBV in the Hardware Setup window (shown in Figure 1.16).

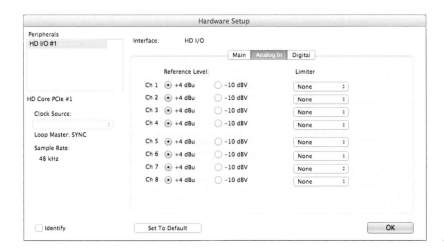

Figure 1.16
Hardware Setup,
Analog In page.

 HD I/O interfaces are factory calibrated so that their +4dBu inputs are set for 20dB headroom above +4dBu/0VU. See Appendix A, "Pro Tools HD-Series Audio Interface Calibration," for more detailed calibration instructions.

Verifying Installation of Additional Pro Tools Software Options

When installing Pro Tools HD software, the Pro Tools installer provides an additional software option called the Avid Video Engine, which supports Avid video record/playback using Avid Mojo or Mojo SDI. To verify if the Avid Video Engine is installed, look for a folder called Video Engine installed in the following directory:

Windows: C:\(or other System Boot Drive)\Program Files\Avid\Pro Tools\DAE\
　　　　Video Engine

Mac: System Boot Drive/Library/Application Support/Avid/Video Engine

In addition to the Avid Video Engine install option, you can also enable and use the Satellite Link option and Machine Control if you purchased the corresponding iLok authorizations. These two options do not require any additional software installation. Instead, they can be enabled in the software only if a valid iLok authorization is found.

The HEAT software option is available for Pro Tools HD DSP-based hardware systems only. HEAT, which stands for Harmonically Enhanced Algorithm Technology, is an add-on installed in the PLUG-INS folder of your system. After installation, HEAT is enabled in the Otions menu, allowing you to apply analog-style harmonic distortion to your mixes. The installer for HEAT is a separate installer that is included as part of the Pro Tools 10 installer package (required iLok authorization sold separately). You should install HEAT only on a supported HD hardware system containing a valid HEAT iLok authorization.

On the Web

Using HEAT is beyond the scope of this book. For more information about HEAT, consult the "HEAT Option Guide" in the Pro Tools documentation folder or visit www.Avid.com (click the Support & Services link).

Windows 7 System Optimization

There are a number of steps that Avid suggests you take to optimize your computer system for use with Pro Tools. Some of these steps are listed in the following sections, but the full steps required to make these adjustments (plus some optional optimizations) can be found in the Mac and Windows 7 optimization guides in the Avid Knowledge Base.

Windows 7 Required Optimizations

In order to ensure that your Pro Tools HD software runs without problems, the following optimizations are required.

Tip: After changing Windows system settings, you will need to restart your computer.

Optimize Hard Disk Performance

This optimization allows your hard drive to work more efficiently when recording and playing back audio files, and can sometimes resolve DAE Error –9073.

To optimize hard disk performance:

1. Open the START menu and choose COMPUTER.

2. Right-click on the C: drive.

3. Choose PROPERTIES.

4. Uncheck COMPRESS THIS DRIVE TO SAVE SPACE.

5. Uncheck ALLOW FILES ON THIS DRIVE TO HAVE CONTENTS INDEXED.

6. Click APPLY and then click OK.

Disable User Account Control (UAC)

Turning off UAC can help with the "Session must be on an audio record volume" error and various issues with launching Pro Tools.

To turn off user account control:

1. Choose START > CONTROL PANEL.

2. Click USER ACCOUNTS AND FAMILY SAFETY.

3. Click USER ACCOUNTS.

4. Click on CHANGE USER ACCOUNT CONTROL SETTINGS.

5. Set the slider to NEVER NOTIFY.

6. Click OK.

7. Restart the computer.

Configuring System Standby and Power Management

When using Pro Tools, the Windows System Standby power scheme must be set to ALWAYS ON. This prevents long record passes from stopping due to system resources powering down.

To configure Windows power management:

1. Choose START > CONTROL PANEL.

2. Click POWER OPTIONS, as shown in Figure 1.17.

3. In the PREFERRED PLANS section, select HIGH PERFORMANCE.

4. Click CHANGE PLAN SETTINGS.

5. Click CHANGE ADVANCED POWER SETTINGS.

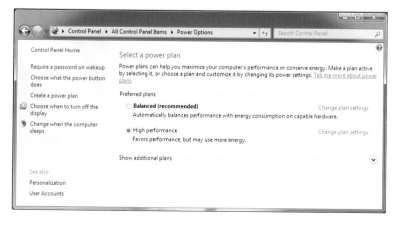

Figure 1.17
Windows 7 Control Panel Power Options.

6. In the POWER OPTIONS dialog box, reveal HARD DISK > TURN OFF HARD DISK AFTER.

7. Click the SETTING option.

8. Select the value in the SETTING (Minutes) field and press BACKSPACE on your computer keyboard or scroll the value to NEVER.

9. Click OK. The hard disk setting will change to NEVER and the POWER OPTIONS dialog box will close.

10. In the EDIT PLAN SETTINGS window, click SAVE CHANGES and close the window.

Note: Pro Tools automatically switches to the High Performance power manage-ment configuration on launch. Windows reverts to previously selected power management settings (if different) when exiting Pro Tools. Consequently, when optimizing the power management settings for Pro Tools, you should only optimize using the High Performance configuration.

Install Latest Device Drivers (Pro Tools 9 and 10 Only)

It is always important to install the latest drivers available for your audio interface to ensure maximum compatibility with Pro Tools.

- If you have an Avid/Digidesign interface, visit http://www.avid.com/drivers to download the latest drivers that are compatible with Pro Tools 10.

- For third-party interfaces, visit the manufacturer's website to download the latest drivers available for your audio interface.

Windows 7 Recommended Optimizations

Pro Tools can also be affected by other software and hardware drivers installed on your computer. For best possible performance, it is recommended (but not required) that you do the following:

- Avoid running any unneeded programs at the same time as Pro Tools.

- Turn off any software utilities that run in the background, such as Windows Messenger, calendars, and disk maintenance programs.

- Turn off any non-essential USB devices while running Pro Tools.

Windows 7 Optional Optimizations

The following system optimizations may help Pro Tools perform better on some systems, although they are not required. It is recommended that you try these optimizations only when necessary, as they may disable or adversely affect the functionality of other programs on your system.

Windows 7 optional optimizations include:

■ Adjust processor scheduling

■ Disable screen savers

■ Adjust display performance

■ Disable USB power management (USB interfaces only)

Disable System Startup Items

The fewer items in use by your computer, the more resources are available for Pro Tools. Some startup applications may be consuming unnecessary CPU resources, and can be turned off.

If you disable any of the following startup items, do so carefully:

■ Portable media serial number (required for some applications that utilize a copy protection key)

■ The Plug-and-Play service

■ Event log

■ Cryptographic services

■ Startup items

To disable system startup items:

1. From the START menu, type **msconfig** in Start Search and press ENTER to open the SYSTEM CONFIGURATION UTILITY.

2. Under the GENERAL tab, choose SELECTIVE STARTUP.

3. Deselect LOAD STARTUP ITEMS and click OK.

4. Click RESTART to restart the computer.

5. After restarting, the computer displays a System Configuration message. Check to see if Pro Tools performance has increased before you deselect the DON'T SHOW THIS MESSAGE AGAIN option. If performance has not changed, run msconfig and return your computer's Startup selection back to NORMAL STARTUP—LOAD ALL DEVICE DRIVES AND SERVICES. Alternatively, try disabling startup items and non-essential processes individually.

Mac OS System Optimization

To ensure optimum performance with Pro Tools, configure your computer first. Before configuring your computer, make sure you are logged in as an Administrator for the account where you want to install Pro Tools. For details on Administrator privileges in Mac OS X, see your Apple OS X documentation.

There are a number of default system settings and keyboard shortcuts for Mac OS that cause conflicts and diminished system performance. Change these settings before using Pro Tools.

Turning Off Software Update

Do not use the Mac OS X automatic software update feature, as it may upgrade your system to a version of Mac OS that has not yet been qualified for Pro Tools.

On the Web

For details on qualified versions of Mac OS, see the latest compatibility information at www.avid.com.

To turn off the Mac software update feature:

1. Choose SYSTEM PREFERENCES from the APPLE menu.

2. Click SOFTWARE UPDATE.

3. Click the SCHEDULED CHECK tab.

4. Deselect CHECK FOR UPDATES.

5. When you are done, close the window to quit SYSTEM PREFERENCES.

Turning Off Energy Saver

Using Energy Saver's default settings can have a negative impact on Pro Tools performance.

To turn off the Energy Saver feature:

1. Choose SYSTEM PREFERENCES from the APPLE menu.

2. Click ENERGY SAVER.

3. Set the COMPUTER SLEEP setting to NEVER.

4. Set the DISPLAY SLEEP setting to NEVER.

5. Deselect PUT THE HARD DISK(S) TO SLEEP WHEN POSSIBLE option.

6. When you are done, close the window to quit SYSTEM PREFERENCES.

Disabling or Reassigning Keyboard Shortcuts

To have the full complement of Pro Tools keyboard shortcuts, you need to disable or reassign conflicting Mac OS X keyboard shortcuts in the Apple system preferences.

Tip: For a complete list of Pro Tools keyboard shortcuts, consult the Keyboard Shortcuts Guide, which can be accessed from within Pro Tools by choosing Help > Keyboard Shortcuts.

Mac OS X 10.7 (Lion)

To disable or reassign Mac keyboard shortcuts used by Pro Tools Mac OS X 10.7 (Lion):

1. From the APPLE menu, choose SYSTEM PREFERENCES.

2. Click KEYBOARD.

3. Click the KEYBOARD SHORTCUTS tab to display the Keyboard Shortcuts page, shown in Figure 1.18.

Figure 1.18
Mac OS X 10.7 (Lion) Keyboard Shortcuts page in System Preferences.

4. You can disable or reassign Mac keyboard shortcuts that conflict with Pro Tools keyboard shortcuts. The following list includes several common Mac keyboard shortcuts that, depending on the make and model of your Mac, may also be used by Pro Tools.

- Under LAUNCHPAD & DOCK

  Turn Dock Hiding On/Off

- Under MISSION CONTROL

  Mission Control

  Application Windows

  Show Desktop

  Show Dashboard

  Mission Control > Move Left a Space

  Mission Control > Move Right a Space

  Mission Control > Switch to Desktop n

- Under KEYBOARD & TEXT INPUT

  Move Focus to the Window Drawer

- Under SERVICES

  Send File to Bluetooth Device

  Search with Google

  Spotlight

  Search Man Pages in Terminal

- Under SPOTLIGHT

  Show Spotlight Search Field

  Show Spotlight Window

- Under UNIVERSAL ACCESS

  Zoom

  Contrast

- Under APPLICATION SHORTCUTS

  Show Help Menu

Mac OS X 10.6 (Snow Leopard)

To disable or reassign Mac keyboard shortcuts used by Pro Tools Mac OS X 10.6 (Snow Leopard):

1. From the APPLE menu, choose SYSTEM PREFERENCES.

2. Click KEYBOARD.

3. Click the KEYBOARD SHORTCUTS tab to display the Keyboard Shortcuts page, shown in Figure 1.19.

Figure 1.19
Mac OS X 10.6 (Snow Leopard) Keyboard Shortcuts page in System Preferences.

4. You can disable or reassign Mac keyboard shortcuts that conflict with Pro Tools keyboard shortcuts. The following list includes several common Mac keyboard shortcuts that are also used by Pro Tools.

- Under DASHBOARD & DOCK

  Turn Dock Hiding On/Off

  Dashboard

- Under EXPOSÉ AND SPACES

  All Windows

  Application Windows

  Desktop

- Under KEYBOARD & TEXT INPUT

  Move Focus to the Window Drawer

- Under SPOTLIGHT

  Show Spotlight Search Field

  Show Spotlight Window

- Under APPLICATION SHORTCUTS

  Show Help Menu

Disabling Spotlight Indexing

The Mac OS Spotlight feature automatically indexes files and folders on local hard drives in the background. In most cases, this is not a concern for normal Pro Tools operation. However, if Spotlight starts indexing drives while recording in a Pro Tools session with a high track count for an extended period of time, it can adversely affect Pro Tools system performance, although the Disk Cache setting in Pro Tools may eliminate most conflicts with Spotlight. You may want to disable Spotlight indexing for all local drives before using Pro Tools for big recording projects.

To disable Spotlight indexing:

1. Choose APPLE MENU > SYSTEM PREFERENCES > SPOTLIGHT.

2. In the Spotlight window, click the PRIVACY tab.

3. To prevent indexing of a drive, drag its icon from the desktop into the list.

Enabling Journaling for Audio Drives

To yield higher performance from audio drives, enable journaling. This is normally done when initializing a drive with Disk Utility and choosing the format option, MAC OS EXTENDED (JOURNALED). However, if the drive is already initialized, you can enable journaling using the following process.

To enable journaling on an existing drive:

1. Launch the DISK UTILITY application, located in System Drive/ Applications/Utilities.

2. Select the volume in the left column of the DISK UTILITY window.

3. Choose FILE > ENABLE JOURNALING or press COMMAND+J.

Non-Administrator (Standard) Accounts

Pro Tools supports both administrator and non-administrator (standard) accounts for Windows and Mac OS systems. This may be useful in facilities or educational institutions where multiple Pro Tools users share workstations. Different engineers or students can work extensively with Pro Tools, while being restricted from installing software, or accessing protected hard disk and server locations.

Implications of Non-Administrator (Standard) Accounts

Pro Tools requires Administrator access for installation. Other considerations apply for Preference settings and disk access.

Pro Tools Preferences

Pro Tools creates individual preference settings files for each user account on the system. Therefore, whenever users log in and launch Pro Tools, they will find Pro Tools preferences configured the same way as when they last logged in. User preferences are stored in the following locations:

- Windows: Documents and Settings\<username>\Application Data\Avid
- Mac: Users/<username>/Library/Preferences

Disk Access and Work Locations

Standard account users are only allowed to save Pro Tools sessions and audio/video files within their own Home directories. This is quite restrictive, as it limits users to working on the system drive. The system administrator should grant Read/Write access to the required external media drives and (on Mac volumes) enable Ignore Ownership on This Volume for normal Pro Tools operation.

Caution: Some third-party software plug-ins, video file formats, and other software options used with Pro Tools might not function properly when run with a non-administrator (standard) account. For further information on possible software incompatibilities with non-administrator (standard) accounts, contact the software developer directly.

Configuring a Non-Administrator (Standard) Account for Pro Tools Users

Note that no special steps are required to configure user accounts to use Pro Tools on Windows computers. During installation of Pro Tools, the installer automatically creates a user group called Pro Tools Users and adds Everyone to the group.

All non-administrator user accounts will have access to Pro Tools, with the limitations outlined previously.

To configure a standard user account on Mac OS:

1. Log in to Mac OS using an ADMINISTRATOR account.

2. Under the APPLE menu, choose SYSTEM PREFERENCES and select ACCOUNTS (Mac OS 10.6) or USERS & GROUPS (Mac OS 10.7).

3. Click the PLUS(+) button to create a new account (shown in Figure 1.20).

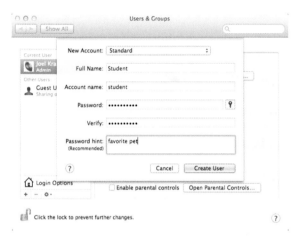

Figure 1.20
Creating a new Standard account using Mac OS 10.7 (Lion).

4. In the NEW ACCOUNT window, choose STANDARD from the pop-up menu, enter the account info, and then click CREATE USER. A new account will appear in the account column.

Pro Tools Session File Interchange

When exchanging Pro Tools sessions between Pro Tools systems using different hardware and software versions, a number of potential pitfalls can occur when opening sessions created on other systems. Pro Tools session files can generally be opened by newer software versions, but not older software versions. To convert a Pro Tools session file to an older format, you must use the Save Copy In command from the File menu, and choose the appropriate software version. The following is a listing of the most current Pro Tools session file formats:

- **Pro Tools 10**: Sessions ending with the file extension .PTX

- **Pro Tools 7.0 through Pro Tools 9.0.5**: Sessions ending with the file extension .PTF

- **Pro Tools 5.1 through Pro Tools 6.9**: Sessions ending with the extension .PTS

Session Compatibility Between Pro Tools HD and Pro Tools

Although sessions created using Pro Tools 10.0 can be opened on Pro Tools HD 10.0, and likewise sessions created on Pro Tools HD 10.0 can be opened on Pro Tools 10, a number of limitations apply.

Opening Pro Tools HD Sessions in Pro Tools

A Pro Tools HD session can be opened with Pro Tools, but certain session components open differently or not at all.

When opening a Pro Tools HD 10.0 session in Pro Tools 10.0, the following occurs:

- Any tracks beyond the first 128 are made inactive.
- Any Instrument tracks beyond 64 are made inactive.
- Any Auxiliary Input tracks beyond 128 are made inactive.
- DSP plug-ins with Native equivalents are converted; those without equivalents are made inactive. (Native plug-ins remain Native plug-ins while running on the host system. If the session is reopened on a Pro Tools HD DSP-accelerated system, the plug-ins will revert back to DSPs plug-ins.)
- Multichannel surround tracks are removed from the session.
- Unavailable input and output paths are made inactive.
- HEAT (if enabled) is deactivated. When re-opened on a HD system, settings are retained, but HEAT must be re-enabled.

Groups:

- Mix groups keep only Main Volume information.
- Mix/Edit groups keep only Main Volume and Automation Mode information.
- Automation overflow information for grouped controls is preserved.
- Group behavior of Solos, Mutes, Send Levels, and Send Mutes is preserved.
- Solo Mode and Solo Latch settings are dropped.

Video:

- Only the main Video track is displayed.
- Only the first QuickTime movie in the session is displayed or played back.
- If the session contains QuickTime movies in the Clip List but no Video track, the session opens with a new Video track containing the first QuickTime movie from the Clip List.
- The Timeline displays and plays back only the video playlist that was last active. Alternate video playlists are not available.

Sharing Sessions Created on Different Pro Tools Software Versions

Pro Tools makes it easy to share sessions between different software versions of a particular Pro Tools system.

Pro Tools 10.0 sessions cannot be opened with lower versions of Pro Tools. To save a Pro Tools 10.0 session so it is compatible with a lower version of Pro Tools, use the FILE > SAVE COPY IN command to select the appropriate session format.

Saving Pro Tools 10.0 Sessions to Pro Tools 7–Pro Tools 9 Format

To save a Pro Tools 10.0 session so it is compatible with Pro Tools version 7.x through 9.x, use the FILE > SAVE COPY IN command to choose the Pro Tools 7–Pro Tools 9 Session format.

When saving a Pro Tools 10.0 session to Pro Tools 7–Pro Tools 9 Session format, the following occurs:

- Any audio tracks beyond 256 are made inactive
- Clip gain settings are dropped. If you want to apply any clip gain settings for the session copy, you must manually render clip gain settings first.
- Fades will be rendered when the session is opened in a lower version of Pro Tools.
- Sessions with mixed bit depths must convert all files to the same bit depth and file format.
- Sessions with files that have a bit depth of 32-bit floating point must be converted to 24-bit or 16-bit.
- For sessions with RF64 files larger than 4GB, these files will be unavailable to lower versions of Pro Tools. (You will manually need to consolidate these files to less than 4GB so that the audio can be available to lower software versions of Pro Tools.)

Opening Pro Tools 9.0 Sessions with Pro Tools 8.5, 8.1, and 8.0

A Pro Tools 9.0 session can be opened with Pro Tools 8.5, 8.1, and 8.0 but certain session components open differently or are removed completely.

Note: When opening a Pro Tools 9.0 session with Pro Tools 8.5, 8.1, or 8.0, you are warned that you are opening a session that was created with a newer version of Pro Tools and that not all session components will be available.

When opening a Pro Tools 9.0 session with Pro Tools 8.5 or 8.1, the following occurs:

■ Any audio tracks beyond 256 are made inactive.

■ Any internal mix busses beyond 128 are made inactive.

■ The stereo pan depth reverts to –2.5dB for the stereo mixer. The pan depth for surround mixer remains at –3.0dB at center.

If the session is opened in Pro Tools 8.0, in addition to the previous, the following also occurs:

■ Output bus assignments are removed.

■ HEAT (if present) is removed.

Review/Discussion Questions

1. What is the maximum number of simultaneous audio tracks that can play back on a Pro Tools|HDX system with two HDX PCIe cards?

2. How many simultaneous audio tracks can play back on Pro Tools 10 software with Complete Production Toolkit installed?

3. What is the maximum number of HD-series audio interfaces that can be connected to a single Pro Tools|HDX PCIe card?

4. Where could you find out if a new model of an Apple Macintosh Intel-based computer will work with Pro Tools?

5. How many microphone inputs are available on an Avid PRE?

6. What four general steps are required to enable remote control of an Avid PRE (or equivalent) from Pro Tools software?

7. What benefits does a Pro Tools|HDX system have over a Pro Tools|HD Native system?

8. What is the name of the cable that is used to connect two Pro Tools|HDX PCIe cards together inside the computer?

9. List at least two system software settings on either a Mac or Windows system that should be changed or disabled when installing a Pro Tools HD system.

10. Name two different settings you will lose when moving a session from Pro Tools 10 HD software to standard Pro Tools 10 software.

11. How would you convert a Pro Tools 10.1 session so that it could be opened on a Pro Tools system running version 9.0.5 software? What files, settings, or session attributes should you consider when saving a Pro Tools 10.0 session so that it could be opened on a Pro Tools system running version 9.x software?

12. What is the file extension on both a Pro Tools 9 and a Pro Tools 10 session file?

Pro Tools HD Hardware Configuration

In this exercise, you will recommend all of the Pro Tools hardware and software that will be needed to satisfy the precise needs of a busy audio production facility. You will also complete a diagram showing the connections required for a professional Pro Tools|HDX system.

Media Used:

None

Duration:

20 minutes

GOAL

- Recommend and list Pro Tools–related hardware and software required to fulfill two specific scenarios

Getting Started

As a certified Pro Tools Expert, you have been hired to specify a new Pro Tools system for a professional musician's private studio. Your goal is to provide a complete list of equipment necessary for a showcase Pro Tools|HDX system that will satisfy any music tracking, editing, or mixing need.

The owner has specified that the system be built on an Apple PowerMac and include the following features and capabilities:

- Play back up to 200 simultaneous tracks of audio at 96 kHz (24-bit or 32-bit)

- Access 4 TB of external FireWire audio storage and 2 TB of internal storage

- Use a synchronization unit for locking to and generating LTC

- Support for stereo and surround sound projects (up to 5.1 surround)

- Provide up to 96 channels of analog I/O

- Provide 32 channels of remote-controlled mic-pres

- Provide 9-pin machine control for 24-track tape machine and satellite link

- Allow mixing using an Avid worksurface with at least 32 faders

- Include additional Native and DSP-based plug-ins required for music production

- Support for opening and saving Pro Tools session in versions 7.0 thru 10.x

Create Your Own Customized Equipment List

Based on the music studio's requirements (listed previously), develop your own list of Pro Tools hardware/software that will fulfill all of the needs of the facility and enter it here or on a separate piece of paper.

Tip: You can look back at this lesson and use the Internet to research the options that are available. It is not necessary to include in your list third-party Pro Tools plug-ins, audio speakers, cables, and other smaller accessories.

Pro Tools|HDX System for Music Production: Equipment List

Apple computer hardware and peripherals (including required OS):

Avid Pro Tools hardware and peripherals:

Avid Pro Tools software options:

Third-party hardware peripherals:

 When you are finished, ask your instructor to check your answers, share your answers with your classmates, or check the answer key in Appendix B, "Exercise Answer Keys."

Making the Connections for a Professional Pro Tools|HDX System

The schematic diagram shown in Figure Ex1.1 is an extended version of the diagram shown earlier in Lesson 1. The components shown in the diagram are typical of what you would find in a professional music studio.

Using the information from Lesson 1 and your own knowledge of Pro Tools, draw and label connections between the components.

A completed diagram needs to include the following types of connections:

- DigiLink (audio interfaces)
- Loop Sync
- FireWire
- MIDI
- USB
- Ethernet
- DigiSerial

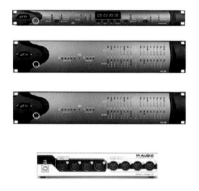

Figure Ex1.1
Schematic diagram to fill in.

Troubleshooting a Pro Tools System

This lesson discusses the proper troubleshooting of a Pro Tools HD-series system.

Media Used: None

Duration: 120 minutes

GOALS

- Troubleshoot a Pro Tools system
- Update firmware for Avid hardware
- Configure Pro Tools Record/Playback settings
- Update I/O settings

This lesson explains the configuration, features, components, and benefits of Avid's hardware-based DSP-accelerated Pro Tools systems—Pro Tools|HDX and Pro Tools|HD. These systems start with the same Pro Tools software covered in the lower-level Pro Tools courses, but add purpose-built PCIe expansion cards and audio interfaces (HD I/O, MADI I/O, and HD OMNI) to meet the needs of professional engineers and producers. By adding dedicated processing power and predictable signal routing, Pro Tools|HDX and Pro Tools|HD provide a reliable and scalable system for any professional audio production environment.

When working under the tight deadlines and demands of a busy professional production facility, it is necessary to keep your Pro Tools system working in peak operating condition. This lesson will show you many of the useful ways to troubleshoot your Pro Tools system, so that you can minimize or avoid any delays that keep you from completing your project.

Troubleshooting Operational Issues

When troubleshooting an operational issue with your Pro Tools system, you'll need to first figure out if the problem is related to hardware failure or software failure. In most cases, software failure or misconfiguration will be the cause. But hardware issues can arise. If you suspect a failure with your Pro Tools HD or HDX hardware, your first stop should be the DigiTest utility.

Using DigiTest to Identify Hardware Problems

DigiTest is a useful diagnostic tool for troubleshooting and updating firmware for Pro Tools HD-series hardware systems. You can also use DigiTest to verify a system after you have changed or added hardware to it.

The DigiTest utility is automatically installed as part of the Pro Tools 10 installation in the Pro Tools Utilities folder, located on your system hard drive, as shown in Figure 2.1.

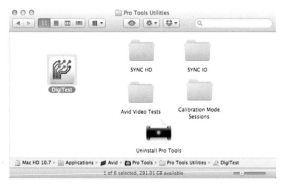

Figure 2.1
DigiTest utility icon.

Run the DigiTest diagnostic application to identify Pro Tools|HD cards and verify that they are correctly installed and working properly.

Tip: Before you run DigiTest, lower the volume of your monitoring system and all output devices. Additionally, be sure to remove your headphones. Very loud digital noise may be emitted during the test.

To run DigiTest:

1. From the **PRO TOOLS UTILITIES** folder, double-click the **DIGITEST** application program. DigiTest opens and lists the supported cards it finds in your system, in their corresponding slot locations. If you have a large number of cards and connected interfaces, it may take a while for the main DigiTest screen to appear, as the application scans the cards and interfaces connected to the system.

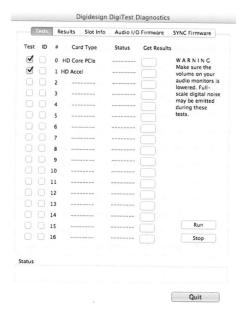

Figure 2.2
The DigiTest main window showing the Tests tab.

2. In the **TESTS** tab of the DigiTest window, verify that all cards you want to test are checked and then click **RUN**.

Tip: An HD-series audio interface must be connected to the first port on the first HDX PCIe card. With previous generation HD Core PCIe hardware, an HD audio interface must be connected to the HD Core card. In addition to being connected, the HD audio interface must be powered on for the test to run properly, since the audio interface supplies the system clock used for testing.

- DigiTest begins by checking the arrangement of your cards.

- After checking card arrangement, DigiTest checks card functionality. The Status box for each tested card will indicate Passed or Failed.

Note: DigiTest reports valid test results for slots containing Avid cards only.

3. After the test is completed, do one of the following:
   - If all of the Avid cards pass, quit DigiTest and restart your computer.
   - If any cards fail, you can review test details by clicking the **RESULTS** tab. Following review, you will need to quit DigiTest, power down your system, and verify proper card seating and card interconnect cable connections.

4. When DigiTest has completed, restart your computer.

Note: After running DigiTest, you must restart your computer. If you attempt to launch Pro Tools without restarting, Pro Tools will start to launch, but will eventually abort the launch and request that your restart your computer.

Avid Knowledge Base

The Avid Knowledge Base is an online database containing thousands of entries that cover common issues, such as DAE errors, and their solutions. Knowledge Base also contains general technical information about Pro Tools and Avid hardware. The most up-to-date version of this database is available on the Avid website.

To use Knowledge Base:

1. From within Pro Tools, select **HELP > PRO TOOLS KNOWLEDGE BASE**, or from your Web browser, go to www.avid.com, click the **SUPPORT & SERVICES** link, and then in the right sidebar (under Pro Tools Support), click **KNOWLEDGE BASE**. You will see the Knowledge Base search field at the top of the page.

2. Enter keywords into the **TYPE YOUR QUESTION** field and then click **SEARCH**.

3. In the **REFINE RESULTS** column, you can refine your search results, as shown in Figure 2.3.

4. Click the text of any of the search results to see the full Knowledge Base entry, as shown in Figure 2.4.

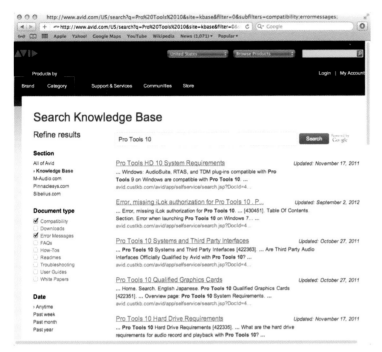

Figure 2.3
Avid Knowledge Base.

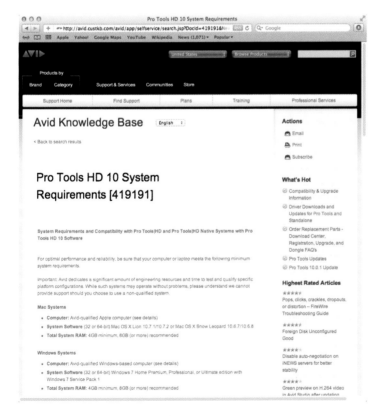

Figure 2.4
Avid Knowledge Base
search result details.

Here are some hints to help with your searches:

■ Do not use full phrases such as "Which records in the Knowledge Base describe 9073 errors?" Use only the words or numbers you want to search for, such as "DAE 9073."

■ Do not use punctuation marks or special characters.

■ Every record that contains all the words entered in the search field will be returned (the text search is an AND search). All fields in the database are searched. For example, searching for "−36 error ATTO" finds this text: "DAE error −36 is thrown when initiating or during playback with the drive connected to an ATTO card."

■ The order of the search text does not matter. Searching for "6042 error" will find "error 6042."

■ Knowledge Base searches are not case sensitive. Searching for "dae" will find "DAE."

Tip: You can access additional help options from within Pro Tools by choosing Help > Avid Audio Forums and Help > Customer Assist.

Updating Avid Firmware

Firmware is the operating software code embedded in a hardware device. Many Avid hardware peripherals (including all HDX cards, worksurfaces, video hardware, audio interfaces, and SYNC Peripherals) contain firmware that can be updated to fix bugs and add new functionality.

HDX Card Firmware

The latest generation DSP-accelerated HDX cards have upgradable firmware that can be updated once the cards are installed in a system. The firmware update code is included in the main Pro Tools software. When Pro Tools is launched, the firmware version is checked. If an update is available, you will be prompted to upgrade the firmware or cancel the upgrade. Once the firmware has been updated, Pro Tools will start normally.

Caution: Early Apple Mac Pro computers ("Harpertown" models) encounter errors when performing Pro Tools HDX PCIe firmware updates. Attempting to update HDX firmware with a "Harpertown" Mac Pro will render the card unusable and should be avoided.

Control Surfaces and Worksurfaces

Each release of Pro Tools software includes the latest versions of firmware for Avid control surfaces and worksurfaces. With the exception of EUCON-enabled control and worksurfaces (which require a separate installation of software), this is part of the basic software package and requires no extra installation. As soon as you declare a control surface or worksurface in the Ethernet Controllers tab of the Peripherals dialog box, Pro Tools will check whether the connected device has current or matching firmware. If not, a dialog box will appear, informing you that new firmware needs to be uploaded to the device. Follow the onscreen instructions, and your control surface/worksurface will be updated. In some instances, a new firmware file will be made available for download separately from a Pro Tools update. In this case, you can replace the file manually, and Pro Tools will prompt you to upload the firmware to the control surface/worksurface when you next launch. Controller files are located in the following locations:

Mac: [*System Disk*]/Applications/Avid/Pro Tools/Controllers/

Windows: [*System Disk*]\Program Files\Avid\Pro Tools\DAE\Controllers

Tip: Avid **EUCON**-enabled control surfaces and worksurfaces do not update their firmware through the Pro Tools software. Instead, their firmware is updated using the EuControl software application (for Artist Series), MC App (for MC Pro or System 5-MC), or eMix (for System 5 and its variants), which autostarts when the computer is turned on. For more information about updating firmware for Avid EUCON-enabled hardware devices, consult the *Pro Tools EUCON User Guide.*

Updating SYNC Peripheral Firmware

As with control surfaces and worksurfaces, SYNC Peripheral firmware may be required for new versions of Pro Tools software. Pro Tools checks that the SYNC Peripheral's firmware is up to date at launch or when you declare a SYNC Peripheral in the Synchronization tab of the Peripherals dialog box. If an update is required, you will be prompted and should follow the onscreen instructions, as shown in Figure 2.5.

Tip: When upgrading from Pro Tools version 9.x to Pro Tools 10.0 software, the Avid SYNC Peripheral will not require a firmware update.

When upgrading the firmware of a SYNC Peripheral, you will be asked to follow several steps, including power cycling the unit while holding down the Set button.

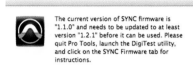

The current version of SYNC firmware is "1.1.0" and needs to be updated to at least version "1.2.1" before it can be used. Please quit Pro Tools, launch the DigiTest utility, and click on the SYNC Firmware tab for instructions.

 OK

Figure 2.5
Sync firmware update warning dialog box.

There are a couple of issues when updating SYNC Peripheral firmware.

SYNC Peripheral Not Connected to DigiSerial Port

The SYNC Peripheral must be connected to the DigiSerial port on either the HDX/HD Core/HD Native PCIe card or the PC COM-1 port (Windows only) for firmware updates.

Firmware Not Found

The latest version of SYNC Peripheral firmware is automatically installed in the Pro Tools Utilities folder when you install the Pro Tools HD software. If you have mistakenly deleted the SYNC Peripheral firmware software since the initial installation, the best course of action is to install it immediately, as this will stop the problem recurring at a later date. If you don't have the Pro Tools 10 installer, you can download the firmware from www.avid.com.

To reinstall the SYNC Peripheral firmware file using the Pro Tools 10 installer:

1. Quit Pro Tools and run the installer.

2. In the PACKAGE NAME column, select only the PRO TOOLS UTILITIES option, as shown in Figure 2.6. This option will install the SYNC Peripheral firmware.

3. Follow the instructions to complete the install.

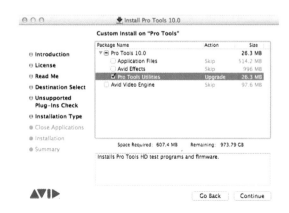

Figure 2.6
Custom Pro Tools 10 install.

Although Pro Tools automatically prompts you to update firmware when required, it's also possible to initiate a firmware update manually. This can be a last resort to try to fix a SYNC Peripheral that is behaving incorrectly, when all other steps have not solved the issue.

To reload the firmware on a SYNC Peripheral manually:

1. Launch the DIGITEST utility and then click the SYNC FIRMWARE tab.

2. If the SYNC Peripheral is connected to the DigiSerial port, select the HD card from the menu.

Tip: **On some Apple Macintosh computers using HD Core/Accel hardware, the Pro ToolsIHD Accel card might be selected by default, requiring you to select the HD Core card in the menu before updating the SYNC Peripheral's firmware.**

3. Select the Serial Port and SYNC type, and then click BEGIN UPDATE, as shown in Figure 2.7.

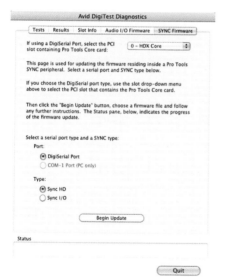

Figure 2.7
SYNC Firmware tab of the DigiTest utility.

Tip: **Follow the onscreen instructions very closely, being careful to power cycle your SYNC Peripheral exactly when instructed.**

Audio Interface Firmware

The firmware in Pro Tools HD-series audio interfaces can be updated using the DigiTest utility (see "Using DigiTest to Identify Hardware Problems," earlier in this lesson).

To update audio interface firmware from DigiTest:

1. Make sure the audio interfaces are connected and powered on.

2. Launch DigiTest.

3. Click the Audio I/O Firmware tab.

4. In the Displaying Information For Slot menu, select the Pro Tools PCIe card that is connected to the HD-series audio interface you want to update, as shown in Figure 2.8.

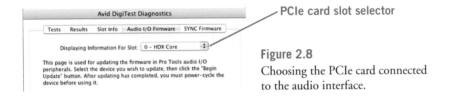

PCIe card slot selector

Figure 2.8
Choosing the PCIe card connected to the audio interface.

Tip: On some Apple Macintosh computers using HD Core/Accel hardware, the Pro Tools|HD Accel card might be selected by default, requiring you to select the HD Core card in the menu before updating audio interface firmware on the first (primary) audio interface.

5. In the Device Selection section, choose between the first and second interfaces (primary or expansion) connected to the HD card. The type of interface will be displayed automatically in the Product section.

6. Mute your speaker monitors.

7. Click Begin Update.

8. When the update is complete, quit DigiTest and restart the computer.

Deleting Pro Tools Settings Files

There are times when the settings files Pro Tools uses become unreadable or corrupted, causing the Pro Tools software to become unstable and behave erratically. After deleting these files and restarting your computer, Pro Tools creates new replacement files that return your Pro Tools system to normal operation.

Deleting settings files will cause the following:

■ Pro Tools Preference options are reset to the factory default settings.

■ Ethernet and MIDI controllers are disabled and must be re-enabled.

■ Machine control will be disabled (if enabled).

- Options and Setup menu options are reset to the factory default settings.

- Satellite Link Option will be disabled (if enabled).

Deleting Settings Files on Mac OS X

On Mac-based Pro Tools systems, all of the files that can be deleted are located in the same directory location.

To locate and delete the settings files:

1. Quit the Pro Tools application (if open).

2. Go to INTERNAL SYSTEM DRIVE/ADMINISTRATOR USERNAME/LIBRARY/PREFERENCES.

Tip: The User Library folder is hidden by default with the Mac OS X 10.7 (Lion) release. To access the User Library folder from within the Finder, press Option and then select Library from the Go menu. Or, open Applications > Utilities > Terminal and type **chflags nohidden/Users/<Username>/Library**.

3. In the PREFERENCES folder, COMMAND-CLICK to select each of the following files:

   - **com.digidesign.DigiTest.plist:** Stores the last position of the DigiTest window on the desktop.

   - **com.digidesign.ProTools.plist:** Stores the last position of various windows (Mix window, Edit window, which windows were visible, and so on) in the Pro Tools application.

   - **DAE Prefs (folder):** Stores a log of what plug-ins are installed on the system and the active plug-in librarian menu choices (for example, the Root Settings folder location).

   - **DigiSetup.OSX:** Stores the last-run hardware state of the Pro Tools environment, including how many DSP cards are installed, the last used sample rate, whether a SYNC HD is present and its last used settings, and so on.

   - **Pro Tools Prefs:** Stores the current user's most recent preference settings that were set in the Pro Tools application.

4. Drag the selected files to the Trash, or press COMMAND+DELETE to move the selected files to the Trash, as shown in Figure 2.9.

5. Empty the Trash and restart your computer.

Note: You must restart the computer after deleting the files listed previously.

Figure 2.9
Deleting Pro Tools preference files on Mac OS X.

Deleting Settings Files on Windows OS

Windows Pro Tools systems have two directories containing the Pro Tools settings files.

To locate and delete the DAE Prefs folder:

1. Quit the Pro Tools application (if open).

2. Choose START MENU > MY COMPUTER > LOCAL DISK (C:) (or correct System Hard Drive). Then click SHOW THE CONTENTS OF THIS DRIVE (if files aren't showing).

3. Navigate to PROGRAM FILES > COMMON FILES > DIGIDESIGN > DAE.

4. Right-click on the DAE PREFS folder and choose DELETE.

Tip: Be sure you are deleting the DAE Prefs folder and not the DAE folder. If you delete the DAE folder, you will need to reinstall Pro Tools and any third-party plug-ins installed.

To locate and delete the Pro Tools Preference file:

1. Go to START MENU > MY COMPUTER > LOCAL DISK (C:) (or correct System Hard Drive) > USERS > (your User file folder) > APPDATA > ROAMING > AVID > PRO TOOLS.

2. If the APPDATA folder is not visible, go to CONTROL PANEL > FOLDER OPTIONS > VIEW tab, and then enable SHOW HIDDEN FILES, FOLDERS, AND DRIVES. Click APPLY and OK.

3. Right-click on the Pro Tools PREFS.PTP file and choose DELETE.

4. You can also delete the DIGITEST.EXE-(8-DIGITS).PF preference file located at the C:\WINDOWS\PREFETCH directory.

5. Empty the recycle bin and restart your computer.

Tip: You must restart the computer after deleting the files listed in this section.

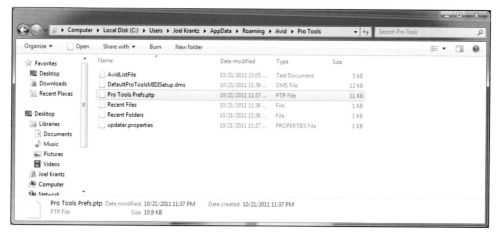

Figure 2.10
Deleting the Pro Tools Preference file in Windows.

Deleting Database Files

Pro Tools creates a media database file for every hard drive connected to the system, including the system drive. If any of these files become corrupt, it can cause unusual behavior such as system slowness or erratic behavior. If in doubt, these files can be deleted and will be regenerated when Pro Tools is relaunched.

To delete media databases on Mac OS computers:

1. Go to [MAC SYSTEM DRIVE]/LIBRARY/APPLICATION SUPPORT/AVID/ DATABASES/UNICODE/VOLUMES.

2. Delete the entire contents of the VOLUMES folder.

Caution: Do NOT delete the whole Databases or Unicode folder, since this would cause all catalogs to be lost.

To delete media databases on Windows computers:

1. Go to C:/PROGRAM FILES/AVID/PRO TOOLS/DATABASES/UNICODE/ VOLUMES.

2. Delete the entire contents of the VOLUMES folder.

Caution: Do NOT delete the whole Databases or Unicode folder, since this would cause all catalogs to be lost.

3. Relaunch Pro Tools. (Restarting the computer is not necessary.)

Note: In previous version of Pro Tools, the Tech Support Utility was included with the software, providing an easy way to delete Pro Tools database and settings files. At the time of print, no such utility was available for Pro Tools 10. Previous versions of the Tech Support Utility are not compatible with Pro Tools 10.

Understanding Voice Allocation

In order for an audio track to play back or record, the track must be assigned a voice. All Pro Tools systems have a maximum number of voices, depending on the hardware configuration. The number of voices supported by your system determines how many simultaneous audio tracks can play back or record. Separate from the voice count of a Pro Tools system, each system also has a maximum number of allowable audio tracks that it will support in a session, referred to as voiceable (or virtual) tracks.

For example, a Pro Tools|HDX system with one PCIe card provides 256 voices (simultaneous channels of audio playback and recording) at 48kHz, whereas a previous generation Pro Tools|HD 2 system provides up to 192 voices of audio playback and recording, at 48kHz. Despite the difference in voice count between the two hardware systems, both of these systems support 768 total voiceable (virtual) tracks in the session.

Track Priority and Voice Assignment

Pro Tools allows you to create many more audio tracks than available voices. Although all audio tracks in a session can record and play back audio, not all of them can be recorded to or played back simultaneously.

When the number of tracks in a session exceeds the number of available voices, the tracks with the lowest priority will not be heard. In these situations, Pro Tools assigns priority to tracks that compete for the available voices. Because there can be more audio tracks than available voices, Pro Tools provides multiple ways of adjusting the playback priority of audio tracks.

Note: Voice allocation works differently on Pro Tools|HDX systems and previous generation Pro Tools|HD systems.

Number of Voices (Pro Tools|HDX Systems Only)

Like the fixed voice count of Pro Tools software with Complete Production Toolkit and Pro Tools|HD Native hardware systems, Pro Tools|HDX hardware systems also have a fixed voice count of 256 voices when using a single card system. Pro

Tools|HDX systems containing two or more cards allow you to expand the voice count, providing 256 voices per HDX PCIe card, with a maximum voice count of 768 total voices (with three HDX cards). For testing session compatibility and performance on systems with lower voice counts, expanded Pro Tools|HDX systems also allow you to change the Number of Voices setting in the Playback Engine dialog box from 256, 512, or 768 voices.

Table 2.1 shows the voice count options that are available when using multi-card Pro Tools|HDX hardware systems.

Table 2.1   Pro Tools|HDX Voice Count Options

Number of HDX Cards	Max Voice Count Options	Playback Engine Voice Count
1	256	256 only
2	512	256 or 512
3 or more	768	256, 512, or 768

One major benefit of the Pro Tools|HDX hardware is that it does not use DSP chips for voices. Instead, each Pro Tools|HDX card has a dedicated FPGA chip, which provides 256 voices per card (as mentioned in Lesson 1, "Pro Tools HD Hardware Configuration"). See Figure 2.11. Since the HDX card's DSP chips are not used for voices, the track count of a session will have no impact on the DSP available for mixing or plug-in processing. This is one major benefit of the Pro Tools|HDX hardware over the previous generation Pro Tools|HD hardware, which shares the Pro Tools|HD card's DSP chips for both voices and DSP plug-ins and mixing.

Note: A Field Programmable Gate Array (FPGA) chip is a circuit that can be re-programmed after it has left the factory. This allows Avid to make changes to the programming of the firmware to increase performance or fix bugs in the future.

Since the HDX card's DSP chips are not used for voices, the track count of a session will have no impact on the DSP available for mixing or plug-in processing. This is one major benefit of the Pro Tools|HDX hardware versus the previous generation Pro Tools|HD hardware, which share the Pro Tools|HD card's DSPs for both voices and DSP plug-ins and mixing.

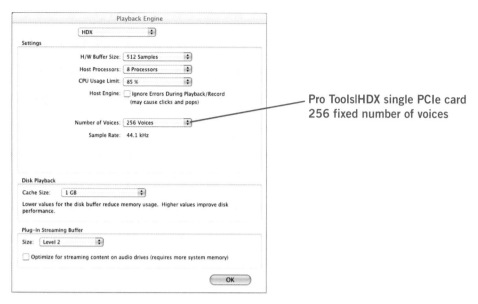

Figure 2.11
Fixed voice assignments with a single Pro Tools|HDX card in the Playback Engine dialog box.

Number of Voices (Pro Tools|HD Systems Only)

In contrast to the high voice counts of Pro Tools|HDX systems, previous generation Pro Tools|HD systems have more limited voice counts but provide more options for managing the voice counts of your session in the Playback Engine dialog box. The total voice count on a Pro Tools|HD system ranges from a minimum of 16 voices to a maximum of 96 voices for a single Pro Tools|HD PCIe card system, doubling to a maximum of 192 voices for a system containing two or more Pro Tools|HD PCIe cards (at 44.1 kHz or 48 kHz).

Tip: When choosing the voice count for previous generation Pro Tools|HD DSP
        hardware, you should select the highest number of voices with the smallest
        number of DSP chips to meet your needs. Increase the number of chips
        (or decrease the number of voices) as needed to avoid PCI bus errors
        (DAE error –6042).

On Pro Tools|HD-series hardware systems, once you select a voice count, the DSP chips used for voices are 100% allocated when the session is opened and cannot be used for anything other than voice count. For example, if you set Number of Voices to 192 voices (6 DSPs) for a session that will only be using 16 voices, you are essentially wasting hardware processing power that could be used for other processes, such as DSP plug-ins or mixing power.

Figure 2.12
Pro Tools|HD Hardware's Selectable Voice Counts in the Playback Engine dialog box.

Note: Unlike previous generation Pro Tools|HD PCIe hardware, Pro Tools|HDX
       hardware systems do not use DSP chips for allocating voices, so the
       maximum voice count is always available, and no DSP processing power
       is wasted on unused voices.

On both Pro Tools|HDX and Pro Tools|HD hardware systems, adding Native
plug-ins on Aux Inputs, Instruments tracks, and Master Faders requires
additional voices. However, using DSP plug-ins on Pro Tools|HDX and Pro
Tools|HD hardware will automatically place the plug-in on the PCIe hard-
ware's DSPs. For more information about how Native plug-in use affects
voice count on Pro Tools|HDX and Pro Tools|HD hardware systems, refer
to Lesson 7, "Pro Tools|HD Mixing Concepts."

Tip: At low and moderate sample rates on Pro Tools|HD PCIe hardware systems,
      you can also choose how many voices will be allocated to each DSP chip.
      This allows for voice load balancing in large sessions to alleviate possible
      system errors related to PCI bus timing conflicts.

Setting Voice Assignment

In Pro Tools, all new audio tracks are assigned (dyn) Dynamic Voicing by default.
Dynamic voicing simply means Pro Tools will allocate the first available voice to

track one, and continue to assign and increment through all of the available voices, until the number of audio tracks in the session exceeds the total number of available voices. When the total number of audio tracks in the session exceeds the available voice count, lower priority tracks will not play back or record. When using dynamic voicing, Pro Tools automatically takes care of the voice management in the background, assigning voices not in use by other tracks.

Track priority, or which track gets a voice, is determined by a track's position in the session relative to the other tracks. The topmost track in the Edit window (or the leftmost track in the Mix window) gets the highest priority. When using previous generation Pro Tools|HD hardware only, track voices can also be assigned to an explicit voice number.

Note: With Pro Tools HD and Pro Tools software with Complete Production Toolkit, when recording using QuickPunch, TrackPunch, and DestructivePunch, additional voices are required. Also, on Pro Tools HD DSP-accelerated systems, the initial insert of a Native (host-based) plug-in on non-audio tracks uses additional voices as well.

Explicit Voice Assignment (Pro Tools|HD DSP Systems Only)

When using a Pro Tools|HD system with a limited voice count, you can conserve voices by sharing voices between multiple tracks. For instance, you may have two different stereo backing tracks that do not play back in the same location in the song. You might choose to place these music cues on separate tracks because, in addition to allowing different clip arrangements, they can then have different plug-in processing as well. Using the default DYN voice assignment, both tracks would utilize two voices each. However, when you assign each of the stereo music tracks to the same pair of voices, as long as there is no overlap between the clips on each track, all clips will play back in their entirety, sharing the same voice pair, thus conserving two voices for use elsewhere in the session. Conversely, if a clip overlap does occur between two or more audio tracks with the same explicit voice assignment, only the highest priority track will play during the overlap.

With Pro Tools|HD systems only, you can assign specific (or *explicit*) voices to multiple tracks, so that the same voices are shared by more than one track. This feature is called *voice borrowing*. For stereo and multichannel tracks, voices appear in pairs and multichannel groups. Voices already explicitly assigned to another track appear in bold in the Voice Selector's pop-up menu. The combination of playback/record tracks and shared voiced tracks comprises the total number of voiceable tracks on a Pro Tools|HD system.

Tip: With Pro Tools|HD, tracks assigned to a specific voice number take priority
      over dynamically allocated tracks and support voice borrowing.

Note: Elastic Audio and Native plug-ins are not allowed on explicitly voiced
       tracks (Pro Tools|HD only). Use only Dynamically Allocated Voicing (dyn)
       for tracks using Elastic Audio or Native plug-ins.

Note: On Pro Tools|HDX systems, explicit voice assignments do not exist. Instead,
       voices are always dynamically allocated automatically by the Pro Tools
       software.

To set the voice assignment for an audio track, you simply click the track's Voice
Selector and select Dyn, Off, or an explicit voice number (Pro Tools|HD hard-
ware only). See Figure 2.13.

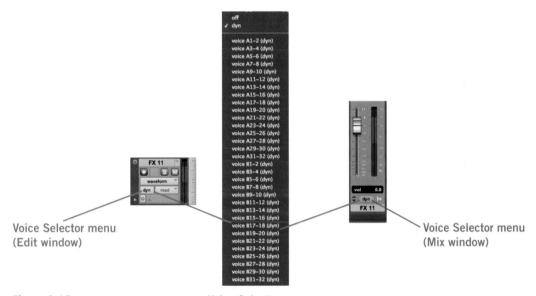

Voice Selector menu
(Edit window)

Voice Selector menu

Voice Selector menu
(Mix window)

Figure 2.13
Pro Tools|HD Voice Selector menu.

In Figure 2.14, two stereo music tracks (MX_01 and MX_02) are assigned to
(explicit) voices A7-8 (and share the same color for the clips). In the empty areas
of the MX_01 track, the audio clips on the MX_02 track will pop through and
play back. This allows you to effectively utilize more tracks in your session than
your maximum number of available voices. Where clips overlap on the MX_01
and MX_02 tracks, only the MX_01 track will play back. This is useful for when
you wish to have an alternate take or different version displayed in the Edit window but don't want the track to be audible.

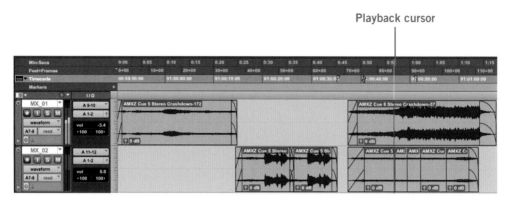

Figure 2.14
Only the MX_01 track is playing at the playback cursor.

Changing the Priority of Tracks

The lowest-numbered (highest priority) audio tracks that are active and have their voice assignment set to dyn (dynamic voicing) are the tracks that play back. (The total number of tracks that play back depends on the maximum number of voiced audio tracks allowed by your system.)

Tracks that are higher-numbered (lower priority) than those with a voice do not play back, and you cannot record to them. Also, their default DYN voice assignments are colored dark blue to indicate there are insufficient voices available for the track to play back or recording.

Note: Tracks do not play back or record when they are inactive, when their voice assignment is set to off, or when all available voices are allocated to higher priority tracks in the session.

If you have more tracks in your session than available voices (which is unlikely when using Pro Tools|HDX hardware), or if you have more than one track assigned to the same voice (Pro Tools|HD hardware only), Pro Tools will allocate the available voices to tracks according to their priority, as shown in Figure 2.15.

Figure 2.15
Audio tracks 257–260 will not play back or record because all available voices are allocated to higher priority tracks.

You can increase the priority of audio tracks in several ways:

- In the Edit window, drag the track up above other tracks in the session.

- In the Mix window, drag the track to the left of other tracks in the session.

- In the Track List, drag the track name to a higher position in the list.

You can free the voice in use by a track in several ways:

- Set the track's Voice selector to Off.

- Deactivate the track.

- Remove *all* of the track's output and send assignments.

- (Pro Tools|HD hardware systems only) If the Mute Frees Assigned Voice option is enabled in the Options menu, mute the track during playback.

Note: On Pro Tools|HD hardware systems only, enabling Mute Frees Assigned
Voice in the Options menu can cause a noticeable muting/soloing delay
on audio tracks, even with Extended Disk Cache enabled.

Deactivating Tracks

Audio tracks, Auxiliary Inputs, Master Faders, and Instrument tracks can be made inactive. Deactivating a track will free any DSP and Native resources (plug-ins, mixing) or voices used by the track. Tracks will automatically be made inactive if a session is opened on a system with fewer available voices and DSP processing power than the originating system.

 Since voices are primarily used by audio tracks, deactivating other types
of tracks (Aux Inputs, Instrument tracks, and Master Faders) will not
usually free voices in your session unless the track is using additional
voices as a result of Native plug-in usage. For more information about
how Native plug-in usage affects voice count on Pro Tools|HDX and Pro
Tools|HD systems, refer to Lesson 7.

To deactivate a track, do one of the following:

- Right-click the track nameplate in the Mix or Edit window and select MAKE INACTIVE, as shown in Figure 2.16.

Figure 2.16
Choosing Make Inactive in the right-click track menu.

- Select the track and select **TRACK > MAKE INACTIVE**. This is useful when you want to make a number of tracks inactive.

- **CONTROL+COMMAND-click** (Mac) or **CTRL+START-click** (Windows) on the track type icon in the Mix window. No confirmation dialog box will appear for this action, as shown in Figure 2.17.

Figure 2.17
Using modifier keys to deactivate a track.

- Click on the track type icon in the Mix window and select **MAKE INACTIVE** (see Figure 2.18). Click again and select **MAKE ACTIVE** to reactivate the track. This is useful when you want to make a single track inactive.

Figure 2.18
Click on a track icon to make the track inactive.

Playback Engine Advanced Options

As you learned in previous Pro Tools courses, the Playback Engine dialog box (shown in Figure 2.19) contains multiple settings that directly affect your Pro Tools system's performance. It is therefore useful to understand how these settings can be configured to correct playback or recording problems.

Optimizing Voice Count Settings (Pro Tools|HD DSP Systems Only)

As you learned earlier in this lesson, voice count determines the maximum number of audio tracks (disk tracks) that can play back or record simultaneously.

The maximum number of voices you can use is limited by your Pro Tools hardware and the sample rate of the session.

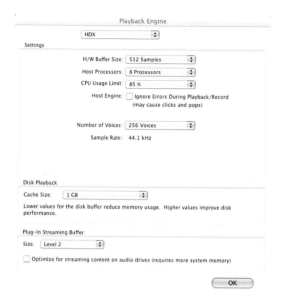

Figure 2.19
HDX PCIe card in the
Playback Engine dialog box.

Note: Refer to the *Pro Tools Reference Guide* for a detailed breakdown of voice
limits by hardware and sample rate.

If your session contains more audio tracks or Native plug-ins than the available
voices for your Pro Tools hardware allows, the error message seen in Figure 2.20
will appear.

Figure 2.20
Insufficient voice allocation warning.

Since Pro Tools|HDX hardware systems have much higher track counts than pre-
vious generation Pro Tools|HD hardware, it is unlikely that you will receive insuf-
ficient voice allocation warnings when using a Pro Tools|HDX hardware system.
If you do receive insufficient voice allocation warnings on a Pro Tools|HDX sys-
tem, increasing the Number of Voices setting (if possible) in the Playback Engine
dialog box will resolve the problem. If the voice count cannot be increased in the
Playback Engine dialog box, then the only remaining option that will resolve the
problem is to change the priority of tracks (as described in the previous section of
this lesson).

When using previous generation Pro Tools|HD hardware, insufficient voice allocations warnings are more common; this can be corrected by increasing the current voice allocation in the Playback Engine dialog box. However, this also increases the total DSP processing usage. Conversely, reducing the voice count on Pro Tools|HD hardware for sessions with unnecessarily high settings frees up DSP processing for other tasks. This is especially true on older HD systems containing a single HD Core card (HD1) or a single Core card with one Accel card (HD2), where available DSP chips are at a premium. Remember that DSP chips are used for voices on Pro Tools|HD hardware, whereas Pro Tools|HD Native and HDX use an FPGA for voices. When attempting to insert DSP plug-ins on a system that has insufficient available DSP-based processing power, the DAE –7204 error message seen in Figure 2.21 will appear.

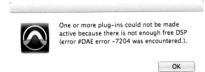

One or more plug-ins could not be made active because there is not enough free DSP (error #DAE error –7204 was encountered.).

OK

Figure 2.21
DAE Error –7204 warning.

Reducing voice count will provide more available processing power for DSP plug-ins on Pro Tools|HD, but it will also reduce PCI traffic for all Pro Tools|HDX and Pro Tools|HD hardware-based systems. This is useful in systems where there is a high level of PCI or FireWire activity caused by other resource-hungry devices being used with your Pro Tools HD cards (for example, Avid Mojo SDI or an Avid ISIS network).

Choosing the Number of DSPs for a Given Voice Count (Pro Tools|HD Hardware Only)

When using Pro Tools|HD hardware, the Number of Voices pop-up menu in the Playback Engine dialog box provides options to choose a number of combinations for voice counts and the number of DSPs used for voices. For example, you can run 96 voices using two, three, or even six DSPs. The reason for this is to enable a Pro Tools operator to optimize the way in which Pro Tools manages its data in different hardware configurations. Certain other PCIe cards in the computer may use the PCI bus in ways that interfere with Pro Tools, especially in large systems containing a PCIe video card or when an Avid ISIS network is used. When you assign high voice counts with fewer DSPs, PCI communication timing becomes more critical. In many situations, you should be able to use the most efficient voice count settings, that is, high voice count with low DSP usage. However, if Pro Tools reports DAE error –6042 (PCI bus too busy), then you can try raising the number of DSPs dedicated to voices.

To optimize the number of voices for the session, select the number of voices from the Playback Engine's Number of Voices pop-up menu, shown in Figure 2.22.

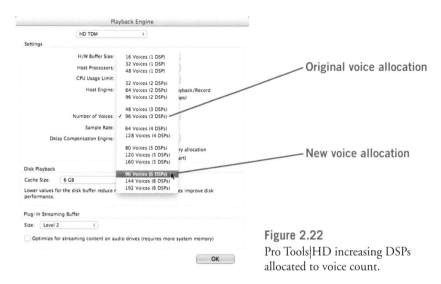

Figure 2.22
Pro Tools|HD increasing DSPs allocated to voice count.

Note: Pro Tools|HD Native and HDX hardware do not use DSPs for their fixed voice counts. However, high track count sessions may lead to PCI traffic errors when competing with other systems that share PCI bus bandwidth, such as the FireWire bus, Ethernet bus, and USB bus.

Disk Playback Cache Size (Pro Tools HD and Pro Tools with Complete Production Toolkit Only)

The Cache Size setting in the Playback Engine dialog box determines the amount of memory DAE allocates to manage disk buffers, affecting audio playback and elastic audio performance. In most cases, the default setting of Normal is an optimized cache size that works well for most sessions. This is the only option available unless you are using Pro Tools HD software or Pro Tools software with Complete Production Toolkit.

Pro Tools HD and Pro Tools software with Complete Production Toolkit let you load audio files used in Pro Tools sessions into RAM for cached playback. Pro Tools prioritizes files closest to the current playhead location. This way, when you start playback, those files are already cached for playback. This is especially useful when working with shared media storage (such as with Avid Unity MediaNetwork and ISIS shared storage systems), since it will improve system performance because it is not streaming as much media directly from the network during real-time playback.

Note: Although Pro Tools 10 now supports the use of any type of local or networked storage, not all storage solutions will work well with Pro Tools.

To determine the maximum amount of RAM available for Disk Cache, Pro Tools polls the computer for the amount of RAM installed and subtracts approximately 3GB with Mac systems or 4GB with Windows systems. (Note that Windows systems reserve more RAM for the system than Mac systems.) For example, if your computer has 10GB of RAM installed, the total amount of RAM available for the Disk Cache will be around 7GB (Mac) or 6GB (Windows) as shown in Figure 2.23.

To set the amount of RAM to be used by the Disk Cache:

1. Choose SETUP > PLAYBACK ENGINE.

2. From the CACHE SIZE selector, select the amount of RAM you want to allocate to the Disk Cache and then click OK. See Figure 2.23.

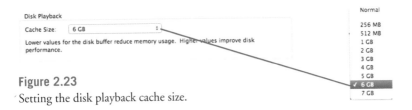

Figure 2.23
Setting the disk playback cache size.

Cache Meters in the System Usage Window

Pro Tools HD software and Complete Production Toolkit provide two additional meters in the System Usage window for monitoring Disk Cache: Disk Cache and Timeline Cached. These meters are present only if the Normal setting is changed to a fixed cache size in the Playback Engine dialog box.

Tip: To access the System Usage window in Pro Tools, select Window > System Usage.

■ **Disk Cache:** Indicates how much of the allocated Disk Cache is filled, as a percentage. For example, if the Cache Size in the Playback Engine is set to 1GB and a session uses 256MB of audio files, the Disk Cache meter reads 25%. If all of the audio in the session is cached (including files in the Clip List that are not on the timeline), the Disk Cache meter appears green.

■ **Timeline Cached:** Displays the amount of audio in the session timeline cached in RAM. If the selected Cache Size in the Playback Engine is the same or greater than the amount of audio on the timeline, the Timeline Cache meter reads 100% and appears green (indicating that all of the audio on the timeline is cached in RAM). This is useful for letting you know how much audio can still be added to the timeline and be cached in RAM.

If the total amount of audio in the timeline is more than the selected cache size in the Playback Engine, the Timeline Cached meter shows the percentage of audio on the timeline that is cached in RAM (see Figure 2.24). For example, if the selected cache size in the Playback Engine is 256MB and the amount of audio on the timeline is 1GB, the Timeline Cached meter reads 25% and appears yellow.

Note: The Disk Cache and Timeline Cached meters are not available in the System Usage window when the disk playback cache size in the Playback Engine dialog box is set to Normal.

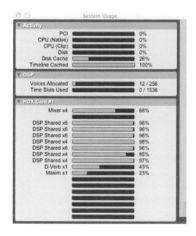

Figure 2.24
System Usage window showing Disk Cache and Timeline Cached meters with 6GB Cache Size setting.

Tip: You can use the cache meters in the System Usage window to determine whether to assign more or less RAM to the Disk Cache for the current session.

The disk playback cache size defaults to Normal, which works well for smaller sessions. However, when session track counts exceed the maximum recommended number of tracks per hard disk (usually above 32–48 tracks), the DAE error –9073 (disk too slow) warning may appear. This warning indicates that the session's hard disk cannot provide the required data throughput rate necessary to play back or record all of the session's tracks. Increasing the disk playback cache size will correct the problem by allowing Pro Tools to cache audio to RAM.

Table 2.2 lists some general guidelines for allocating higher and lower Disk Cache settings in the Playback Engine dialog box for resolving some playback and recording issues.

Table 2.2   Disk Cache Settings Guidelines

Disk Cache Setting	Advantages	Disadvantages
Normal	Pro Tools dynamically allocates Disk Cache RAM automatically based on the number of tracks in the session.	Pro Tools does not buffer as much audio in RAM, so high track count sessions could cause disk playback errors. Also higher disk usage in the System Usage window.
User Selected Fixed RAM Amount	More of the session's timeline audio is loaded into RAM, providing better performance in high track count sessions and sessions utilizing networked storage.	Utilizes more of the computer's total available system RAM.

Note: Video files are not cached with audio files when using Extended Disk Cache and are always streamed from hard disk. This can cause the system to not be as fast and responsive as one might expect, even when 100% of the timeline is cached in RAM.

Monitoring DSP Resources (Pro Tools|HDX and Pro Tools|HD Systems Only)

In the previous section of this lesson, you learned how the System Usage window is used to monitor the Disk Cache settings you configured in the Playback Engine dialog box. For Pro Tools|HDX and Pro Tools|HD system, the System Usage window also provides DSP usage gauges that help you monitor the DSP usage on your system. See Figure 2.25.

■ **Voices Allocated:** Displays the total number of disk voices that can be allocated and the number of voices currently allocated. This includes all voices, whether they are allocated explicitly or dynamically, as well as any voices used for routing Native plug-in processing.

■ **Time Slots Used (Pro Tools|HD):** Time slots are like patch points on a patch bay. Pro Tools|HD uses Time Slots for passing signals between DSPs. The Time Slot gauge displays a total number of 512 time slots available and the number of time slots currently used.

■ **Time Slots (Pro Tools|HDX):** Pro Tools|HDX hardware uses time slots differently than Pro Tools|HD hardware. Pro Tools|HDX hardware uses "crossbars" to move data between DSP chips on the HDX card. When moving data between cards in a multiple card system, time slots are used as a dedicated multiplexed bus (via the HDX TDM cable) for intercard communication. Therefore, in a single HDX card system (or when a second or third HDX card is "idle"), no time slots will be used, and the System Usage Time Slots meter will display 0/1536.

■ **DSP Usage:** For Pro Tools|HDX or Pro Tools|HD DSP hardware, this meter displays (in percent) how much of the total system's DSP processing power card is currently being used for mixing and DSP processing.

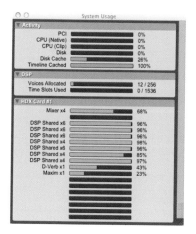
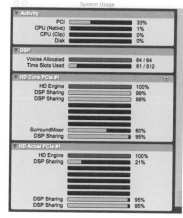

Figure 2.25
System Usage window using a single Pro Tools|HDX PCIe card (left) and Pro Tools|HD Core/Accel PCIe cards (right).

Monitoring Native Resources (Recap)

As you learned in previous Pro Tools 100-level and 200-level courses, the System Usage window also includes activity meters that indicate how much of your system's CPU processing power is being used to process Native audio plug-ins, process Elastic Audio, and write and play back automation and MIDI.

Very rarely does automation, MIDI, or non-DSP activity by itself cause DAE errors, although high track count sessions containing dense areas of automation can cause CPU overload and errors that are not the result of Native plug-in processing. Pro Tools provides separate meters allowing you to monitor the processing activity hitting the main processors.

To monitor the usage of Native resources during a Pro Tools session, choose Window > System Usage (see Figure 2.26).

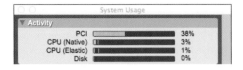

Figure 2.26
System Usage window activity meters.

The System Usage window includes the following meters related to Native resource usage:

- **CPU (Native):** Displays the amount of CPU processing activity for host-based plug-in processing, as well as automation and MIDI playback.

- **CPU (Elastic):** Displays the amount of processing activity for real-time Elastic Audio processing and clip gain.

- **Disk:** Displays the amount of hard disk processing activity.

As these meters approach their limits, host processing and recording or playback of audio, MIDI, and automation data can be affected. If CPU or PCI activity is high, a system error may occur. If disk activity is high, Pro Tools may play automation data late (plug-in automation being the most susceptible), such as while using the Bounce to Disk command, and result in a DAE error.

To reduce CPU processing load in a session, do some of the following:

- Reduce the density of automation in places where it shows the most activity.

- Turn off meters in Sends view, if enabled (by deselecting Show Meters in Sends View in the Display Preferences page).

- Reduce the number of instances of Native plug-ins, or convert the Native plug-ins to DSP plug-ins.

- Reduce the overall amount of Elastic Audio real-time processing by switching to rendered processing.

Advanced Pro Tools I/O Setup

In the Pro Tools 110 and Pro Tools 201 courses, you learned how the I/O Setup window can be used to configure and manage the various interface and bus path assignments in your sessions. This section discusses how to exchange sessions between Pro Tools HD software-based systems that do not have identical audio interfaces.

Remapping

Where possible, when a session is opened on a system with different I/O, session paths are reassigned to the currently available hardware.

For example, a session that was recorded using a Pro Tools|HD-series hardware system and a single 192 I/O audio interface and a single 96 I/O interface would include 32 output paths spread across the two 16-channel interfaces. If that session were taken to a different Pro Tools HD system, such as an HD I/O-based system, the first 16 outputs would be mapped to the HD I/O's available output channels, as shown in Figure 2.27.

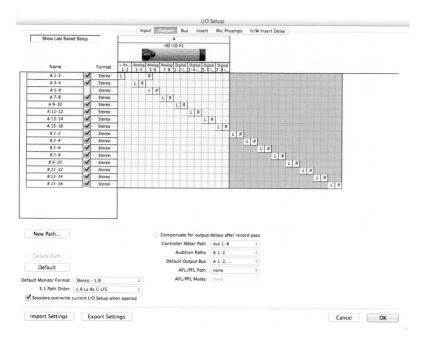

Figure 2.27
Output paths remapped on an HD I/O system.

Unavailable I/O is shown in dark gray. Any tracks assigned to unavailable output paths will have the output paths grayed out and inaudible. If the automatic remapping is not suitable to your session's requirements, you can manually shift paths to more appropriate I/O and make unused paths inactive.

Show Last Saved Setup

When I/O remapping has occurred, the Show Last Saved Setup button appears in the top left corner of the I/O Setup window. Clicking on this button displays the audio interfaces used in the original session. This temporary display lets you check the original I/O configuration for reference when reconfiguring the session for your system, even if the session came from a different version of Pro Tools or from a different Pro Tools hardware platform. See Figure 2.28.

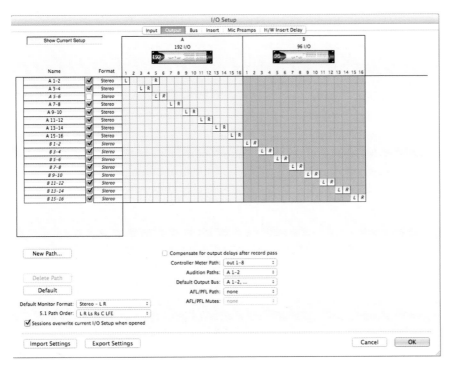

Figure 2.28
Show Last Saved I/O Setup.

Sessions Overwrite Current I/O Setup When Opened

The Sessions Overwrite Current I/O Setup When Opened option (introduced in Pro Tools 8.1) was added to the I/O Setup dialog box, in order to solve session interchange issues (such as maintaining studio settings on different Pro Tools systems) and to provide better overall workflows for session interchange. This setting determines whether the current input, output, insert, mic preamps, and hardware insert delay settings configured on your system will be overwritten by any of the I/O settings stored within a session, when opened.

Because different Pro Tools systems often use different channel outputs for speakers, disabling this checkbox will allow you to replace the original settings, mappings, and input/output assignments saved with the session with your own studio's default settings, mappings, and input/output assignments. See Figure 2.29.

☐ Sessions overwrite current I/O Setup when opened

Figure 2.29
Sessions overwrite current I/O Setup when opened option from I/O Setup (disabled).

In versions of Pro Tools earlier than Pro Tools 8.1, I/O settings are recalled from the Pro Tools session document, so studio settings corresponding to your hardware could potentially change each time a session is opened, resulting in a temporary loss of audio monitoring paths. In the most recent versions of Pro Tools, I/O settings such as Input, Output, Insert, Mic Preamps, and H/W Insert Delay can be recalled from the system, while busses are always saved and recalled with the session file. Since busses are specific to the mixer configuration in Pro Tools, you want to retain your bussing when you open a session on any system. The ability to apply your studio's system settings to any session you open, while maintaining the bussing configuration saved with the session, allows you to quickly and easily exchange sessions between many different Pro Tools systems.

- **Sessions Overwrite Current I/O Setup When Opened (disabled by default)**: Disabling this setting is the recommended default setting when exchanging sessions with other Pro Tools systems running Pro Tools version 8.1 or higher. When disabled, Pro Tools recalls I/O assignments from the system (rather than the session), with all output bus paths of the session automatically remapping to the system output paths. Disabling this option allows you to overwrite the session's I/O settings and apply your preferred studio I/O assignments, names, and routings, allowing you to maintain your studio output monitoring path assignments for any sessions you open.

Tip: Enabling or disabling the Sessions Overwrite Current I/O Setup When Opened option in any page of the I/O Setup dialog box affects all of the other pages as well.

- **Sessions Overwrite Current I/O Setup When Opened (enabled)**: Recommended for session compatibility with Pro Tools sessions earlier than Pro Tools 8.1. When enabled, Pro Tools recalls I/O assignments, names, and routings from the session file (rather than the system), with the output bus paths of the session remaining mapped to the output paths saved with the session. When enabled, any custom settings saved with the session that do not match your system may need to be reconfigured in the I/O Setup dialog box. Be aware that using this option uses the originating session's I/O Setup mappings, ignoring your default system I/O Setup mappings (inputs, outputs, busses, and so on).

Tip: Due to changes in the I/O Setup window bussing options first introduced in Pro Tools 8.1, it is recommended that you enable the Sessions Overwrite Current I/O Setup When Opened option for legacy Pro Tools session behavior and full compatibility with Pro Tools sessions created in software versions earlier than 8.1. When exchanging sessions with other Pro Tools systems running Pro Tools 8.1 or higher, this option should be disabled. This option is disabled by default.

Review/Discussion Questions

1. What is the DigiTest utility used for?

2. What Avid Audio products are supported by DigiTest?

3. What is Knowledge Base used for?

4. How do you update an Avid SYNC HD's firmware?

5. What is hardware firmware?

6. What are the 5 key Pro Tools preference files?

7. Where are DigiBase index database files for volumes stored, and why is it sometimes necessary to delete them?

8. How many audio tracks can exist in a session?

9. What are "explicit voices" and which Pro Tools systems support them?

10. How is the Disk Cache setting in the Playback Engine dialog box useful?

11. What is affected by checking/enabling the Sessions Overwrite Current I/O Setup When Opened checkbox?

Troubleshooting a Pro Tools System

In this exercise, you will use the Avid Online Knowledge Base to find possible causes and solutions to several common errors. You will open a Pro Tools session with missing media and other problems that must be corrected. After correcting the problems with the session, you will import I/O settings and replace the IO labels with your own.

Media Used:

310M Exercise 02.PTXT (Pro Tools session file)

Duration:

30 minutes

GOALS

- Use Avid Knowledge Base to investigate error messages
- Learn to use DigiTest
- Open and play a session
- Import I/O setup pages

Getting Started: Using Avid Knowledge Base

Assuming you have a computer with an Internet connection, use the Avid Online Knowledge Base to try to find possible causes of and solutions to the errors listed in Table Ex2.1 when using Pro Tools 10.x (or higher).

Tip: Feel free to write on a separate piece of paper instead of writing in your book.

Table Ex2.1   Pro Tools Error Messages

Error	Possible Cause	Solution
Pro Tools failure to launch	_____	_____
DAE Error –36	_____	_____
DAE Error –9073	_____	_____
DAE Error –909x	_____	_____

Using DigiTest

If you have never run DigiTest on your hardware, you should do so now.

1. Quit Pro Tools if it's open.

2. Navigate to the **PRO TOOLS UTILITIES** folder on your system (located one subfolder below where Pro Tools is installed).

3. Be sure to lower the volume on your monitoring system, as DigiTest can sometimes emit full code, or loud pops when running.

4. Launch **DIGITEST**. The main DigiTest screen will appear as shown in Figure Ex2.1.

5. Click the **RUN** button. The test will take approximately eight minutes for each HDX card, four minutes for each Pro Tools|HD card, and a few moments for the Pro Tools|HD Native card.

Figure Ex2.1
DigiTest main screen.

Opening and Playing a Session

1. Open **310M EXERCISE 02.PTXT**, located on the book DVD at directory:

   EXERCISE MEDIA/310M CLASS FILES V10/310M EXERCISE 02
   (or other location specified by the course instructor).

2. In the **SAVE NEW SESSION AS** dialog box, name the session as desired, saving into an appropriate location on a valid storage volume.

When the session opens, a basic session structure will be displayed. Be aware there are no effects, the song has not been mixed, tracks are labeled incorrectly, tracks are sometimes out of order, and the labeling may not make sense. This can be a common issue when receiving files from another Pro Tools system. Your first task as a Pro Tools Expert is to put the session right, including the following:

1. Play and familiarize yourself with the session.

2. Rename the **CHOIR** tracks to **HEAVY GUITARS**.

3. Open the I/O setup window (**SETUP > I/O**), click the **BUS** tab, and delete all busses. Click **OK** to confirm delete.

4. Click **DEFAULT** (or press **COMMAND+D** [Mac] or **CTRL+D** [Windows]) to use the default busses and click **OK**. You can choose to rename the main stereo output path or leave it as is. Close the I/O Setup window when you're finished.

5. Use Pro Tools' **ROUTE TO TRACK** function in the **OUTPUT** tab of each track to reroute tracks to their appropriate submasters. This will conveniently rename all I/O bus labels to what is actually used in the session. Then route the submasters to the main monitors.

6. For the Acoustic Guitar tracks, use the **ROUTE TO NEW TRACK** function, creating a stereo Aux Input track in the process.

7. Lower all tracks that are clipping. Lower groups of tracks so that the submasters are not clipping.

Tip: Remember, it is always preferred to lower the source tracks feeding an auxiliary submaster rather than lower the auxiliary submaster to keep gain stages in order. Remember that inserts are pre-fader on the auxiliary sub master, meaning you could be clipping the input to a plug-in and not know it from the output level of the auxiliary submaster.

8. When you can play back the session with all tracks playing and nothing clipped, save the session (but do not close it).

Importing I/O Setup Pages

Your last task is to import a specific page of I/O setup. The input labels on the session do not correspond to anything meaningful. An I/O setup file has been supplied to replace the inputs with labels of a hypothetical studio. As a Pro Tools Expert, you should get into the habit of keeping a global I/O setup for your entire studio and replacing specific I/O pages when necessary.

1. Open the I/O Setup window (choose **SETUP > I/O**). Click the **INPUTS** tab (or press **COMMAND+1** [Mac] or **CTRL+1** [Windows]).

2. Highlight all paths (**COMMAND+A** [Mac] or **CTRL+A** [Windows]) and delete all paths (**BACKSPACE/DELETE**). Next, you will import a hypothetical input list.

3. Click **IMPORT SETTINGS** and navigate to the **EXERCISE 2 SESSION** folder that you previously copied from the DVD.

4. Select the **INPUTS ONLY.PIO** file. All input labels should now be changed.

Lesson 3

Tactile Control of Pro Tools

This lesson describes how a standard alphanumeric keyboard can be used to greatly increase the speed with which you use Pro Tools.

Media Used: None

Duration: 45 minutes

GOALS

- Understand the theory and application of modifier keys
- Understand Keyboard Focus shortcuts and use them in practice
- Understand and control the Keyboard Focus mode
- Understand the usefulness of different numeric keypad modes

Introduction

Using a keyboard to access the functions you use regularly increases both speed and precision. As you become more familiar with Pro Tools (and dedicated to implementing these shortcuts into your workflow), you will start to develop "strings" of key combinations that will allow you to "touch-type" routine tasks. Just like standard typing, becoming efficient at controlling Pro Tools with an alphanumeric keyboard requires time and practice. In this lesson, you'll explore seldom used keyboard commands, review the general theory behind modifiers, and learn Focus key functions you may have not known even existed in Pro Tools.

Tip: It is highly recommended to use an extended keyboard while reviewing this chapter and performing the associated exercise. This chapter relies heavily on the numeric keypad of an extended keyboard for numbers and special characters (*, /, +/-, etc). Also note, numeric keypad numbers are referred to in brackets (e.g., [3]) whereas alphanumberic keyboard numbers do not have brackets (e.g., 3).

Parts of the Keyboard

There are four ways to access Pro Tools functions on an extended keyboard:

- Modifier keys
- Focus keys
- Function keys
- Numeric keypad

This lesson is divided into sections focused on each of these areas. Take time in each section to think about how to apply these shortcuts to your everyday workflows.

Modifier Keys

As you have encountered in lower-level Pro Tools books in the Avid Learning Series, many keyboard shortcuts in Pro Tools use *modifier keys*. By holding modifier keys while performing a key press or mouse action, you can access a variety of Pro Tools functions. Although keyboard modifiers are available on both Macintosh and Windows platforms, they have different names. Once you are familiar with which Macintosh and Windows modifier keys are equivalent, using keyboard shortcuts on either platform will be second nature, regardless of the platform you started on.

Many common modifier and key combination listings are directly available through Pro Tools by clicking on the menu Help > Keyboard Commands. However, numerous key combinations do not have menu equivalents and some are contextual in nature.

Modifier Keys and Menus

One use of modifier keys is to access menu functions. Many menu functions, but not all, that have a keyboard shortcut will have the key combination listed to the right of the function within the menu. See Figure 3.1.

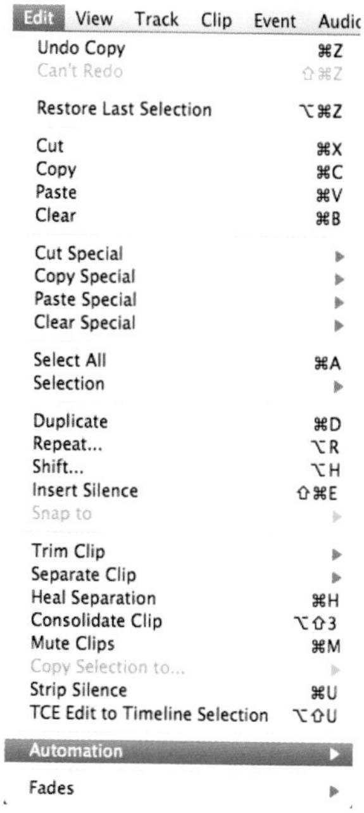

Figure 3.1

Edit menu with modifier key equivalents.

Modifier Keys and Track Parameters

A number of functions are accessed by holding down modifier keys while clicking on track controls in the mixer or while changing track parameters. These functions include the following:

- Modifiers that allow you to change a parameter across a number of tracks simultaneously

- Modifiers that change parameters on tracks containing the Edit cursor

- Modifiers that change the state or display of a parameter when clicked

Changing Parameters on Multiple Tracks Simultaneously

As you have encountered in previous courses, the Option key (Mac) or Alt key (Windows) is the root modifier for applying changes to all/multiple tracks at the same time. For example, Option/Alt-clicking on the Record Enable button on any audio track will attempt to place all audio tracks into Record Ready mode. The following parameters and track functions behave in this way:

- Mute and Solo buttons

- Record Enable and TrackInput Monitor buttons

- Input and Output assignments

- Send assignments

- Voice assignments

- Plug-in/Insert assignments

- Automation modes

- Meter Clips (clearing)

- Volume/Peak/Delay display mode assignments

- Track height (Edit window)

- Track View display (Waveform, Pan, Automation, and so on, in the Edit window)

- Playlist pop-up selectors

To apply a parameter change to all tracks, you simply Option-click (Mac) or Alt-click (Windows) on the appropriate parameter control or pop-up selector on any track.

Tip: When using the Option/Alt modifier, only tracks of the same type will be affected. For example, holding Option/Alt while changing an output of a mono audio track will affect only mono audio tracks in the session.

To apply a parameter change to a selection of tracks:

1. Select all the tracks you want to be affected.

2. OPTION+SHIFT-CLICK (Mac) or ALT+SHIFT-CLICK (Windows) on the parameter control or pop-up selector on any of the selected tracks.

Changing Parameters on Tracks Containing the Edit Cursor

Pro Tools includes a collection of commands that allow you to toggle the Record Enable state, TrackInput Monitoring mode, and Mute and Solo status across all tracks containing the Edit cursor. These key commands act as toggles, meaning repeat presses alternate between enabling and disabling the action.

To apply a track status change to all tracks containing the Edit cursor:

1. Place the **EDIT** cursor within all tracks you want to change. A quick way to do this is to click and drag through the tracks with the **SELECTOR TOOL**. To add the **EDIT** cursor to non-adjacent tracks, **SHIFT-CLICK** within the Edit playlist for each desired track. If **LINK TRACK AND EDIT SELECTION** is enabled, you can also simply select tracks to add them to the Edit selection.

2. Hold **SHIFT** and press the appropriate alpha key for the parameter to toggle. Each key is simply the first letter of the parameter, as listed in Table 3.1. See Figure 3.2.

Table 3.1 Keyboard Shortcuts for Common Tasks

Keyboard Shortcut	Parameter Toggled on Tracks Containing Edit Cursor
Shift+R	Record Enable
Shift+I	TrackInput Monitoring Mode
Shift+M	Track Mute
Shift+S	Track Solo

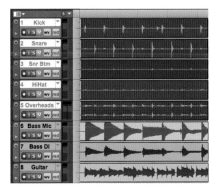

Figure 3.2
Muting multiple tracks with the Shift+M modifier.

Table 3.2 lists special functions accessed by clicking with a modifier key.

Table 3.2   Changing Parameter States

Mac	Windows	Parameter	Behavior
Command	Ctrl	Record Arm	Initiate Safe Mode
Command	Ctrl	Solo	Solo Safe
Command	Ctrl	Plug-ins in Inserts view	Bypass Toggle
Command	Ctrl	Send Name (Assignments or Single Send View)	Send Mute Toggle
Command	Ctrl	Track data display	Toggle volume/peak/delay display
Command	Ctrl	Volume, Pan, Plug-in parameter, Send level, Automation playlist	Fine resolution mouse control
Command	Ctrl	Send assignment pop-up selector	Switch to Single Send view or between Send Assignment views (depending on current state)
Option	Alt	Volume, Pan, Plug-in parameter, Send level	Set to default value
Option+Command	Ctrl+Alt	Input/output assignments, Send assignments, Interface input and output assignments in I/O setup	Cascade paths (selects ascending I/O assignments for all tracks starting with the track you change). Add Shift to affect selected tracks only.

Focus Keys

The Keyboard Focus system in Pro Tools assigns a vast array of functions to the main alphanumeric section of your keyboard. Each of these functions can be accessed with a single keypress; you don't need to hold down a modifier key. The keyboard can be focused on one of several areas of the Pro Tools user interface. Each focus mode maps the keys to a different set of functions.

Pro Tools provides three Keyboard Focus modes:

- **Commands Focus**—Provides single-key shortcuts from the alphanumeric keyboard for editing, navigation, and playback. This is the mode used much of the time in Pro Tools.

- **Clip List Focus**—Allows clips and clip groups to be located and selected in the Clip List by typing the first few letters of a clip's name.

- **Group List Focus**—Allows Edit and Mix groups to be enabled/disabled by typing a group's corresponding ID letter.

Assigning Keyboard Focus

You can set the Keyboard Focus mode using the mouse or using keyboard shortcuts. To set the Keyboard Focus with the mouse, you simply click the a–z button for the focus you want to enable, as shown in Figure 3.3.

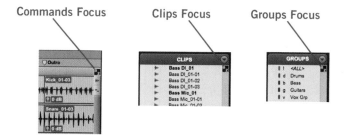

Figure 3.3
Keyboard Focus buttons.

To switch between the different Keyboard Focus modes using keyboard shortcuts, press Option+Command (Mac) or Ctrl+Alt (Windows) and numbers 1–3 on the alpha keyboard.

Table 3.3 shows the shortcut for each focus button.

Table 3.3   Shortcuts for Changing Keyboard Focus

Mac	Windows	Behavior
Option+Command+1	Ctrl+Alt+1	Activates Commands Keyboard Focus
Option+Command+2	Ctrl+Alt+2	Activates Clip List Keyboard Focus
Option+Command+3	Ctrl+Alt+3	Activates Group List Keyboard Focus

Note: You can enable only one Keyboard Focus at a time. Enabling a Keyboard Focus will disable the previously selected one.

Active Window for Keyboard Focus

Keyboard Focus mode shortcuts are always directed toward the active window in the software interface. The windows that support Keyboard Focus commands are the Edit window, Mix window, MIDI Editor windows, and the docked MIDI Editor window.

Not all Keyboard Focus modes are available in each window type:

- **Edit window**—All three modes are available.

- **Mix window**—Group List Focus only.

- **MIDI Editor windows**—Commands Focus and Group List Focus.

- **Docked MIDI Editor**—Commands Focus only.

Different Focus modes can be set in each open window. For example, the Edit window may have Clip List Focus selected at the same time that a MIDI Editor window has Commands Focus selected. However, only the active window (highlighted title bar) will respond to Focus shortcuts. To make a window active, click on it, or use a window selection shortcut—such as Command+= (Mac) or Ctrl+= (Windows)—to toggle between windows.

Edit Window with the Docked MIDI Editor

When the docked MIDI Editor is present in the Edit window, two distinct areas in the Edit window can respond to Commands Focus keys and toolbar shortcuts. These areas behave similarly to two separate windows, with only one active at any time for the purposes of Commands Focus and toolbar shortcuts. The active section is indicated by a yellow outline around its toolbar. See Figure 3.4.

Has yellow highlight indicating it is the focused editor for key commands

Figure 3.4
Docked MIDI Editor focused for shortcuts and Commands Focus keys.

Tip: If Group List or Clip List Focus is selected in the Edit window, they will remain active whether the docked MIDI Editor is focused or not.

Switching Focus Between the Docked MIDI Editor and the Main Edit Window

Clicking anywhere in the docked MIDI Editor will focus it for keyboard shortcuts; clicking elsewhere in the Edit window returns focus to the main area. There are also two keyboard shortcuts for switching focus, as shown in Table 3.4. These follow on from the main focus selection shortcuts from Table 3.3 (which are included again here in italics).

Table 3.4 Switching Focus Between Edit and MIDI Editor Windows

Mac	Windows	Behavior
Option+Command+1	*Ctrl+Alt+1*	*Activates Commands Keyboard Focus*
Option+Command+2	*Ctrl+Alt+2*	*Activates Clip List Keyboard Focus*
Option+Command+3	*Ctrl+Alt+3*	*Activates Group List Keyboard Focus*
Option+Command+4	Ctrl+Alt+4	Moves focus to the Edit window from the MIDI Editor
Option+Command+5	Ctrl+Alt+5	Moves focus to the MIDI Editor from the Edit window

Shortcuts That Follow Edit Window Focus

The shortcuts listed next can be re-focused to the docked MIDI Editor.

Commands Focus Functions

■ Most single-key functions described in the following section also apply to the MIDI Editor.

Tip: Some commands are only relevant to audio clips (such as fades) so they are not applicable in MIDI Editor views.

Toolbar Functions

■ Edit Tool selection

■ Edit Mode selection

■ Grid and Nudge Value selection

Navigation and View Functions

■ Zooming

■ Paging (Page Up/Down, and so on)

■ Track Heights (automation lanes only in MIDI Editor)

Commands Keyboard Focus Mode Shortcuts

Commands Keyboard Focus mode enables all the single-key functions that are printed on custom Pro Tools keyboards (such as the optional built-in Pro Tools keyboard on a D-Control). The Commands Focus keys are color-coded into groups of keys with related functions, as follows (see Figure 3.5):

- **Yellow**: Zoom, Display, and Numeric time-entry functions

- **Pink**: Edit functions (fades are typically a different color but still considered edit functions)

- **Blue**: Transport and Locate functions

- **Green**: MIDI functions

- **Peach/Orange**: Tool or Mode selection

- **Red**: Record functions

Figure 3.5
Keyboard with color-coded shortcuts based on function.

Tip: With Commands Keyboard Focus disabled, you can still access the same set of functions by pressing Control (Mac) or Start (Windows) along with the associated alpha key.

Note: The numeric keypad functions are determined by the Numeric Keypad operation preference and are not affected by enabling/disabling Commands Keyboard Focus mode.

Zoom and Numeric Time-Entry Functions

These yellow color-coded Commands Focus keys allow single-key zooming and numeric time-entry. The zoom and numeric entry functions are shown in Figure 3.6. Table 3.5 lists the zoom and numeric entry command functions.

Figure 3.6
Commands Focus keyboard shortcuts: Zoom and Numeric Entry.

Table 3.5   Zoom and Numeric Command Functions

Key(s)	Function	Notes
1, 2, 3, 4, 5	Recall Zoom Presets	Zoom values must be stored with the mouse and software.
- (minus)	Track View Toggle	Toggles the track view between two different states: • Audio tracks: Toggles between Waveform and Volume views. • MIDI/Instrument tracks: Toggles between Notes and Clips views.* • VCA tracks: Toggles between Volume and Trim value • Aux/Master tracks: N/A.
= (Alphanumeric)	Capture Timecode	Auto-enters the current incoming LTC timecode when a timecode field is highlighted in a dialog box (such as Spot mode start time)
= (Numeric Keypad)	Capture Timecode	Same as previous but when no timecode is being received, activates the Main Counter in the Edit window for numeric entry (similar to * on the numeric keypad).
E	Zoom Toggle	Activates Zoom Toggle based on your preferences.
R, T	Zoom In/Out	Zooms waveforms and MIDI data horizontally in/out.
/ (Keypad)	Start/End/Length	Activates numeric entry for the Start/End/Length fields in the Edit window.
* (Keypad)	Enter Main Time	Activates the Main Counter in the Edit window for numeric entry.

* Track View Toggle: On MIDI or Instrument tracks, switches between Notes and Clips (non-Zoom Toggle mode) or Notes and Velocity (Zoom Toggle mode).

Edit Functions

The pink color-coded Commands Focus keys allow single-key access to various edit functions (see Figure 3.7). Table 3.6 lists the editing shortcuts.

Figure 3.7
Command Key Focus editing shortcuts.

Note: Several of the pink keys require that the Timeline and Edit selection be unlinked in order to work.

Table 3.6   Edit Command Functions

Key(s)	Function	Notes
A and S	Clip Trim	Trims clip to current cursor location: • A = Trim Start to Insertion • S = Trim End to Insertion
D,F,G	Fade In/Out/Crossfade	Fades a clip in/out based on the current cursor location. When clips overlap, the F key crossfades the clips together. These commands use the fade preset curve and duration from Preferences.
X,C,V	Cut, Copy, Paste	Standard cut, copy, and paste using single keystrokes.
B	Separate Clip	Separates (breaks) clips at current cursor location.
N	Insertion Follows Playback	Places the Edit Insertion cursor where playback is stopped.*
, and .	Nudge Forward/Back	Nudges forward or back by nudge amount.
+ and -	Nudge Forward/Back	Nudges forward or back by nudge amount.
M and /	Nudge by Next Value	Nudges forward or back by the next larger nudge value in Nudge List.

Table 3.6   Edit Command Functions *(continued)*

Key(s)	Function	Notes
Up/Down	Mark In/Out	Moves the mark in/out point during playback.
H,J,K	Snap Clip	Snaps the selected clip to timeline location**:
		• H = Snap head of clip to the cursor
		• J = Snap clip sync point to the cursor
		• K = Snap tail of clip to the cursor
Y,U,I	Snap Clip to Timecode	Snaps the selected clip to incoming timecode***:
		• Y = Snap head of clip to current timecode location
		• U = Snap clip sync point to current timecode location
		• I = Snap tail of clip to current timecode location

* Insertion Follows Playback is also represented by an icon in the toolbar in Pro Tools 9 and later. See Figure 3.8.

** Requires that the Timeline and Edit selections be unlinked.

*** Requires that incoming timecode be present (also Timeline and Edit selection recommended to be unlinked).

Figure 3.8
Insertion Follows Playback toggle on/off.

The Snap to Play keys (H, J, and K) move the currently selected clip(s) to the timeline cursor position. These keys allow you to snap a single clip or a whole group of clips to a new location, which you can't do with the standard Snap technique (that is, Control-click on Mac, Start-click on Windows). This advanced way of moving clips to timeline locations works only if the Edit and Timeline selections are unlinked.

To snap a collection of clips to a new location:

1. Unlink the Timeline and Edit selections by clicking the **LINK TIMELINE AND EDIT SELECTION** button in the Edit window toolbar to disable it, as shown in Figure 3.9.

Link Timeline and Edit Selection button

Figure 3.9
Link/Unlink Timeline and Edit Selection button in the toolbar.

2. Select all the clips you want to move. Use the **OBJECT GRABBER** to select non-continuous clips.

3. Place the cursor in a Timebase ruler at the position where you want the group of clips to start. (Note: Do not click in a track playlist.)

4. Press the **H** key (**SNAP START TO PLAY**). All the clips will be shifted so that the first clip begins at the new time. The **J** and **K** keys also work with multiple clips.

Navigation and Transport Functions

The blue color-coded Commands Focus keys allow single-key access for navigation and transport functions (see Figure 3.10). Table 3.7 lists these command functions.

Figure 3.10
Navigation and Transport keyboard focus keys.

Note: Several of the blue keys require that the Timeline and Edit selection be unlinked in order to work.

Tip: The numeric keypad Transport shortcuts listed in Table 3.8 are independent of Commands Keyboard Focus mode and are instead enabled when the Operation Page Preference's Numeric Keypad mode is set to Transport (see the "Numeric Keypad" section later in this lesson).

Table 3.7 Navigation and Transport Command Functions

Key(s)	Function	Notes
Q and W	Center Timeline Selection	Centers the current Timeline selection start (Q) or end (W) in the center of the Edit window.
Left and Right Arrow	Center Edit Selection	Centers the current Edit selection start (Left Arrow) or end (Right Arrow) in the Edit window.
[	Play Edit Selection	Plays the current Edit selection.
]	Play Timeline Selection	Plays the current Timeline selection.
P and semicolon (;) L and single quote (')	Navigation keys	Moves the cursor up/down tracks (P/;), or to previous/next clip boundaries (L/')*.
6, 7, 8, 9	Audition keys	Plays a short duration of audio based on the pre/post-roll amount (see the "Audition Commands" section later in this lesson).
Spacebar/[0]	Play/Stop	The numeric [0] can be used as a separate stop play command, as set in preferences.
[1] [2]	FF/REW	Numeric [1] activates Rewind; numeric [2] activates Fast Forward; to hear audio during FF/REW, select the option in preferences.
[4]	Enable Loop Playback	Toggles Loop Playback On/Off.
[5]	Enable Loop Record	Toggles Loop Record On/Off.
[6]	Enable QuickPunch	Toggles QuickPunch On/Off.
[.]	Recall Memory Location	Type period, memory location number, period on the numeric keypad to recall.
[Enter]	Store Memory Location	Press Enter for next available memory location or press period, memory location number, [Enter] to store a specific memory location.
[3] & F12	Immediate Record	Enables record on the transport and starts recording immediately.

* Moves to next transient if Tab to Transients is enabled.

Table 3.8   Navigation and Transport Command Functions

Function	Focus Key	Mac	Windows
Play up to edit start by the pre-roll amount	6	Option+Left Arrow	Alt+Left Arrow
Play from edit start by the post-roll amount	7	Command+Left Arrow	Ctrl+Left Arrow
Play up to edit end by the pre-roll amount	8	Option+Right Arrow	Alt+Right Arrow
Play from edit end by the post-roll amount	9	Command+Right Arrow	Ctrl+Right Arrow
Play through edit start by the pre/post-roll amount	N/A	Option+Command+ Left Arrow	Ctrl+Alt+Left Arrow
Play through edit end by the pre/post-roll amount	N/A	Option+Command+ Right Arrow	Ctrl+Alt+Right Arrow

Audition Commands

The alphanumeric keys 6–9 on the main keyboard (not on the numeric keypad) are used for auditioning (playing back) using pre- and post-roll settings for the current edit selection in several ways.

Note: There is no way to access the "play through" functionality from the single-stroke Commands Focus keys.

MIDI Functions

The green color-coded Commands Focus keys shown in Figure 3.11 allow single-key access to MIDI recording functions. The MIDI command functions are listed in Table 3.9.

Figure 3.11
MIDI Keyboard Focus keys.

Table 3.9   MIDI Command Functions

Key(s)	Function	Notes
Numeric [7]	Toggle Metronome On/Off	Enables/disables the Click or TLMetro Plug-In metronome click based on session tempo.
Numeric [8]	Countoff	Enables countoff before playback/record based on setting in Preferences.
Numeric [9]	MIDI Merge	Enables/disables MIDI merge mode (merge vs. overwrite) when recording or step inputting MIDI data.
F11*	Wait for Note	Enables/disables Wait for Note.

* To use F11 for Wait for Note you must enable the key in Preferences > MIDI.

Function Keys

Using the Function (F) keys on your computer keyboard, you can easily switch between the four Edit modes and six Edit tools.

Edit Mode Function Keys

To access an Edit mode, simply press the corresponding Function key: F1–F4. See Figure 3.12.

Figure 3.12
Edit mode Function key shortcuts shown in orange.

Snap to Grid

You can use a keyboard shortcut to enable the Snap to Grid option (see Table 3.10). To enable Snap to Grid while in an Edit mode other than Grid, do one of the following:

- Shift-click the Grid mode button.

- Press Shift+F4 to enable Snap to Grid while in another Edit mode.

Table 3.10   Snap to Grid Shortcuts

Snap to Grid Mode	Keyboard Shortcut
Shuffle	F1+F4
Slip	F2+F4
Spot	F3+F4

Edit Tool Function Keys

To access one of the six Edit tools:

- Press the corresponding Function key (F5–F10).

- Repeat presses of the Function key corresponding to the Zoomer, Trim, Grabber, or Pencil tool will toggle through the alternate modes for each tool. This can be disabled with Options > Edit Tool/Mode Keyboard Lock.

- Repeat presses of F4 will switch between Absolute and Relative Grid mode (unless Keyboard lock is engaged).

- You can access the Smart Tool by pressing any two of the Function keys F6–F8 simultaneously.

Note: The Function key shortcuts (F1–F12) are always available and do not change when Commands Keyboard Focus mode is enabled or disabled.

 In the Mac OS, some of the Function keys may be in use for system tasks, such as Dashboard, Spotlight, and Exposé. Refer to Lesson 1, "Pro Tools HD Hardware Configuration," for instructions on how to resolve this issue.

Numeric Keypad

The numeric keypad can take on one of three different modes—Classic, Transport, or Shuttle. The numeric keypad mode preference (found under the Setup > Preferences > Operation dialog box and shown in Figure 3.13) determines how the numeric keypad will function. No matter which numeric keypad mode is selected, you can always use the keypad to select and enter values in the Event Edit area, Location Indicators, and Transport fields.

To set the numeric keypad mode:

1. Choose **Setup > Preferences** and click the **Operation** tab.

2. Under the option for **Numeric Keypad** mode, select a keypad mode (Classic, Transport, or Shuttle).

Figure 3.13
Numeric keypad preferences.

3. Click **OK**. The selected numeric keypad mode is always available and is not affected by the keyboard focus.

Classic Mode

This mode emulates the way Pro Tools worked in versions earlier than 5.0. With the numeric keypad mode set to Classic, you can:

■ Recall memory locations by typing the memory location number, followed by a period.

■ Play up to two tracks of audio in Shuttle Lock mode. Press **Start** (Windows) or **Control** (Mac) followed by 0–9 for different play speeds. Press **+** (plus) or **–** (minus) on the numeric keypad to reverse direction.

Shuttle Lock Mode

Shuttle Lock mode allows you to playback audio forward or backward at various speeds. This is useful for long-format program material (such as live recordings or classical recordings) where you want to listen for certain cues or problems without listening in real-time. For example, you may want to edit two different takes of a classical performance or a live performance together but the edit point is not visually obvious.

Transport Mode (Default)

This mode allows you to set a number of record and play functions and also operate the Transport mode from the numeric keypad. See Table 3.11.

Table 3.11 Numeric Keypad Mapping for Transport Control

Function	Key
Click On/Off	7
Countoff On/Off	8
MIDI Merge/Replace Mode	9
Loop Playback On/Off	4
Loop Record On/Off	5
QuickPunch Mode On/Off	6
Rewind	1
Fast Forward	2
Record	3
Play/Stop	0

With the numeric keypad mode set to Transport, you can also:

- Recall memory locations by typing period, the memory location number, and period again.

- Play up to two tracks of audio in Shuttle Lock mode. Press Control (Mac) or Start (Windows) followed by 0–9 for different play speeds. Press + (plus) or – (minus) on the numeric keypad to reverse direction.

- Use Separate Play and Stop keys: When enabled, this option lets you start playback with the Enter key and stop playback with the [0] (Zero) key on the numeric keypad. When this option is disabled, the numeric keypad Zero key will toggle between playback and stop.

Shuttle Mode

Shuttle Mode with Pro Tools HD software and Complete Toolkit, offers an alternative to Shuttle Lock mode. With the Numeric Keypad mode set to Shuttle, playback from the current Edit selection is triggered by pressing and holding the keys on the numeric keypad—playback stops once the keys are released. Selections can also be made in this mode by holding Shift as well. Various playback speeds are available in both forward and reverse. In this mode, pre- and post-roll are ignored. See Table 3.12.

Table 3.12   Numeric Keypad Mapping for Shuttle Mode

Function	Key
1x Forward	6
1x Rewind	4
4x Forward	9
4x Rewind	7
1/4x Forward	3
1/4x Rewind	1
1/2x Forward	5+6
1/2x Rewind	5+4
2x Forward	8+9
2x Rewind	8+7
1/16x Forward	2+3
1/16x Rewind	2+1
Loop Selection (1x)	0

With the numeric keypad mode set to Shuttle, you can also recall memory locations by typing period, the memory location number, and period again.

Note: Shuttle Lock mode is not available when the numeric keypad mode is set to Shuttle.

Review/Discussion Questions

1. In your own words, what do the different modifier keys typically control?

   (Mac/Windows order) Command/Ctrl = ? Option/Alt = ? Control/Start = ?

2. What is the modifier used to Solo Safe a track?

3. How many different keyboard focus options are available in the Mix and Edit windows?

4. What is the key command for activating Commands Keyboard Focus mode?

5. What do the different colors (yellow, pink, and blue) on a coded keyboard refer to?

6. With Commands Keyboard Focus enabled in the Edit window, which key would you press to switch a track containing the cursor from Waveform view to Volume view?

7. What are the Commands Keyboard Focus shortcuts for fade-in, fade-out, and crossfade?

8. What is the keyboard shortcut for enabling Loop Playback?

9. What is the keyboard shortcut to enable Loop Record and QuickPunch?

10. Why would you change the numeric keypad preference from Transport to Shuttle?

11. Explain the difference between Shuttle Lock and Shuttle mode using the numeric keypad.

Tactile Control

This exercise is designed to improve your general knowledge of keyboard shortcuts, focus keys, and modifiers. Some of the following tasks will use shortcuts that are familiar to you. For other tasks, you may need to look up the appropriate shortcut or construct a command using two or more modifiers. This is an opportunity for you to identify the aspects you are comfortable with and the areas where you need practice.

Media Used:
310M Exercise 03.PTX (Pro Tools session file)

Duration:
30-45 minutes

Getting Started

Open the 310M Exercise 3 session. Take a few moments to look over the session and familiarize yourself with what is on the tracks.

Editing Shortcuts:
Commands Keyboard Focus Mode

Using ONLY the keyboard (you shouldn't touch the mouse in this section), perform each of the following tasks within the suggested times, and then enter the commands used to achieve the task using the column provided. As an example, the key commands for Step 1 have been filled out for you. (Other key commands not covered in Lesson 3 are also filled out for you.)

Tip: Feel free to write on a separate piece of paper instead of writing in your book.

Before starting, switch to the Edit window.

Description: Editing with Commands Keyboard Focus shortcuts
Total time to complete: 5 minutes

Table Ex3.1 Editing Shortcuts

Step #	Task Description	Commands Used to Complete Task
1	Recall memory location 2	Press Period+[2]+Period (numeric keypad)
2	Enable Commands Keyboard Focus mode	
3	Move the cursor with nudge commands to right before audio begins	
4	Fade the start of the clip	
5	Move the Edit cursor down to the GtrTheme1 track	
6	Trim the start of the clip	
7	Disable Tab to Transients	Command+Option+Tab (Mac) or Ctrl+Alt+Tab (Windows)
8	Navigate to the beginning of the next clip	Tab or ' (single quote) key
9	Re-enable Tab to Transients and navigate to the first transient	Command+Option+Tab (Mac) or Ctrl+Alt+Tab (Windows), Tab
10	Trim the front of the clip to the current cursor location	
11	Select the entire clip	Control+Tab (Mac) or Start+Tab (Windows)
12	Trim out the clip start using nudging until the attack is restored	Option+ – (Mac) or Alt+ – (Windows)

Editing Keyboard Modifiers and Shortcuts

For the following tasks, you will use *only* the Commands Focus keys or keyboard modifiers with mouse clicks (except where noted). Perform each of the following tasks within the suggested times and then enter the commands used to achieve the task using the column provided. (Shortcuts not covered in Lesson 3 are filled out for you.)

Description: Editing with modifier keys

Total time to complete: 5 minutes

Table Ex3.2   Keyboard Shortcuts

Step #	Task Description	Commands Used to Complete Task
1	Recall memory location 3	Press Period+[3]+Period (numeric keypad)
2	Zoom out to see the entire selection (in one move)	Option+F (Mac) or Alt+F (Windows)
3	Open the Strip Silence window	Edit menu command equivalent
4	Zoom In enough to see the start and end pad edit preview	
5	Adjust the start and end pad settings to ensure you have all audio	Mouse only
6	Navigate down the track to the right using key commands to see all the hits	Option+Pg Down (Mac) or Alt+Pg Down (Windows)
7	Zoom to your selection again	Option+F (Mac) or Alt+F (Windows)
8	Click Strip to strip the silent areas from the selection	Mouse only
9	With the resulting clips still selected, apply batch fades with a length of 10ms	Edit menu command equivalent
10	Using the appropriate modifier, show all tracks quickly from the Track List	
11	Place the cursor across all tracks quickly	Click in the Timeline ruler
12	Select from Bar 83|1|000 to Bar 99|1|000 using the numeric keypad	
13	Open the Time Operations window	Option+[1] (Mac) or Alt+[1] (Windows) on the numeric keypad
14	Apply the Cut Time operation	Command+Up/Down Arrow (Mac) or Ctrl+Up/Down Arrow (Windows) to navigate to Cut Time; Return or Enter to apply the change and close the window

Mixing Keyboard Modifiers and Shortcuts

Using ONLY the keyboard or keyboard modifiers and mouse clicks, perform each of the following tasks within the suggested times and then enter the commands used to achieve the task using the column provided. (Shortcuts not covered in Lesson 3 are filled out for you.)

Description: Mixing with modifier keys

Total time to complete: 5 minutes

Table Ex3.3   Commands and Modifiers: Mixing

Step #	Task Description	Commands Used to Complete Task
1	Recall memory location 4	Press Period+[4]+Period (numeric keypad)
2	Bypass the compressor on the LdVc track without opening the plug-in	
3	Bypass all dynamics on Insert position A throughout the mixer	
4	Select all the Drum tracks quickly	Click to the left of group name in the Group List or click on Kick and Shift-click on Room-R in the Track List
5	Record-safe all selected tracks	Command-click (Mac) or Ctrl-click (Windows) on each Record Enable button or Option+Command+Shift-click (Mac) or Ctrl+Alt+Shift-click (Windows) on any Record Enable button
6	Clear all clips (if any)	Option+C (Mac) or Alt+C (Windows)
7	Select both drum auxiliary submasters	Shift-click
8	Reset drum auxiliary faders to unity	
9	Navigate to the Keys tracks. Disable both tracks with a single click.	Shift-click to select, Control+Option+Command+Shift-click (Mac) or Ctrl+Start+Alt+Shift-click (Windows) on track icon to deactivate
10	Deactivate all plug-ins at Insert position A	Command+Option+Control-click (Mac) or Ctrl+Start+Alt-click (Windows) on any Insert A

Importing and Recording Audio

This lesson contains a collection of advanced pre-production topics, including file interchange formats, session templates, and several recording scenarios.

Media Used: None

Duration: 90 minutes

GOALS

- Understand the AAF, OMF, and MXF file formats

- Import AAF/OMF/MXF files into Pro Tools

- Manage I/O changes when moving sessions between differently configured systems

- Work with Pro Tools session templates

- Use grouped playlists to speed up and simplify multitrack recording sessions

- Connect Pro Tools to Avid VENUE systems

Introduction

In modern production workflows, it is commonplace to move sessions between different audio platforms and systems. This lesson starts by explaining the concept of platform-independent file interchange formats. You then learn how to import these files into Pro Tools.

The lesson moves on to look at some advanced techniques for setting up and managing recording sessions, such as remapping I/O setups between systems, working with session templates, and using grouped playlists for multitrack recordings.

At the end of the lesson, you are introduced to Avid's VENUE live sound platform, including the steps and methods required to record directly to Pro Tools from a VENUE system.

Importing AAF or OMF Sequences

Although the AAF and OMF file formats were originally developed for use in the television and film post-production fields, they have been adopted by music production professionals because of the ease with which they allow projects to be moved between different software platforms. Understanding the use of these formats is a valuable asset and broadens the range of possible projects you can work on as a Pro Tools operator.

Overview of OMF

The Open Media Framework Interchange (OMFI, or just OMF) was developed by Avid Technology as a standard file format to enable content creators to share metadata (project or session edit information) and media data (audio and video files) across platforms and between software applications. Although the standard was developed by Avid, it was made freely available to any other manufacturers who wanted to support the standard.

For the first time, the industry had a standard that promised to enable projects to originate in one manufacturer's editing system and at any time migrate to a different manufacturer's system with all edits, timeline positions, and media intact.

Although the OMF standard offered great promise, it never really achieved wide industry implementation and success. One of the main obstacles was that OMF is not a true industry standard developed by a consortium of independent manufacturers. The OMF file format also contains Avid-specific features that make it difficult for some manufacturers to support. Despite these limitations, OMF export and import are still widely used today and are still supported by a number of companies (in addition to Avid). However, OMF has largely been replaced by AAF.

Overview of AAF

In contrast to OMF, the Advanced Authoring Format (AAF) is an industry-driven, open standard for multimedia authoring and post-production, created by a consortium of developers and broadcasters called the AAF Association. The association changed its name to the Advanced Media Workflow Association, Inc. or AMWA in 2007 to better reflect the association's focus and mission (see http://www.amwa.tv/).

Typically, multimedia-authoring applications save projects to their own proprietary file format. This approach generally makes the reuse or repurposing of media extremely difficult. In particular, the project metadata (for example, information from within the Pro Tools session file) is not transferable between authoring applications.

AAF provides a file format that includes the data that all audio and video work-stations are likely to have in common. This includes the raw media (video and audio files) and the edit information (how the media are cut up and assembled onto tracks). More complicated information (such as video clip transitions) can be included but can be ignored by any platform that doesn't support it.

Embedded or Referenced Media

When an editor creates an AAF or OMF file, he/she can select whether to include the media as part of the file. There are therefore two types of OMF/AAF transfer scenarios that you may encounter:

- **With media (embedded)**—This includes all the edit and track information, along with all the raw audio and video media wrapped up in one (large) file.

- **Without media**—This is a much smaller file that contains just the edit information and other metadata. The video and audio files are supplied separately (in a MediaFiles folder) and are referenced by the OMF/AAF file in the same way that a Pro Tools session references separate media files.

Importing AAF or OMF Tracks into Pro Tools

Pro Tools handles both AAF and OMF files in the same way: using the Import Session Data dialog box. When you receive AAF/OMF exports from other editing systems, you have two options available in Pro Tools:

- Open the AAF/OMF sequence/tracks as a new session.

- Import the AAF/OMF sequence/tracks into an existing Pro Tools session.

To open an AAF or OMF sequence as a new session:

1. Select FILE > OPEN SESSION.

2. Select the AAF or OMF sequence you want to import.

3. Click OPEN. The Pro Tools New Session dialog box will appear, showing the audio file format, sample rate, and bit depth used in the original AAF/OMF project. You can choose to keep the same file format or to change any of the parameters.

Tip: You can also double-click the AAF or OMF sequence that you want to import in any DigiBase browser, or double click the AAF/OMF file in the Finder/Explorer, or simply click and drag the AAF/OMF file on the Pro Tools icon.

4. In the NEW SESSION (SAVE AS) dialog box, enter a name for the converted AAF/OMF sequence, select a directory location, and click SAVE. The Import Session Data dialog box will open with OMF-specific choices.

5. Configure the Import Session Data options as described in the section entitled "Translation Options," later in this lesson.

To import AAF or OMF tracks into an existing Pro Tools session:

1. Create a new Pro Tools session or open an existing session.

2. Select FILE > IMPORT > SESSION DATA.

3. Select the AAF or OMF sequence that contains the tracks you want to import and click OPEN. The Import Session Data dialog box will open, as shown in Figure 4.1.

Tip: You can also import tracks from a DigiBase browser by either double-clicking the AAF or OMF sequence or dragging and dropping the file into the Pro Tools timeline.

4. Select the tracks to import by doing one of the following:

   - Select tracks for import by clicking on them. Clicking subsequent tracks does not deselect previous ones.

   - SHIFT-CLICK to select multiple adjacent tracks.

   - Select all tracks for import by pressing COMMAND+A (Mac OS) or CTRL+A (Windows). You can also OPTION-CLICK (Mac) or ALT-CLICK (Windows) on any track name.

5. Use the DESTINATION pop-up menus to decide whether to import to new tracks or import into existing tracks in your session.

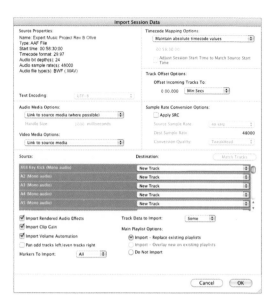

Figure 4.1
The Import Session Data dialog box.

6. Click **OK** to import the selected tracks or configure additional options, as detailed in the next section.

Note: If there are any errors, a dialog box will appear, asking if you want a detailed report. If so, click Yes and select where you want to save the log.

Translation Options

When opening or importing AAF or OMF sequences, Pro Tools provides several import options through the Import Session Data dialog box:

- AAF/OMF Translation settings
- Audio Media options
- Sample Rate Conversion options
- Timecode Mapping options
- Track Offset options

AAF/OMF Translation Settings

These settings are aimed at projects coming from an Avid video editing workstation to audio post-production systems such as Pro Tools. For music-only production, some of these settings are not necessary. Others have a bearing on music productions, as shown in Figure 4.2.

Figure 4.2

AAF/OMF translation settings, from the Import Session Data dialog box.

Audio Media Options

This menu lets you select how to handle the audio media that come with the project. Depending on the type of AAF/OMF file you receive and the other options you have chosen, some of these choices may be unavailable (grayed out). See Figure 4.3.

Figure 4.3

Source Media pop-up (AAF or OMF to Pro Tools), from the Import Session Data dialog box.

- **Link to source media (where possible)**—If you select this option, Pro Tools will read the audio files as they were given to you (whether external or embedded) when it opens the session, without copying or moving them. Therefore you need to make sure the audio files are on the drive you intend to use for production and the audio files bit depth and sample rate are supported with Pro Tools.

- **Copy from source media**—Use this setting to copy referenced audio to a new drive or folder in their original format. If you want to convert the files to the current Pro Tools session format, use Force to Target Session Format (covered later in this lesson).

- **Consolidate from source media**—This setting will copy audio media to a new drive location but will discard data that is not actually being used in the timeline. For example, if only 20 seconds of a 5-minute vocal take are used in a clip, the rest of the take will not be copied when you import, other than the handle size (see the next topic). Use this setting if you need to reduce the amount of drive space the project will take up, similar to how Compact Selected works in the Clip List.

- **Handle size (ms)**—*Handles* are small amounts of audio before and after clips that are retained when you select Consolidate from Source Media. Handles let you keep some editing options open, such as trimming clips and creating crossfades; these possibilities are lost if you consolidate only what was in the timeline. The standard practice is to keep handles of at least 2000ms with video projects, however Pro Tools defaults for 1000ms. You can set a handle size up to 10,000ms.

■ **Force to target session format**—This is a quick way to have Pro Tools convert all audio media to match the bit depth, sample rate, and audio file type set for the currently open session. Any files that are converted will be generated in a new location, but files that do not need converting will be referred to directly by the session.

Sample Rate Conversion Options

When importing audio into an existing session, Pro Tools 10 will allow you to import different sample rates. However, Pro Tools will not autocorrect for pitch. For example, importing 48kHz audio into a 44.1kHz session will result in the audio playing three semitones lower than normal. Using the Force to target session format will alleviate any issues with mismatched sample rates.

In addition, there may be times you want to import a session done at 48kHz but want all the files to be converted at 44.1kHz. The vast majority of choices in the Sample Rate drop-down are mainly for video and film post-production when subtle pitch changes are required for source audio and post-production audio to match pitch due to pull-up and pull-down workflows. Figure 4.4 shows the sample rate conversion options.

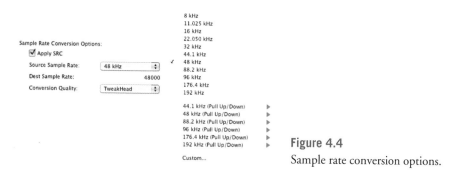

Figure 4.4

Sample rate conversion options.

Timecode Mapping Options

These settings let you select what to do when the start time of the tracks you are importing is different from the current session.

■ **Maintain absolute timecode values**—This option places clips at the same timecode locations where they were located in the source session. If the start time of the session you are importing from is earlier than that of the current session, this option will not be available. If the start time of the current session is earlier than that of the session you are importing from, your tracks may not line up with the bars and beats grid correctly, as this location is based solely upon timecode locations. Therefore, this option is not recommended for music projects unless the exact same timecode start was used in each session.

- **Maintain relative timecode values**—This option places tracks at the same offset from session start as they had in the source session. For example, if the source session starts at 01:00:00:00 and contains a track that starts at 01:01:00:00, and the current session start is 02:00:00:00, the track will be placed at 02:01:00:00 in the current session. This option is usually appropriate for most music projects.

- **Map start timecode to**—This option places tracks relative to their original session start time. For example, if the current session starts at 00:01:00:00 and the session from which you are importing starts at 10:00:00:00, you can reset the start timecode to 00:01:00:00 to avoid placing files 9 hours and 59 minutes from the start of your session.

- **Adjust session start time to match sequence start time**—When selected, this option automatically sets the start time of the current Pro Tools session to match the start time of the session, AAF, or OMF sequence being imported.

Track Offset Options

These options (shown in Figure 4.5) allow you to specify a track offset in addition to any offset incurred with the Timecode Mapping options. Any imported audio is offset in the current session's timeline by the specified amount. Values can be entered in minutes:seconds, bars|beats, samples, timecode, or feet/frames.

Figure 4.5
Track Offset options from the Import Session Data dialog box.

Importing MXF Audio

MXF (Material eXchange Format) is a media file format, in that it contains actual audio and video media. It is often referred to as a *media wrapper,* because it conceptually "wraps" the raw media inside a well-defined data structure, allowing applications to understand the contents. Unlike many other media wrappers in current use, it was designed from the ground up for professional applications and compatibility with AAF. MXF files can be associated with AAF compositions or they can function on their own. MXF can contain any kind of raw media format, such as WAV, AIFF, MPEG, AVI, or DPX, making it useful for many purposes, and also maintaining the extensible nature of AAF and MXF by allowing future media formats to be accommodated within its data structure.

Together, AAF and MXF offer video/film post-production professionals the prospect of complete data interchange between picture, audio, and effects systems.

For music production, MXF is not widely employed today, but may offer more potential than the ubiquitous AES31 BWAV file format that is widely used in music production.

MXF audio files can be imported in the same ways as normal audio files:

- Using the File > Import > Audio command.
- By dragging from a DigiBase browser.
- By dragging to the Pro Tools icon.

MXF audio files can also be edited in the same ways as other audio files.

Updating the Pro Tools I/O Setup

Pro Tools sessions store information about the type and order of audio interfaces available when the session was last saved.

Remapping

Where possible, when a session is opened on a system with different I/O, session paths are reassigned to the currently available hardware. For example, a session tracked to a Pro Tools HD-series system through two 192 I/O audio interfaces would typically include 32 output paths spread across the two 16-channel interfaces. If that session were taken to a different Pro Tools system, for example, an HD I/O-based system, the first 16 outputs would be mapped to the HD I/O's available output channels. See Figure 4.6.

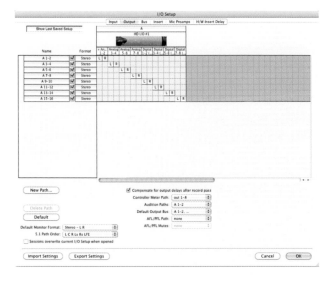

Figure 4.6

Output paths remapped on an HDX system with HD I/O.

Unavailable I/O is shown in dark gray. Any tracks assigned to unavailable output paths will be grayed out and inaudible. If the automatic remapping is not suitable to your session's requirements, you can manually shift paths to more appropriate I/O and make unused paths inactive.

Show Last Saved Setup

When I/O remapping has occurred but the current Pro Tools system is unable to remap all the paths, the Show Last Saved Setup button appears in the top-left corner of the I/O Setup window. This button displays the audio interfaces used in the original session. This temporary display lets you check the original I/O configuration for reference when reconfiguring the session for your system. See Figure 4.7.

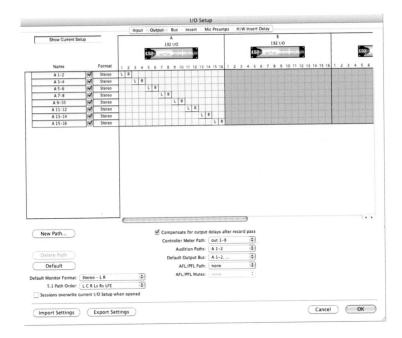

Figure 4.7
Displaying the last saved I/O setup.

Using Session Templates

Pro Tools 8.0 introduced a file format for session templates. Pro Tools 10 session template files use the .PTXT extension (lower versions use the .PTT extension) to differentiate templates from regular Pro Tools session files, which have the .PTX extension for Pro Tools 10 or .PTF and .PTS for lower versions.

With session templates, you can save and reuse session settings, configurations, and media as starting points for new sessions you create. Pro Tools 8 and later include a number of session templates that are available from the Quick Start and

New Session dialog boxes. You can also create and share your own custom session templates using the Save As Template command in Pro Tools or the Make Template command in the Workspace browser.

Saving a Session as a Template

Often you will want to create a template file that includes common settings and configurations that you can reuse in multiple sessions so that you do not have to configure the same setup repeatedly. Consider the case of recording an album for a particular band. You can configure the I/O setup and path labels, your favorite window configurations, custom disk allocation settings—even the basic tracks and routing—all in a starter session that you save as a template. For each song on the album, you simply use the template as a starting point, thus ensuring that each song uses the same setup.

To create a custom Pro Tools session template:

1. Do one of the following:

    • Create a new Pro Tools session and configure it with the settings you want.

    • Open an existing session that you want to reuse.

2. Select **FILE > SAVE AS TEMPLATE**. The Save Session Template dialog box opens, as shown in Figure 4.8.

Figure 4.8
The Save Session Template dialog box.

3. Select a template location using the following options:

    • **Install template in system**—Select this option to save the template file in the default template location (the Session Templates folder in the Pro Tools Application folder). This folder is referenced by the Quick Start and New Session dialog boxes. When you select this option, you also need to select a category for the template from the Category pop-up menu.

    • **Select location for template**—Select this option to save the template file to a directory location of your choice. In this case, the saved session template will not appear in the Pro Tools Quick Start or New Session dialog box (unless you save it in a subdirectory of the Session Templates folder).

- **Include media**—Select this option if you would like audio, MIDI, and video media that exist in the session to be included in the template.

Note: When the Include Media option is enabled, all audio, MIDI, and video files in the session will also be included in the template. When using this option, be sure that the session contains only the media files that you want to reuse (or share, if you distribute the template). Also note that any media included with the template will be copied to the new session.

4. Click **OK**.

System Template Categories

If you select the Install Template in System option in Step 3, your template will be available in the Pro Tools session Quick Start dialog box and the New Session dialog box. When you select this option, you also need to choose a category for the template from the Category pop-up menu and provide a name for the template. See Figure 4.9.

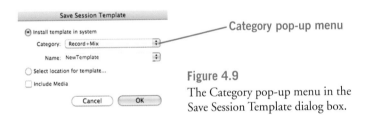

Category pop-up menu

Figure 4.9
The Category pop-up menu in the
Save Session Template dialog box.

You can add a new subdirectory by selecting Add Category from the bottom of the Category pop-up menu. This allows you to save your template in a new category folder or create additional categories for future use.

Manually Managing System Template Files

To install a template in your system manually, you can navigate to the Session Templates folder from the Save As Template dialog box when saving from within Pro Tools, or you can copy an existing template into the Session Templates folder using the Mac Finder or Windows Explorer.

On Mac OS systems, the Session Templates folder is located at System HD/ Applications/Avid/Pro Tools/Session Templates. On Windows systems, the Session Templates folder is located on the system drive at C:/Program Files/Avid/Pro Tools/ Session Templates.

For your template files to be available in the Quick Start or New Session dialog box, they must be installed inside a subdirectory within the Session Templates folder. Subdirectories in the Session Templates folder correspond to template Categories in the pop-up menu within the associated dialog boxes. Adding a new folder (subdirectory) inside the Session Templates folder thus creates a new Category in the pop-up menu. You can create folders as needed to install templates under new categories. You can also add folders to create additional categories for future use. See Figure 4.10.

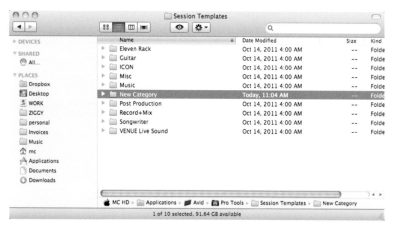

Figure 4.10
Subfolders created within the Session Templates folder correspond to Categories in the Quick Start dialog box.

Revealing the Session Templates Folder

With a session already open, you can automatically display the Session Templates folder.

To automatically display the Session Templates folder:

1. Select FILE > SAVE AS TEMPLATE.

2. Click on the CATEGORY pop-up menu and select REVEAL SESSION TEMPLATES FOLDER at the bottom of the menu.

The Session Templates folder will appear in a Finder window (Mac OS) or Explorer window (Windows). Despite being initiated by the Save As Template command, this action does not create a session template file.

Creating New Sessions from Templates

As you have no doubt experienced, you can create a new session based on an installed template simply by selecting the template from the Quick Start or New

Session dialog box. However, you can also open a Pro Tools Session Template file on any available drive or volume to start a new session based on that template.

To open a Pro Tools session template and save it as a new session:

1. Do one of the following:

   • Select FILE > OPEN, navigate to the session template file you want, and open it.

   • Navigate to the session template in the Mac OS Finder or Windows Explorer and double-click on the file to open it.

2. In the New Session From dialog box, select the AUDIO FILE TYPE, SAMPLE RATE, and BIT DEPTH for the new session that will be created from the template.

3. Click OK.

4. In the Save New Session As dialog box, navigate to the location where you want to save your new session and click SAVE.

Converting Files Between Sessions and Templates

Pro Tools makes it easy to convert an existing session into a template or convert an existing template back into a session. You may want to do this, for example, if you have already created a session with settings that will be useful for subsequent projects (in which case you can convert the session into a template) or if you have already created a template but find that you need to modify it (in which case you can convert the template into a session to make the changes and then re-save it as a template again).

To convert a session file to a template or vice versa:

1. From within Pro Tools, open the Workspace or Volume browser.

2. In the browser, navigate to the file that you want to convert.

3. Right-click on the file and select MAKE TEMPLATE (to convert a session file to a template file) or MAKE SESSION (to convert a template file to a session file). The file extension will change to correspond to the new file format.

Using PRE in Standalone Mode

Although PRE, first covered in Lesson 1, "Pro Tools HD Hardware Configuration," is designed to be integrated into Pro Tools systems, it can also function as a stand-alone mic preamp. In these cases, you control the unit entirely from the front panel.

To use PRE as a standalone preamplifier:

1. Connect AC power to PRE.

2. Power on PRE. At power up, PRE units will default to the settings they had when last powered down.

To connect audio sources—microphones:

1. Press the **CHANNEL SELECT** switch for the mic input you will be using.

2. Change the Input source to **MIC** by pressing **SOURCE** one or more times.

3. Make sure the gain is turned down, especially if the monitors are up.

4. Verify 48V Phantom power is disabled. Press **48V** so that the LED is off.

5. Plug a microphone directly into the mic input on the back of the PRE. These inputs accept XLR connections.

6. If your microphone requires phantom power, press 48V.

7. Turn the **GAIN/PARAM** control to raise the gain. Use the peak meter to determine the proper level.

To connect line- and instrument-level sources:

1. Press the **CHANNEL SELECT** switch for the Line/Inst input you will be using.

2. Change the Input source to **LINE** or **INST**, by pressing **SOURCE** one or more times.

3. Plug a line-level source (such as a synth) or a DI source (such as a guitar) into a Line/Inst Input on the front or back of PRE. These inputs accept balanced/unbalanced TRS connectors.

Editing Channel Controls

As you can see, each PRE parameter can be changed on a channel-by-channel basis. However, you may want to change multiple channels simultaneously.

To edit channel controls:

1. Press the **CHANNEL SELECT** switch for the channel you want to edit. You can select multiple channels for simultaneous editing by holding **SHIFT** while selecting channels.

2. Press a channel control switch to change its current setting. For example, if the 48V LED is off, pressing **48V** will enable phantom power for all the selected channels.

3. Multiple channel selections will stay enabled until you select another single channel. When done adjusting settings, be sure to select a single channel to disengage selected channels.

Adjusting Input Gain

To set the input gain on a channel:

1. If the Gain/Param display currently shows a MIDI channel, press **MIDI**. The display should now show an input gain level.

2. Press the **SELECT** switch for the channel you want to adjust. Rotate the **GAIN/PARAM** control to adjust the input gain.

 For more detailed information about using, configuring, and declaring PRE, refer back to Lesson 1.

Grouped Playlist Synchronization

When grouping a number of tracks, it becomes imperative for all the group tracks to retain a common name as playlists are added. This is automatically done for you when you create an Edit (or Mix and Edit) group in Pro Tools. Once the tracks are linked creating a new playlist on any of the group member tracks creates a similarly named playlist on other grouped tracks. You have seen in other courses how this is useful during the editing phase of a project. But it can also benefit you when tracking a multi-mic'ed source such as a drum kit.

Multitrack Recording Using Playlists

Pro Tools playlist functionality provides an ideal way to store and manage multiple takes within tracks. Playlists on tracks that are grouped are synchronized, so multi-track recordings can be handled in the same way as mono recordings. This is particularly relevant to multi-mic drum recordings or using a group of backing vocalists.

To record multitrack takes using synchronized playlists:

1. Create an Edit group (or Mix and Edit group) of all the tracks you want to synchronize for multi-playlist recording.

2. In any track in the group, select **NEW** from the Playlist Selector or press **CONTROL+** (Mac OS) or **START+** (Windows). New playlists will be created in each track in the group. The new playlists will have the track's name with the suffix .01 for Take 1.

3. Record Take 1 into the tracks.

4. Again, select **NEW** from any track's Playlist Selector, and all tracks in the groups will get new playlists.

5. Record Take 2 into the new .02 playlists.

6. To go back and audition any take, switch a track to the playlist from that take and all other tracks will follow.

Tip: After creating, naming, and grouping your tracks for the session, immediately create a new playlist. By doing so, your playlists will have the same number as the take (for example, Take 1 = Kick.01). At the end of recording, you can use the original unnumbered playlist (for example, Kick) to comp the takes.

Adding Tracks During a Recording Session

Pro Tools is capable of handling a situation in which you may decide to expand an existing Edit group, even after you've already recorded takes, and subsequently keep all tracks with the same playlist number. This simply requires adding one or more new tracks to your existing Edit group. Subsequent takes will increment normally across all tracks. If you select an earlier take that did not include the newly added track, Pro Tools will create empty "dummy takes" on the new tracks so that the playlists stay synchronized across all the tracks in the group.

To add a new track to the group:

1. Create the new track(s).

2. Right-click on the group in the **GROUP LIST** and select **MODIFY GROUP**. The Modify Groups dialog box will appear, as shown in Figure 4.11.

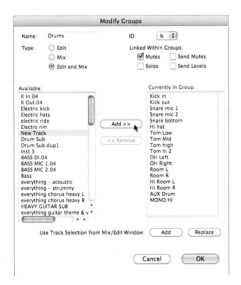

Figure 4.11
The Modify Groups dialog box.

3. Select the new track(s) in the left-side list.

4. Click the **ADD** button.

5. Click **OK**.

6. From any track in the group, create a new playlist. The new track(s) will get a new playlist with a suffix number matching the rest of the group.

Connecting Pro Tools to VENUE

VENUE is Avid's family of live sound mixing consoles. One principal feature of any VENUE system is its seamless integration with Pro Tools for recording, playback, or both. There are two possible interconnect cards used on VENUE to connect to Pro Tools: HDx and FWx (discussed later in this lesson).

This section provides a brief primer on the VENUE family, the options available, and how those options affect the requirements necessary to capture an entire VENUE performance. You do not need to study VENUE systems as part of Pro Tools Expert certification; however, a general understanding of the Pro Tools connectivity may help you in situations where you are required to set up Pro Tools recording or playback with VENUE.

Introduction to VENUE

The term *VENUE* applies to both consoles and the entire system in general. In this section, you learn about the different console bundles and their Pro Tools interconnect options. Figure 4.12 shows dual-VENUE D-Shows in action.

Figure 4.12
Dual-VENUE D-Shows in action.

No matter which VENUE system you find yourself working behind, the system will include the following:

- VENUE software

- A control surface

- DSP mix engines

- Analog and digital I/O

VENUE Software

At the heart of each VENUE console lays the VENUE software. This is where you will patch channels (if necessary) from the VENUE console to Pro Tools. See Figure 4.13.

Figure 4.13
The VENUE software interface.

A standalone version of the software is available as a download from Avid's website. Even without a VENUE console, you can use the VENUE standalone software to experiment with how to patch channels to a connected Pro Tools system. Patching (routing to Pro Tools) is controlled via the Patchbay page in the VENUE software (top-center tab in the VENUE software interface).

Tip: VENUE standalone software is available only for the Windows platform (Windows XP, Vista, Windows 7). VENUE operators will often use a Mac with virtualization environment software such as VMware Fusion or Parallels Desktop to run Windows on their Mac or simply install Windows on a BootCamp partition.

VENUE Console Configurations

As mentioned, VENUE refers to both the entire platform as well as consoles. The VENUE family offers several console configurations at different price points. However, they all share the same software interface. This means how to route to/from Pro Tools is identical with any of the consoles. However, as a Pro Tools Expert, you should understand the major differences between the console and what Pro Tools interconnect options are available with each.

VENUE D-Show

Released in 2005, the VENUE D-Show console (see Figure 4.14) is the original as well as the largest of the three VENUE consoles available. A base system includes 24 input faders, a Focus fader on the main unit, and eight output faders on the main unit. The VENUE D-Show is the only control surface that is expandable (up to 56 channels using two additional 16-channel sidecars). A fully featured VENUE console is capable of mixing up to 128 inputs, 24 busses, and 43 output busses comprised of aux, group, matrix, stereo matrix, and main LCR busses. There are no inputs, outputs, or processing power directly on the VENUE D-Show console; they use different rack-mount solutions: Stage rack/FOH rack, or Mix rack (see next section).

Figure 4.14
VENUE D-Show console.

VENUE Profile

Released in 2007, the VENUE Profile console (see Figure 4.15) offers the same features as a D-Show–equipped VENUE system in a more compact control surface format. It also has 24 input faders and 8 output faders, but the control surface is not expandable and is much smaller than the D-Show control surface. VENUE Profile systems offer the same feature set for mixing, inputs, outputs, and processing power as VENUE D-Show, using the same rack mount units for inputs/outputs and processing power. The VENUE Profile can also be bundled with a Mix rack configuration.

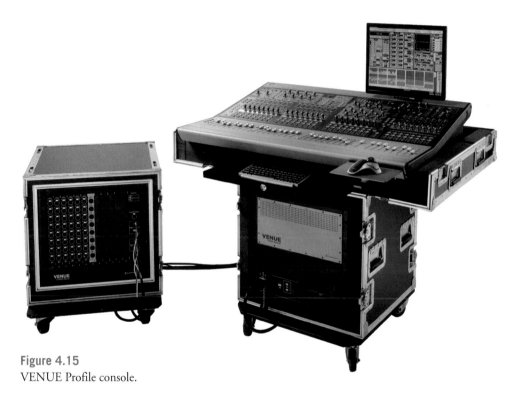

Figure 4.15
VENUE Profile console.

VENUE SC48

Released in 2009, the VENUE SC48 console is the smallest format-mixing console (see Figure 4.16). Unlike its bigger siblings, the base unit SC48 has all equipment inside the console—DSP, control computer, I/O, and control surface (no additional rack-mount unit is required). However, a separate IO rack, called the VENUE Stage 48, is available to offload the IO closer to the stage.

Figure 4.16
VENUE SC48 console.

VENUE Stage Rack (D-Show and Profile Only)

The Stage rack (see Figure 4.17) is a rack-mount unit that houses the input and output cards of the VENUE D-Show or Profile system. A standard Stage rack configuration consists of 48 inputs and at least 8 outputs, expandable up to 48 outputs. If more inputs are required, a second Stage rack can be added for a total of 96 stage inputs.

Figure 4.17
VENUE Stage rack.

Front of House (FOH) Rack

The FOH rack, shown in Figure 4.18, is a separate rack-mount unit that houses the following:

■ DSP mix engines used with the VENUE system

■ Control computer

■ Additional I/O for FOH needs (for example, external effects units, main outs for speaker management systems, and so on)

■ Pro Tools interconnect option cards—HDx or FWx

■ Digital Snake card—Used to connect to the Stage rack

■ FOH cable port—For connecting to the control surface (D-Show or Profile)

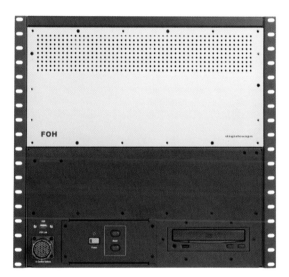

Figure 4.18
On the left is the front view of the VENUE FOH rack; on the right is the rear view of the VENUE FOH rack with an FWx card installed.

The important point for Pro Tools users is that the interconnect options for Pro Tools are installed in the FOH rack (HDx and FWx cards—see the section entitled "Pro Tools Connectivity with VENUE" that follows for more detail).

Note: Do not confuse the VENUE HDx interconnect card with the Pro Tools|HDX card. The HDx card in VENUE can interconnect to Pro Tools|HD, Pro Tools|HD Native, and Pro Tools|HDX cards.

Mix Rack

The Mix rack, shown in Figure 4.19, combines the attributes of the Stage rack and FOH rack into a single rack-mount solution housing all I/O, DSP processing, and control computer into a single rack-mount unit. Although used primarily with VENUE Profile consoles, it can be used with a VENUE D-Show console (however, this is rare). Be aware that the Mix rack uses the same Pro Tools interconnect cards as the FOH rack—the HDx and FWx cards.

Figure 4.19
Mix rack IO.

Stage 48

The Stage 48 rack allows you to move your SC48-based IO into a small format remote rack, eliminating the need for analog snakes or harnesses from the stage to the mix position. When used with the companion Ethernet Snake card in the SC48, a simple pair of redundant Ethernet cables links the Stage 48 to the SC48 console.

Pro Tools Connectivity with VENUE

Two expansion options are available for VENUE that enable recording to (and playback from) Pro Tools. They are described as follows:

■ **HDx Card**—Connects a VENUE FOH or Mix rack system to Pro Tools|HDX, Pro Tools|HD, or Pro Tools|HD Native system. A single VENUE HDx card offers 64 channels of Pro Tools I/O—48 inputs from the Stage rack or 48 playback tracks/outputs from Pro Tools—plus 16 HDx assignable channels of I/O (which can be any input/output on VENUE and additional outputs from Pro Tools). An additional VENUE HDx card can be installed for up to 128 inputs/outputs from Pro Tools. See Figure 4.20.

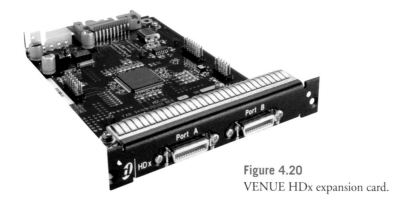

Figure 4.20
VENUE HDx expansion card.

■ **FWx Card**—Connects a VENUE FOH/Mix rack/SC48 to a laptop or desktop computer with Pro Tools software installed (prior to Pro Tools 9, this was called Pro Tools LE). The FWx card offers 32 channels of I/O entirely routable from VENUE's Patchbay page. See Figure 4.21.

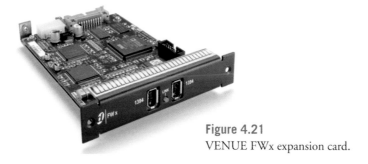

Figure 4.21
VENUE FWx expansion card.

Note: The 32 channels of I/O across FWx connections require VENUE 3.0 software on the console and Pro Tools 9.0.3 or later. Prior to VENUE 3.0 software, 18 channels of I/O was the maximum offered by FWx.

SC48 has the capabilities of the FWx card included as a standard part of the console on the rear of the unit.

By installing these option cards in a VENUE system, your VENUE becomes the audio interface for Pro Tools. No other audio interface is necessary to record or play back from Pro Tools into your VENUE. Each interconnect has advantages and limitations.

Connecting Pro Tools with FWx

Connection between a computer with Pro Tools software installed and VENUE with the FWx card installed is made via a standard 6-pin FireWire/IEE 1394 cable or a 9-pin to 6-pin Firewire cable.

The FWx card provides 32 assignable bi-directional channels of I/O between VENUE Pro Tools. This means you can record 32 individual input channels of VENUE, or a combination of inputs, auxes, groups, FX returns, and so on, by using the patchbay of VENUE to route to Pro Tools.

Note: Only one FWx card can be installed in the FOH rack or Mix rack. Therefore, FWx configurations cannot be expanded (unlike HDx configurations).

Once the connection is made and Pro Tools is launched, VENUE appears as a 32-channel interface in the Pro Tools I/O Setup dialog box. Pro Tools 9.0.3 or later on both Macintosh and Windows computers is supported. Once Pro Tools is launched, routing to/from VENUE is through the I/O Setup dialog box. VENUE will appear as the audio interface for the system.

Tip: Audio from the FWx link is 24-bit/48kHz, so you must use these settings for your Pro Tools session.

FWx Routing Options from VENUE

Numerous routing options are available from VENUE to Pro Tools via the Patchbay page of the VENUE software:

■ Direct Outputs let you record discrete VENUE input channels or any output from the pickoff point you select.

■ Output busses such as main, aux, group, matrix, or PQs can be recorded, up to the number of available FWx channels.

Tip: When recording to Pro Tools with earlier versions of VENUE software, using stereo group submixes is useful for fitting large mixes into the 18 available record channels. However, upgrading the VENUE to v.3.0 software may eliminate most of this need.

Connecting Pro Tools Using HDx

VENUE's HDx card option provides 64 channels of I/O to Pro Tools HD systems via two 32-channel DigiLink ports (using the same cables as are used to connect the original HD series audio interfaces). Two HDx cards can be installed in a single VENUE for a maximum total of 128 channels of I/O. HDx cards are compatible with both the FOH rack and Mix rack but are not compatible with SC48 consoles (see Figure 4.22). HDx configurations are required if:

■ You need to record more than 32-channels of live input

■ You need more than 32-channels of pre-recorded playback into VENUE

■ You want to simplify a *virtual soundcheck* (the ability to feed a performance back in and treat it as live signals to VENUE is called a virtual soundcheck)

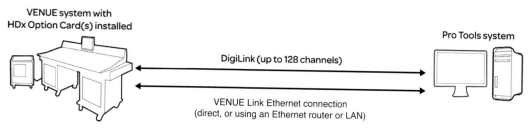

Figure 4.22
Diagram of VENUE HDx connection to Pro Tools|HD 2.

Tip: Each HDx card on VENUE consists of two DigiLink ports supporting 32 channels of Pro Tools I/O each. To record 64 channels of I/O you would need a single Pro Tools|HDX card or Pro Tools|HD Native card. If you have Pro Tools|HD hardware, you need at least a Pro Tools|HD 2 system to support all 64 channels. To record all 128 channels, you need two Pro Tools|HDX, or four Pro Tools|HD series cards.

Tip: An FWx option card cannot be used simultaneously with an HDx option card.

Setting Up a Session for Recording via HDx

As with the FWx card, HDx channels appear in Pro Tools Hardware Setup and I/O Setup pages in the same way as normal HD-series audio interfaces.

Tip: Audio from the HDx link is 24-bit/48kHz, so you must use these settings for your Pro Tools session.

HDx Routing Options from VENUE

HDx inputs into Pro Tools are somewhat different from FWx inputs. Essentially, the 48 "Stage" inputs of your VENUE (whether via Stage rack or Mix rack) are routed directly to Pro Tools *without* patching in VENUE's Patchbay page. In other words, these are considered "fixed" inputs in which Stage inputs show up as the first 48 inputs in Pro Tools. This routing cannot be modified or swapped for any other inputs.

These inputs will show up as "HDx1" inputs 1–48 in Pro Tools.

If you want to route other sources (for example, FOH rack inputs, L-R bus, aux return, and so on), you must use the 16 HDx assignable channels available on the second DigiLink connection. These sources must be routed through the VENUE Patchbay page as outputs or directs.

Note: It is imperative that if you want to capture the board mix or any other signal other than the first 32 inputs of the Stage rack, you must have the second HDx connection connected to a DigiLink port on your Pro Tools system. HDx assignable channels are only available on DigiLink channels 49–64.

These inputs will show up as "HDx Assignable" inputs 1–16 in Pro Tools, as shown in Figure 4.23. Table 4.1 lists the HDx channel mappings.

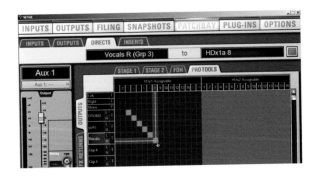

Figure 4.23
HDx assignables being used to route group outputs for recording.

Table 4.1   HDx Channel Map

HDx Card	Port	Pro Tools I/O Channel#
HDx Card 1	A	HDx1 #1–32
HDx Card 1	B	HDx1 #33–48 and HDx1 Assgn #1–16
HDx Card 2	A	HDx2 #1–32
HDx Card 2	B	HDx2 #33–48 and HDx2 Assgn #1–16

Recording from VENUE

Once you have connected your Pro Tools system to VENUE and created a new session in Pro Tools, you have to create new tracks and route the inputs. You can do this manually or use VENUE Link (part of VENUE 2.9 and later).

Auto Session Configuration with VENUE Link

Available on VENUE systems running VENUE software 2.9 or later is a useful feature for automatically setting up a Pro Tools session to record a VENUE show called VENUE Link. The configuration requires the following:

- VENUE software 2.9 or later

- Pro Tools HD 8.1 or later

- An active Ethernet connection between your Pro Tools system and your VENUE console

- An HDx, FWx, or MADI card installed in your VENUE console

To use VENUE Link between Pro Tools and VENUE you must make an Ethernet connection between the two. This can be as simple as connecting one end of a Cat5 cable to VENUE and the other end to your Pro Tools computer and setting each system to unique IP addresses. Once the Ethernet connection is made between the two, you can create a new session and select from the choices shown in the dialog box that appears.

If you've already created a Pro Tools session or are working from an existing session template and want to ensure that its track names match the latest VENUE channel lineup, use the Import VENUE Channel Names as Track Names feature to update your Pro Tools session.

Manual Session Configuration

If you choose to configure your Pro Tools session manually, you will need to set the input of a track in Pro Tools to the corresponding channel you want to record in VENUE.

Manually Routing HDx Channels

With HDx, this is somewhat simple in that the first 48 inputs of the Stage rack or Mix rack inputs will automatically show up as inputs 1–48.

To record the show with HDx:

1. Create a new session.

2. Add 48 mono tracks (or combination of mono and stereo tracks that mirror the mono and stereo inputs on VENUE).

3. Click **RECORD+PLAY**.

Tip: VENUE uses 20dB of headroom to prevent clipping in the live program material, so signals from FWx and HDx may be at a lower level than those you would normally set when recording into Pro Tools.

If you want to record other sources that are not inputs on the Stage rack or Mix rack (stage inputs), you must use the HDx assignables. These are located in VENUE's Patchbay > Directs > Pro Tools tab. You can choose to route practically anything in VENUE through these outputs, including mains, auxes, groups, FX returns, input channels, matrix and PQ outputs, and so on.

To route a channel directly to a Pro Tools input channel:

1. On VENUE, navigate to the **PATCHBAY > DIRECTS > PRO TOOLS** page.

2. On the left side of the Patchbay grid, select which channel you want to record. For the main L-R bus, select **OUTPUTS** and then scroll to Main L and Main R.

3. Hover the mouse over the HDx-assignable channel you want to send the **MAIN L-R** bus to and click.

4. In Pro Tools, create a stereo track and set the input for **HDxAssign x-x**.

Manually Routing FWx Channels

With FWx, you will always have to route channels via the Directs page in VENUE to record in Pro Tools. There is no automatic channel assignment using the FWx card. However, this means you can record any source to any of the available 32 inputs on Pro Tools.

To record the show with FWx:

1. Create a new session.

2. Add 32 mono tracks (or a combination of mono and stereo tracks that mirror the mono and stereo inputs on VENUE).

3. Route the FWx channels using **PATCHBAY > DIRECTS**.

4. In Pro Tools, click **RECORD+PLAY**.

If you choose to record other sources, simply change the routing for the channels you want to record. Remember, only 32 channels are available with FWx. It is recommended to submix non-critical channels in VENUE with PQ mixers to reduce channel count and keep critical channels used for remixing (for example, drum kit, guitars, vocals) as their own direct channels.

Recording and Playing Back Through VENUE

Both the HDx and FWx cards for VENUE allow you to record to and play back from a Pro Tools system. For the most part, routing is done in the Patchbay tab of the VENUE software. However, there are instances when you'll need to know about other pages and whether you are simply routing signals or trying to do a virtual soundcheck.

Virtual Soundcheck

Routing tracks to VENUE from Pro Tools is done the same way as recording but in reverse signal order. If you keep your tracks in Pro Tools as a mirror of the input channels on VENUE, you can easily simulate a "virtual soundcheck" of the performance you recorded by simply swapping input channels with Pro Tools playback channels.

Intelligence is built into the HDx and FWx expansion cards and it enables you to feed the recorded signal back into the input channels at the same pickoff point. In other words, if a microphone going to Channel 1 on VENUE is recorded to Pro Tools, that channel input can be routed back from Pro Tools as an input to Channel 1. The FWx card performs a gain adjustment that sends the recorded signal back into the VENUE input channel at the same gain as the mic level and at the same pickoff point, allowing you to tweak the VENUE mix and processing.

FWx Playback to VENUE

To play back Pro Tools tracks through VENUE with FWx:

1. Configure output paths in Pro Tools using the I/O Setup window. The FWx appears as a Pro Tools interface along the top of the path matrix in the Output page of I/O setup.

2. Route track output assignments in the mixer to paths going to the required FWx channels.

3. Route the Pro Tools channels in **VENUE's Patchbay > Input** page. FWx inputs are found under the **Pro Tools** subtab and may be routed to any input or FX return channel on the board. Assigning an input from Pro Tools will bring up a dialog box in VENUE asking to confirm a change in routing from an existing input to that channel or return from other sources such as the Stage racks and auxes. See Figure 4.24.

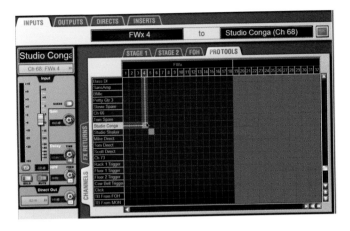

Figure 4.24
Routing inputs from Pro Tools to D-Show channels.

HDx Playback to VENUE

Routing from Pro Tools via HDx is slightly different from FWx, as some channels have fixed destinations, and some are flexible. The first 48 channels from the HDx card are routed directly to the first 48 Stage inputs, effectively replacing the Stage rack when switched in. When switched in, the Stage rack inputs are disabled (this is called virtual soundcheck). However, if you have recorded a submix and want to hear that back through the VENUE, it must be brought in as input channels or FX returns. In this case, you need to route these channels through Patchbay > Inputs > Pro Tools using the HDx-assignable channels.

If you need to record more than 48 input channels, the VENUE system is often configured with two HDx cards. If using two HDx cards on VENUE, you need at least two Pro Tools|HDX or four Pro Tools|HD cards to see all inputs. Furthermore, since the first 48 channels are fixed from the Stage rack, you require an additional Stage rack on VENUE for inputs 49 to 96. If you want to record 48 tracks while playing back 48 tracks, this also requires two HDx cards on VENUE (typically, channels 1–48 are used for recording, channels 65–112 are used for playback into VENUE, and HDx assignables are used for board mixes, group mixes, audience mics, and for capturing the reverb return signals to be used as reference for studio remix).

To play back Pro Tools tracks through VENUE with HDx:

1. Configure output paths in the I/O Setup (click **DEFAULT** to create all HDx channels automatically).

2. Route track output assignments in the mixer to paths going to the required HDx channels. It is often quicker to use the Cascade Outputs shortcut (**COMMAND+OPTION-CLICK** on the Mac or **CTRL+ALT-CLICK** on Windows) to route all tracks quickly.

3. In the VENUE software, open **OPTIONS > SYSTEM** to select HDx inputs as
   inputs 1–48 (rather than Stage 1 inputs). See Figure 4.25.

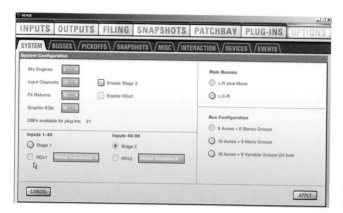

Figure 4.25
Routing inputs from Pro Tools
to D-Show channels.

4. If using HDx-assignable channels, route those inputs through **PATCHBAY >
   INPUTS** to available input channels or FX returns.

Recording and Playing Back Simultaneously

There may be times when a VENUE operator asks you to record the show but also
play back tracks from Pro Tools along with the show. In these cases, having the
act play to a click track is vital so that the backing tracks and the live performance
are in sync. This means a Pro Tools session will last as long as the performance. In
addition, MIDI Timecode (MTC) can be used to sync Pro Tools and VENUE
snapshots.

Although an FWx connection may suffice for a simple show with only a few backing tracks, most larger shows require dual HDx cards in the VENUE as well as a
multi-card Pro Tools|HDX or Pro Tools|HD system. This is due to the fact that
HDx channels 1 to 48 can be used as either playback or virtual soundcheck but
not both simultaneously. In these cases, the HDx#1 card on the VENUE may be
used for recording, while the HDx#2 is used for backing tracks (this will come up
as inputs 49–64 on the console). Also, with two HDx connections, you have 32
HDx assignables that can be used for anything you want.

*In the Avid
Learning Series*

For more information on advanced synchronization between
VENUE and Pro Tools, see the Synchronization and Snapshots
chapter in the **VENUE 210V course.**

Review/Discussion Questions

1. What are AAF or OMF files used for in music production?

2. Explain the difference between an embedded AAF file and an externally referenced AAF file.

3. Name three ways to open an AAF/OMF file in Pro Tools.

4. What are MXF audio files? How do they differ from a WAV file?

5. The Show Last Setup button in the I/O Setup window appears under what conditions?

6. How do you convert a session to a template? And vice versa?

7. What are the two Pro Tools interconnect options for VENUE? How many channels of Pro Tools I/O for each?

8. Where do you configure which channels go to which Pro Tools channels in VENUE for FWx connections?

9. Explain the concept between fixed channels and assignable channels when using HDx connections with Pro Tools.

10. What is required in order for Pro Tools to use channel names from VENUE for track names in Pro Tools?

Importing/Exporting and Session Interchange

This exercise is designed to improve your knowledge of the AAF/OMF file interchange as well as advanced import options of Pro Tools session data.

Media Used:

310M Exercise 4.PTTX (Pro Tools session file), Backing-vocals-Everything.AAF (AAF Media file), PT310M Ex.4 Other Song-no media.PTX (Pro Tools session file)

Duration:

25 to 30 minutes

Overview

In this exercise, you explore the different options for importing attributes of a song from other Pro Tools sessions as well as from an AAF file. In modern music production, the entire production is rarely done on a single Pro Tools system. For example, in this exercise, the female vocal backing tracks were recorded at another studio using another digital audio workstation. You will use Import Session Data to import the AAF as well as plug-in settings from a different Pro Tools mixing template session. At the end of the exercise, you save your session as a template and learn how to create a template category, enabling you to quickly select the template when creating new sessions.

Getting Started

Open the 310M Exercise 4.PTTX session and save the session in the student folder you created with earlier exercises. Take a few moments to play the session and look over the track layout.

Importing an AAF

This session is similar to the one you used in Exercise 3. However, you'll notice there are no backing tracks, nor are there any choir tracks. You'll start by importing the AAF that contains these tracks.

To import the AAF and associated media:

1. Select FILE > IMPORT > SESSION DATA, as shown in Figure Ex4.1.

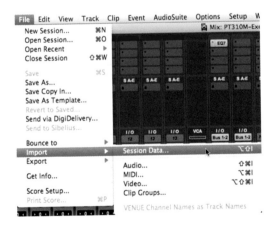

Figure Ex4.1
You import session data from the File menu.

2. Navigate to the **PT310M Ex.4** folder on your audio drive and open the **AAF Import Session** folder. Inside of the folder is an AAF file called **Backing-vocals-Everything.AAF** (see Figure Ex4.2). Select the file and click **Open**.

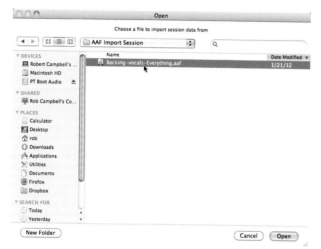

Figure Ex4.2
The AAF file as it appears in the Finder.

The Import Session dialog box will appear. All the source tracks should correspond to a new track in the destination column, as shown in Figure Ex4.3.

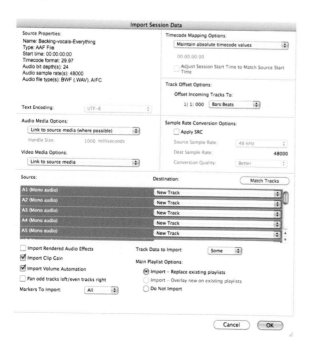

Figure Ex4.3
The Import Session Data dialog box with correct attributes selected.

3. Check the following options:

   - **Audio media options**—Link to source media (where possible)

   - **Timecode mapping options**—Maintain absolute timecode values

4. Next, select to import only the media and ignore all volume and pan automation. Start by unchecking the following in the Import Options section:

   - Import Rendered Audio Effects

   - Import Clip Gain

   - Import Volume Automation

   - Pan Odd/Even Tracks Left/Right

   In a real-world situation, you may want to keep some of these attributes. However, for this exercise, let's assume that there is no data to import, or that you don't want any previous volume or pan automation. See Figure Ex4.4.

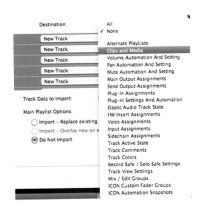

Figure Ex4.4
Unchecking automation and processing options.

5. Next, click on TRACK DATA TO IMPORT in the lower-right side of the dialog box and select NONE. Notice that the Main Playlist Options button below the drop-down switches to DO NOT IMPORT. Click on the list and select CLIPS AND MEDIA, as shown in Figure Ex4.5. Do not click OK at this point. You must re-enable the appropriate playlist options first. Otherwise nothing will import.

Figure Ex4.5
Choosing to import just audio
without any automation.

6. Under **MAIN PLAYLIST OPTIONS**, click on **IMPORT—REPLACE EXISTING PLAYLISTS** (see Figure Ex4.6). If you do not do this, you will import only blank tracks into your session.

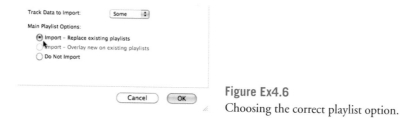

Figure Ex4.6
Choosing the correct playlist option.

7. Click **OK** to complete the process. Fourteen tracks with generic names will import into your session.

8. Listen through each track and familiarize yourself with each part. The first two tracks are a stereo mic pair of the entire choir at close range. The next three tracks are overdubs of individual parts. The next two tracks are a stereo mic pair at a distance from the choir. The last four tracks are background vocals of a quieter section.

9. Label each track, set their pans to suit your taste, and rebalance them to match the stereo pairs. Also, bus the tracks to an appropriate submaster and solo-safe the Aux Input submaster.

Importing Session Data

At times while mixing an album project you will find it helpful to import all the plug-ins and their settings from one session to another. In this example, the drums have been mixed for another song. You'll use Import Session Data to bring in just the plug-in assignments and settings to reuse them on the existing drum tracks for this song.

To import the session data from another Pro Tools session:

1. Select **FILE > IMPORT > SESSION DATA**. Navigate to your **EXERCISE 4** folder and open the **SESSION DATA IMPORT** folder. Select the file **PT310M EX.4 OTHER SONG-NO MEDIA.PTX**, as shown in Figure Ex4.7. This session has no media in it, just plug-in settings and attributes.

2. The Import Session Data dialog box is almost identical to when you opened the AAF, but with subtle differences, as you can see in Figure Ex4.8. At the top it tells you the Pro Tools version number, and at the bottom the Import Options are different. Also notice that none of the tracks are highlighted.

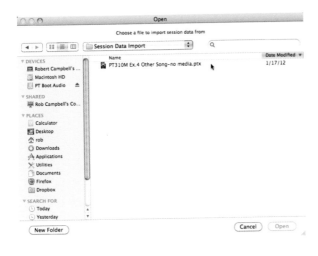

Figure Ex4.7
Opening another Pro Tools
session with data to import.

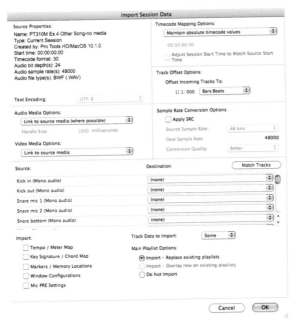

Figure Ex4.8
Import Session Data dialog box
when importing attributes from
another Pro Tools session.

3. At this stage, you do not want to import any of these tracks as new tracks; you just want the plug-in assignments. Click on the **MATCH TRACKS** button to have Pro Tools try to match up tracks from the template mix session to the tracks in your current session.

Tip: Match Tracks is based on track names, track types, and channel format. Sometimes it will match tracks that should not be matched, so be sure to review the matching.

4. After clicking **MATCH TRACKS**, some of the tracks will not match correctly. Notice in Figure Ex4.9, for example, that the Snare Bottom track tried to line up with B3 Bottom.

Figure Ex4.9
Match Tracks tries to match tracks based on the names.

5. Go through your tracks and make sure each track lines up with the corresponding track in the session. You are using only drum tracks at this point, and this template mix session has more drum tracks than the session you are working with. Click the Destination track drop-down for each track in your session and make sure it matches Table Ex4.1.

Tip: Clicking between the source track name and the destination track name on a matched track will toggle it to None. If the track is not previously matched, clicking here will select New Track.

Table Ex4.1   Matching Tracks

Source Track	Destination Track	Source Track	Destination Track
Kick In	Kick	OH Left	OH-L
Kick Out	None	OH Right	OH-R
Snare Mic 1	SnTop	Room L	Room-L
Snare Mic 2	None	Room R	Room-R
Snare Bottom	SnBot	Hi Room L	None
Hi Hat	Hat	Hi Room R	None
Tom Hi	None	Aux DRUM	None
Tom Mid	None	MONO HI	None
Tom Low	None	Drum Sub	Drum Sub
Tom hi 2	None		

6. Under **Track Data to Import**, select **None**. Then click on the drop-down again and select **Plug-In Assignments** and **Plug-In Settings and Automation**. Leave the Main Playlist option set to **Do Not Import**. Finally, click **OK**. See Figure Ex4.10.

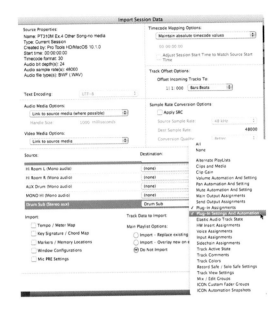

Figure Ex4.10

Track Data to Import settings.

Notice that the kick and snare tracks now have different plug-in assignments in the session. Figure Ex4.11 shows this result.

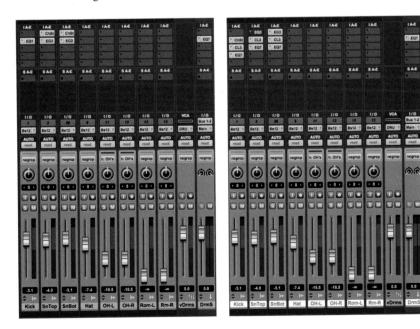

Figure Ex4.11

Kick, SnTop, and SnBot tracks have new plug-in assignments.

Saving a Session as a Template

Now that you have all the elements of your song, you can use this session as a starting point for all other songs on the album. To simplify the process, you can save the session as a template. That way all the track names, their routing, their submixing, and any plug-in assignments will be ready for the other songs.

To save a session as a template:

1. Choose FILE > SAVE AS TEMPLATE, as shown in Figure Ex4.12.

Figure Ex4.12

Save As Template is in the File menu.

In the Save Session Template dialog box, you can choose to save the template into the system templates that appear with the Quick Start dialog box and the New Session dialog box. You can add the template to an existing category or create your own, which is what you will do for this project.

2. Click on CATEGORY and select ADD CATEGORY, as shown in Figure Ex4.13.

Figure Ex4.13

Creating a new template category when saving a session template.

Type **PT310M EXERCISES** for the category name and click **OK**.

3. After creating the category, you will be returned to the Save Session Template dialog box with the new category chosen. At this point, change the name of the session to indicate it is a template (**PT310M ALBUM**). In some instances you may want to include media, but in this case you will not include media as it is just a template file.

4. Click **OK**. Your template will be saved.

Creating a New Session from a Template

Now that you have created a template for your album project, you can quickly create new sessions with the same layout and track names.

To create a session from your template:

1. Click on FILE > NEW SESSION and click on CREATE SESSION FROM TEMPLATE.

2. Click on the CREATE SESSION FROM TEMPLATE drop-down and select PT310M EXERCISES, as shown in Figure Ex4.14.

3. The dialog box will change to reflect the session names in your PT310M Exercises template category. Select the template file you saved previously and click OK to open a new session based on the template. See Figure Ex4.15.

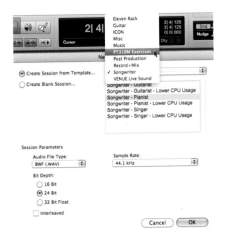

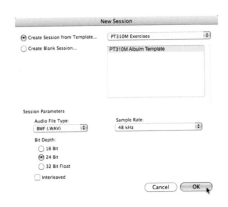

Figure Ex4.14
The Create Session from Template drop-down.

Figure Ex4.15
Choosing a template session to create a new session.

4. If you are in a session, you will be prompted to save changes. Select to SAVE or DON'T SAVE. The session will close, and the Save New Session As dialog box will appear. Type in a new name, such as PT 310M ALBUM SONG 2.

5. Select your student folder where you saved your session earlier. Click on SAVE; your session will open with empty tracks and all routing and plug-in assignments in place. Use FILE > IMPORT > SESSION DATA to import audio from another song into this template and start your mix.

Advanced Editing

This lesson covers advanced MIDI concepts, as well as the most advanced aspects of Beat Detective and Elastic Audio.

Media Used: None

Duration: 60 minutes

GOALS

- Use the Select and Split Notes MIDI function
- Understand sample-based MIDI tracks
- Record, edit, and transmit SysEx events using Pro Tools
- Use Beat Detective Collection mode
- Use Elastic Audio to adjust the timing of multi-mic'ed drum recordings
- Understand advanced Elastic Audio parameters

Introduction

In this lesson you return to some areas of Pro Tools that will be familiar from previous courses. Here, you learn the most advanced functions and concepts within these areas—specifically MIDI, Beat Detective, and Elastic Audio.

Advanced MIDI

The other Avid Learning courses have dealt extensively with MIDI. This lesson caps off those earlier courses by discussing several advanced MIDI techniques—Split Notes and SysEx.

Select and Split Notes

Select and Split Notes (accessed from Event > Event Operations > Select/Split Notes, as shown in Figure 5.1) allows you to select a subset of MIDI notes within a selection based on pitch, velocity, duration, position, or a combination of those criteria. This command can be used for the following purposes:

- To identify a range of notes for selective processing by another MIDI operation.

- To split pitch ranges to different tracks to use different sound sources. For example, the left-hand notes can be split from the right-hand notes in a performance.

- To split chords into separate monophonic clips.

- To split polyphonic drum tracks onto separate tracks.

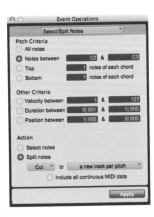

Figure 5.1
The Select/Split Notes window.

To select or split notes:

1. Make a selection of MIDI clips. Choose **EVENT > EVENT OPERATIONS > SELECT/SPLIT NOTES**.

2. Configure the **PITCH CRITERIA** as desired.

3. Configure the **OTHER CRITERIA** (Velocity, Duration, and Position) as desired.

4. Enable the **SELECT NOTES** or **SPLIT NOTES** option as desired.

5. When the **SPLIT NOTES** option is selected, choose **COPY** or **CUT** from the Split Notes pop-up menu and select the desired Copy or Cut destination.

   - **The clipboard**—Cuts or copies the selected data to the clipboard only.

   - **A new track**—Cuts or copies all selected data to a single, new track. If the selection includes multiple tracks, that same number of tracks will be created. The new tracks will duplicate the original track type (Instrument or MIDI).

   - **A new track per pitch**—Cuts or copies all selected data to multiple new tracks (one new track for each pitch). If the selection includes multiple tracks, each track will have its data split separately.

6. If desired, enable **THE INCLUDE ALL CONTINUOUS MIDI DATA** option. Enabling this option will include all controller data associated with the split notes in each newly created track. Leave this option unchecked to split only the note data to new tracks.

7. Click **APPLY**.

Note: The Select/Split Notes command cannot be undone.

Note: Any Real-Time MIDI Properties associated with the track or clips are copied to the new tracks or clips created by Select/Split Notes.

Sample-Based MIDI Tracks

Just like Audio tracks, MIDI tracks are interchangeable between sample-based and tick-based timebases. When a MIDI track's timebase is set to samples, all MIDI events in the track are anchored to locations in absolute time, instead of to relative Bar|Beat locations.

Sample-based MIDI tracks can be used to:

- Keep a MIDI track safe from changes to the session tempo map.

- Start a song from a free MIDI performance and build the session's tempo map around that, instead of recording against a predetermined grid and click track.

With sample-based MIDI tracks, tempo changes in the session will not affect sample-based MIDI clips. In fact, changing the tempo may expand or contract the tempo ruler but will have no effect on a sample-based MIDI track; thus, the sample-based MIDI clip will maintain its absolute time (such as Mins:Secs or timecode). With tick-based MIDI tracks, tempo changes will affect tick-based MIDI clips, keeping MIDI data relatively locked to the bars and beats grid. If the tempo is slowed down or sped up, the MIDI data will expand or contract, thus changing its timing.

MIDI tracks can be designated as tick-based or sample-based when they are created, as shown in Figure 5.2.

Figure 5.2
Timebase choices when creating new tracks.

MIDI tracks can also be switched at any time using the track's timebase selector pop-up menu, as shown in Figure 5.3.

Figure 5.3
Changing a track's timebase.

SysEx Events

SysEx (short for System Exclusive) data is an umbrella term for any proprietary data sent using the MIDI protocol. Effects devices and MIDI instruments can send SysEx data "dumps" (or "bulk dumps") that contain all the information about their current settings, or portions of their data as defined by the source device. Pro Tools can record this data to MIDI tracks and resend it when you want to reload the environment on your MIDI device. This provides a way of archiving and recalling the settings of your studio equipment when you return to a session.

SysEx Dumps

To record a SysEx dump at the beginning of a MIDI track:

1. Make sure that the MIDI In and Out for the device sending the SysEx is connected to a MIDI In and Out port on your MIDI interface.

2. Configure a MIDI or Instrument track for recording.

3. In the Options menu, make sure that **DESTRUCTIVE RECORD**, **LOOP RECORD**, and **QUICKPUNCH** are disabled.

4. In the MIDI Input Filter dialog box (choose **SETUP > MIDI > INPUT FILTER**), enable recording of System Exclusive data.

5. Record-enable the MIDI track.

6. Enable **WAIT FOR NOTE** in the Transport window or press F11 (must be enabled in **PREFERENCES > MIDI**; it is disabled by default).

7. Make sure that you are at the beginning of the session or another place in the session you want to have the external device change with SysEx data.

8. When you are ready to begin recording, click **RECORD** in the Transport window. The Record, Play, and Wait for Note buttons will flash, indicating that Pro Tools is waiting for MIDI data.

9. Initiate the SysEx transfer from the external device, according to the instructions in the reference guide for the device. When receiving the MIDI data, Pro Tools automatically begins recording.

10. When the transfer is complete, click **STOP** in the Transport window.

The newly recorded MIDI data will appear as a MIDI clip in the track's playlist and in the Clip List. MIDI clips that contain SysEx data appear blank when the MIDI or Instrument Track View selector is set to Clips. To see the SysEx event blocks, which indicate the location of the data, set the Track View selector to SysEx.

To resend the SysEx from Pro Tools:

1. Make sure the MIDI Out of your MIDI interface is connected to the MIDI In of the device. Also make sure the device is set to receive SysEx. Some devices require that memory protect be off.

2. In Pro Tools, click the track's **MIDI OUTPUT SELECTOR** and assign the device from the pop-up menu.

3. Locate to the beginning of the session.

4. Press **PLAY**. Pro Tools will transmit the previously recorded SysEx to the assigned MIDI device.

Moving/Deleting SysEx Events

SysEx events appear in the track's playlist as blocks when the Track View selector is set to SysEx. See Figure 5.4.

Figure 5.4
SysEx event block.

Although the contents of recorded System Exclusive events cannot be directly edited in Pro Tools, the events can be moved or nudged, copied and pasted, or deleted.

To move a SysEx event:

1. Set the MIDI or Instrument track's display to SysEx using the Track View selector.

2. With the Grabber tool, drag the SysEx event left or right.

To delete one or more SysEx events:

1. With the track view set to SysEx, click the SysEx event with the Grabber tool to select it.

2. Choose EDIT > CLEAR to remove the selected events from the track.

Tip: Individual SysEx event blocks can also be deleted by Option-clicking (Mac) or Alt-clicking (Windows) on them with the Pencil tool.

Advanced Multitrack Drum Editing

This section explains how to use Beat Detective's Collection mode and discusses the differences between editing multi-mic'ed drums with Beat Detective and Elastic Audio.

Beat Detective Collection Mode

In Pro Tools 210M you learned how to detect beats in the kick and snare tracks of a multitrack drum recording and then apply the beat markers to all the other tracks. This technique can work well for generating a tempo map and for working with reasonably well played performances. However, if there are beats on other tracks that are not detected (such as hi-hats and tom patterns), these will not be corrected if you're conforming, or included in a groove template when you're extracting grooves.

Another option is to include all the tracks when detecting transients. However, it can be difficult to find detection settings that include all the quieter beats on certain tracks without generating false triggers on other tracks. You could analyze only the overheads, which contain all the beats, but the hits will also be later in time due to acoustic latency, as seen in Figure 5.5.

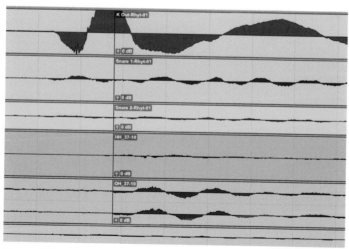

Figure 5.5
Detecting triggers on the overheads can cause close-mic'ed sources to be cut late.

Collection mode offers a solution to this situation by allowing you to collect beat markers from several tracks using different detection settings.

Collection Mode

Collection mode is available in Bar|Beat Marker Generation, Groove Template Extraction, or Clip Separation mode and is accessed from the pop-up menu at the top of the Detection section of the Beat Detective window. See Figure 5.6.

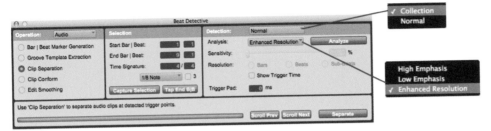

Figure 5.6
Beat Detective window with Collection and Analysis drop-down menus.

Used to refine the Analysis step of Beat Detective, Collection mode allows you to analyze the transient hits on each of the drum kit tracks, adjust the sensitivity slider for each track individually, choose different detection algorithms (such as High Emphasis, Low Emphasis, or Enhanced Resolution), and then add the triggers from each of the tracks together into a collection to be used for Clip separation, Marker Generation, or Groove Template Extraction across all the tracks as a group. See Figure 5.7.

Figure 5.7
Collection mode controls.

To use Collection mode:

1. In the Edit window, select a whole number of bars (typically 4–8 bars) of a single drum track (best to start with the Kick drum). Remember, the selection's start and end points should be made right before the transient, irrespective of where the bar line is. Be sure to listen to your selection to make sure it is musically correct.

2. In the Beat Detective window, select one of the following modes:

   • Bar|Beat Marker Generation

   • Groove Template Extraction

   • Clip Separation

3. Enter the Start and End locations in the Selection section of Beat Detective (for example, start is bar 1 beat 1, and end is bar 9 beat 1 for an 8-bar selection).

Tip: As you learned in 210M, the Capture button in Beat Detective enters the start and end times automatically. However, these values can be wrong because the Capture button is based on the Bar|Beat grid. If a hit is earlier than your minimum detection value (e.g., 1/8 note) then the start time may come up as Beat 4 instead of Beat 1. If using the Capture button, always be sure to check that start/end times are correct before proceeding.

4. Click **ANALYZE**.

5. Experiment with the **ANALYSIS** mode and the **SENSITIVITY SLIDER** to detect all the beats on the track without creating false triggers. You may need to add/remove triggers by hand at this point.

Tip: A good rule of thumb is to set the Analysis mode to Enhanced Resolution and press Analyze. Return the Sensitivity slider to 0 and then slowly raise the slider until you see just the triggers you are looking for (for example, on a kick track, raise the sensitivity slider until you see just the kick transients).

6. Click on the **DETECTION**-drop-down menu and choose **COLLECTION**.

7. Click **ADD ALL** to add all of the current beat triggers to the collection. You will see the display update to show all the triggers you just detected.

8. Switch back to **NORMAL** mode and move the selection to the next track (for example the snare track) you want to analyze. Be sure to keep the selection range exactly the same for each track.

Tip: With Commands Keyboard Focus enabled, press P to move the selection up or semicolon (;) to move the selection down. If Link Track and Edit Selection is enabled, simply select each track in turn.

9. Click **ANALYZE** again. Return the Sensitivity slider to 0 and raise it slowly until you see the transients detected that you want for the track (for instance, on a snare track, raise it until you see just the snare hits).

10. Switch back to **COLLECTION** mode again.

11. In the Detection (Collection mode) section, click **ADD UNIQUE** to add the unique triggers detected on this track to the collection. When you choose to add unique triggers, Beat Detective looks for triggers that are close to triggers already collected from other tracks (those that are assigned to the same trigger location). Where triggers already exist, the newly detected triggers are discarded.

Tip: It is important that you analyze close-mic'ed tracks first (kick, snare, hats, toms) to ensure that the earliest trigger in time at any beat location is added to the pool. Otherwise, some beats will be cut late when you separate. If you are uncertain whether the earliest triggers were added to the pool, consider adding a start pad when separating to avoid cutting any beats in two.

12. Repeat Steps 8–11 for each track you are analyzing.

Tip: Don't analyze room mic tracks, as these do not normally contain any unique triggers. Only analyze overhead mics if they are being used to pick up sources that are not close-mic'ed (or covered by other physically closer mics).

13. When all tracks have been analyzed, extend your edit selection to cover all the tracks. Better yet, group your drum tracks. If the group is already enabled, simply re-enable the group. You will see all the beat triggers you collected, color-coded by which track generated them, as shown in Figure 5.8.

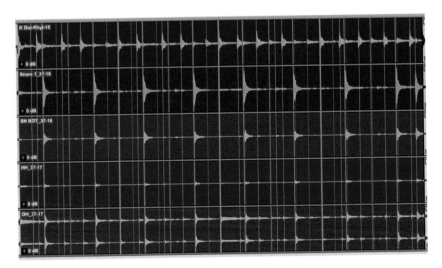

Figure 5.8
Color-coded triggers in Collection mode.

14. Finally, with Beat Detective's Collection mode still active, apply Bar|Beat Marker Generation, Groove Template Extraction or Clip Separation.

Tip: Make sure your selection covers all the required tracks before separating.

Elastic Audio Versus Beat Detective for Multi-Mic'ed Drums

For many years, Beat Detective had been the primary tool in Pro Tools for editing multitrack drum recordings. However, the introduction of Elastic Audio in Pro Tools 7.4 added another option. This section discusses the Elastic Audio approach to drum editing and highlights the issues that affect the decision whether to use Elastic Audio or Beat Detective in a project.

Using Elastic Audio for Multi-Mic'ed Drums—Workflow

The following workflow outlines the procedure for tightening a multi-track drum performance with Elastic Audio.

1. **Group tracks:** It's important that your drum mic tracks are grouped. During analysis, different event markers may appear across the different transient events in a multi-track performance. If they are grouped, only the event marker closest to the most significant transient in the group will be promoted to a Warp marker (see Figure 5.10) and all grouped tracks moved in relation when quantized. If they are not grouped, conforming may sound erratic as each individual track will be quantized to the grid with no regard to the timing of other tracks.

2. **Enable Elastic Audio on the tracks:** Enable the Rhythmic Elastic Audio plug-in on any of the drum tracks. With the tracks grouped, they will all switch when one is set for Elastic Audio. See Figure 5.9.

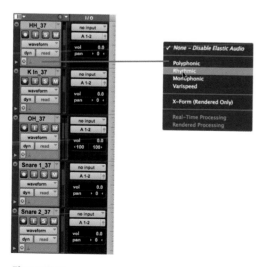

Figure 5.9
Choosing Rhythmic algorithm for Elastic Audio.

3. **Switch to Warp view:** This allows you to view the transient analysis and also the results of any quantization that you apply. Transient detection is also shown in Analysis view.

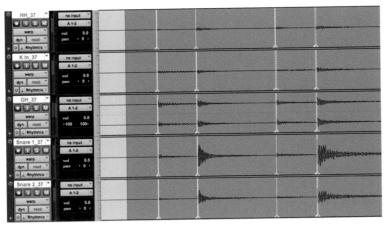

Figure 5.10
Drum tracks after quantizing with Warp markers.

4. **Verify analysis:** Zoom in on a section of drums to check how successfully the beats have been detected by the Elastic Audio transient detection. In most cases, you should see event markers at every hit, and hopefully no false triggers (see Figure 5.11). Many hits will be detected in more than one track due to mic bleed, and others will only be detected on their close mic track. This does not affect the outcome.

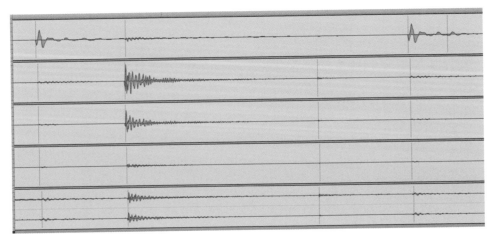

Figure 5.11
Event markers in Warp view.

As with Beat Detective's transient analysis, there is the possibility that the Elastic Audio analysis may either miss some hits or generate false triggers. A quick scan through the tracks should tell you whether this is an issue with a particular recording.

Tip: Unlike Beat Detective, Elastic Audio always defaults for Sensitivity at 100%. Most false triggers can be eliminated by slightly reducing the timing sensitivity to 90–95% while maintaining enough Warp markers to successfully quantize a drum performance.

5. **Add or remove event markers:** If there are false or missing event markers, switch the tracks to Analysis view so that you can directly edit them. To add a marker to a drum hit, right-click with the GRABBER (or any tool) at the transient in the waveform and choose ADD EVENT MARKER. To delete a false trigger, OPTION-CLICK (Mac) or ALT-CLICK (Windows) on the marker with the GRABBER or PENCIL tool. You can select and delete multiple markers by selecting them with the SELECTOR tool and pressing the BACKSPACE or DELETE key.

Tip: Remember, you don't need to delete markers that are the result of mic spill.

6. **Select an area to quantize:** As with Beat Detective, you may decide to break the song down into shorter sections to work on. However, if transient analysis appears to have worked successfully, you may be able to get good results quantizing large sections at a time. To isolate sections of your drum tracks for Elastic Audio Quantization, you should separate them into clips.

Tip: Although Quantization is applied only to the selected area of a clip, any change to the last transient in the selection will have a knock-on effect on all subsequent transients unless you Separate clips.

7. **Open the Quantize window:** Select EVENT > EVENT OPERATIONS > QUANTIZE or press OPTION+0 (Mac) or ALT+0 (Windows). Choose the appropriate settings, as shown in Figure 5.12.

   In the What to Quantize pop-up menu, choose ELASTIC AUDIO EVENTS. Select other quantization options as needed.

Tip: Depending upon the style of music you are quantizing, you may want to retain more of the original feel than a full quantized sound. For this, adjust the Strength slider to a setting that quantizes the performance yet retains the original feel of the performance. As a rule, 65–85% should retain the original feel yet result in a near perfect quantization of the performance.

Figure 5.12
Event Operations: Quantize window.

8. **Apply the quantization**: Click the APPLY button in the Event Operations: Quantize window.

9. **Listen to the results:** Press the SPACEBAR to hear the results of the Quantization operation. If you zoom in on the tracks, you will be able to see how Pro Tools applied quantization to Elastic Audio events on grouped tracks. See Figure 5.13.

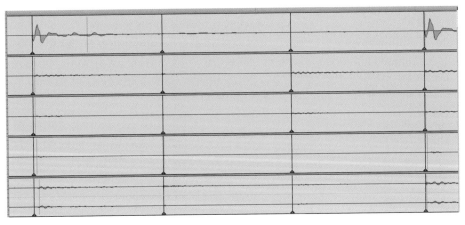

Figure 5.13
Warp markers applied during quantization of Elastic Audio events.

All Warping Applies to All Tracks

Warp markers appear in the clips wherever Elastic Audio events have been moved. Notice that whenever an event is moved, the same warp is applied to all tracks in the group, even if the event marker was only on one of the tracks. This is how Pro Tools attempts to maintain phase coherency between the tracks.

Nearby Events on Multiple Tracks Are Treated as One Event

When there are events on multiple tracks that fall closely together, only the earliest event is used. This is the same behavior as Beat Detective. The co-existent events keep their relative positions, so as audio is moved around, it is moved around together when grouped. This allows Elastic Audio a good chance to maintain phase relationships. However, due to the nature of stretching or compressing sounds, phase accuracy may not be maintained. Using the earliest event avoids having Warp markers placed in the middle of any drum hits. As with Beat Detective, this scheme can fail in some circumstances.

Fixing Problems After Quantizing with Elastic Audio

As with Beat Detective, certain situations can be problematic when conforming drums with Elastic Audio. After applying Quantize settings in the Event Operations window, you should check through the results to identify any problems.

Tip: Many of these issues also occur when using Beat Detective, with slightly different symptoms and solutions.

Problem: Simultaneous Hits Played Out of Time

In Figure 5.14, a kick drum and hi-hat were both meant to occur at the same time on the beat, but they were played out of time with respect to each other. However, because they both fall within the same quantization grid unit (one 1/16th note in this case), they are treated as one event, and the relative timing remains. In this example, the hi-hat was actually played in time, but the kick was early. After quantization, the kick is in time, and the hi-hat is pushed late.

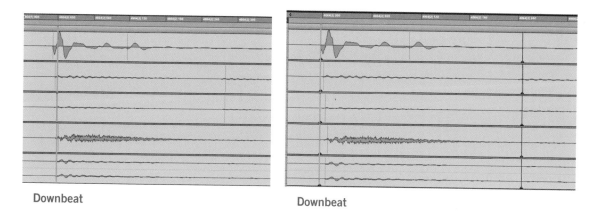

Downbeat   Downbeat

Figure 5.14
Relative timing between coincident drum hits may not be fixed by Elastic Audio (or Beat Detective).

Solution

You should not manually warp the two events in this situation, as you will put the tracks out of phase. The best solution is to replace the audio at this location with a similar section from elsewhere in the song.

Problem: Quantization in the Wrong Direction

As with Beat Detective and MIDI note quantization, any hits that are played further out of time than the quantization grid will be moved even further out of time than they were played.

Solution

This problem may be resolved by manually moving the grouped Warp markers for this event to the correct grid location. If this causes excessive warping to be applied, consider replacing the audio.

Problem: Coincident Hits Treated Separately (Split Notes)

Two hits that were supposed to be coincident were played out of time with one another. However, they are far enough apart that Pro Tools treats them as separate events. This is more likely to happen if you use smaller quantization grid values (such as 1/16th notes). Because all tracks must be warped equally, this can cause dramatic warping effects to occur between two adjacent events, often with one event being warped in the middle of its decay.

Solution

To fix this problem, delete one of the two Warp markers and adjust the remaining one for the best result. This usually means placing the earliest event at the grid. If the timing discrepancy between the two events is audible, consider replacing.

Beat Detective or Elastic Audio?

The decision whether to use Beat Detective or Elastic Audio to edit multitrack drums is dependent on the circumstances and personal preference. Here are some considerations:

- **Speed and ease of use:** In most cases, using Elastic Audio is faster than using Beat Detective. This is because getting the best results with Beat Detective usually requires careful work on short sections at a time, followed by editing to clean up the results. With Elastic Audio, you can often work with longer sections of time and then fix any problems during a careful listen-through.

■ **Sound quality:** Some differences in sound can occur when using Elastic Audio instead of Beat Detective. Beat Detective does not change the audio in any way and guarantees phase coherency between grouped tracks. Elastic Audio, on the other hand, works by time-stretching audio and has the potential to create different "micro-timings" that may be audible by altering the stereo field of the entire drum kit.

■ **Warping artifacts:** In most cases, the warping applied when quantizing recorded drums is rather small, and the nature of the Rhythmic algorithm minimizes changes to the program material as much as possible. However, with audio that requires significant quantization (particularly sounds with long decay times), changes to the sound may be audible.

■ **Phase:** As you have seen, Elastic Audio processing seeks to maintain the phase relationship between tracks by applying Warp markers equally to all tracks. However, time-stretching is not a wholly linear process, so tiny shifts (micro-timings) can still occur between tracks. Some listeners may be able to hear this as a subtle narrowing or blurring of the stereo image and/or pitch modulation.

■ **Switching to X-Form:** The X-Form Elastic Audio plug-in offers an additional level of time of detail when stretching audio, but it cannot be used for real-time processing. However, a trick you can use is to work with the Rhythmic plug-in while editing the drums and then switch, or render the track with X-Form when you're finished. The same warping will be applied, using the higher quality algorithm. When you switch to X-Form, the drum tracks will be rendered as new audio files. This may take several minutes or more, so you should schedule this for the end of a session.

Advanced Elastic Audio

Elastic Audio is covered in some depth in earlier Avid Learning courses. In this course, we will look in detail at some of the parameters and settings that affect the results achieved with Elastic Audio.

Elastic Properties

Any clip that has undergone Elastic Audio analysis has Elastic Audio properties associated with it. These properties are stored with the clip, so they are preserved when copying the clip or dragging it from the Clip List to any track with the same Elastic Audio configuration (plug-in and timebase).

To view a clip's Elastic Audio properties, do one of the following:

■ Right-click on the clip and choose **ELASTIC PROPERTIES** from the pop-up menu. See Figure 5.15.

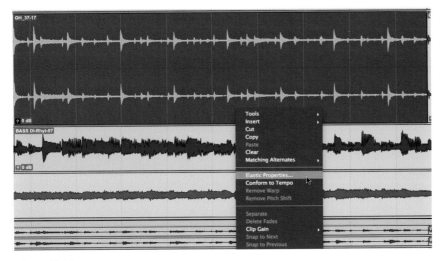

Figure 5.15
Opening the Elastic Properties window from a clip.

■ Select the clip, and choose **CLIP > ELASTIC PROPERTIES**.

■ Press **OPTION+[5]** (Mac) or **ALT+[5]** (Windows).

The Elastic Properties window will open.

The Elastic Properties window shows the Elastic properties for the selected clip(s). The number of parameters shown differs, depending on whether the selected clip is on a track that is tick-based or sample-based. See Figure 5.16.

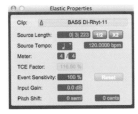

Figure 5.16
Elastic properties window.

If multiple clips are selected, the Elastic Properties window displays the value of any parameters that the clips have in common. Parameters that differ between the selected clips are displayed as an asterisk, as shown in Figure 5.17.

Figure 5.17
Elastic Properties window with different Source Length and BPM values for selected clips.

When multiple clips are selected, you can change Elastic properties for all of them at once.

Property Specifics

Most users may not have the time to truly understand the intricacies of the Elastic Audio properties window. However, a full understanding of this window can give you the knowledge you need to fix issues detected improperly by Elastic Audio or creativity options that may not be readily apparent.

Source Length and Tempo

These two linked properties describe the original un-stretched length and tempo of the clip. When a clip is first analyzed, Elastic Audio attempts to detect these properties automatically. For clearly rhythmic sections of audio that conform to the meter defined for the session, the detected values are often correct. If the detection yields an incorrect result, you can enter the correct values manually. This is often the case when the music has a double time feel or a hemiola (two over three [2:3] or three over 2 [3:2])

1/2 and x2 Buttons

In some cases, analysis results in a detected tempo that is half or twice the correct value. In these cases, you can quickly correct the Source Length parameter by clicking the 1/2 or x2 button.

Tip: Although intended as a way to correct the nominal tempo of a clip, you can also use these buttons creatively to force the audio to play at half or double speed.

Meter

Elastic Audio analysis does not attempt to detect the meter of audio, and this parameter always defaults to 4/4. If a different time signature is used, you must enter it manually.

TCE Factor

This parameter simply displays the amount the clip is being time-stretched, expressed as a percentage of the original audio length. This value is not directly editable; rather, it shows you the net result when adjusting other elastic properties or after quantization.

Event Sensitivity

This parameter is covered in detail in earlier Avid Learning courses. It is used to adjust the sensitivity of the Elastic Audio analysis to transients. Event Sensitivity defaults to 100% and can be reduced if false triggers cause Elastic Audio warping to function incorrectly.

As explained in earlier courses, by switching a track to Analysis view and then clicking and dragging up and down in the Event Sensitivity field, you can follow visual cues to find the optimal setting that produces no false triggers. See Figure 5.18.

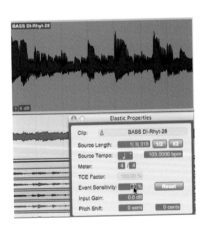

Figure 5.18
Lowering Event Sensitivity limits detection to just bass note attacks.

Input Gain

This parameter allows you to attenuate the gain of a clip. This option is provided because in some cases, Elastic Audio warping can result in a gain increase and may cause clipping. This can sometimes happen when two slices of audio must be crossfaded together (specifically when drastically speeding up a performance).

Elastic Audio Plug-Ins and Parameters

Pro Tools approaches time manipulation of audio, or warping, in several different ways, represented by the different algorithms used by the Elastic Audio plug-ins. In this section, you'll look at the plug-ins and their settings and explore their strengths and weaknesses for different types of material.

Time Compression Expansion (TCE) Modes

There is one unavoidable truth when you want to change the length/tempo of recorded audio without changing its pitch: You must either cut audio out (when compressing) or add audio in (when expanding). This should be done intelligently with regard to the program material to achieve the most transparent results. Therefore, Pro Tools provides different algorithms (plug-ins) for different circumstances.

Rhythmic Mode

Rhythmic mode uses TCE techniques that work best with drums and percussion. The audio is assumed to consist primarily of non-pitched transients followed by decays, interspersed with essentially non-program material (the gaps between the beats). This kind of material can be stretched and compressed more effectively than any other, as there are areas between the hits that can be removed (when compressing) or expanded (when stretching). See Figure 5.19.

Figure 5.19
The Rhythmic Elastic Audio plug-in.

Rhythmic mode attempts to preserve the integrity of individual percussive events, moving them apart or closer together as necessary to achieve time warping. As is generally the case with all warping, speeding up the audio is less problematic than slowing it down. Skipping sections of audio is relatively simple. When stretching, Pro Tools must generate audio to fill the gaps. If the beats are clearly separated by silence, this does not present a huge problem, but this is rarely the case, as decays will often overlap, and there will be background ambience. The audio that is generated is based on the surrounding material, so it blends in, but it will sound unnatural and "looped" when the tempo is significantly slowed.

Decay Rate

In order to reduce unnatural-sounding artifacts when material is slowed down, the audio can be gated with a decay after each transient. The Decay Rate control gives you manual control over how fast the program material (in most cases, a drum attack) is decayed or, put another way, how much program material (the drum strike) is considered in the algorithm. By applying a shorter decay, you can capture the main transient and original decay of the performance while disregarding the tails of the decay and removing them from the filler (the part that repeats when stretching). A longer decay rate maintains a continuous audio recording (that is, it includes more of the original transient's decay), but it may expose more of the filler material used to stretch out the hits.

Tip: You can use the Rhythmic Elastic Audio plug-in to isolate individual hits in a loop by setting the decay rate to 0% and slowing down the tempo tremendously to isolate each hit. This effectively keeps the original transient intact and inserts silence between the hits.

Monophonic Mode

Monophonic mode uses an algorithm suited to pitched (tonal) monophonic material such as bass guitar, vocals, solo woodwind, and so forth. Unlike Rhythmic mode, this approach cannot rely on obvious points in the program material that can be removed or duplicated. Instead, the audio must be treated in a more uniform way.

Monophonic mode preserves the formant of the audio. This is the overall frequency response shape that gives any instrument or voice its timbre (see "X-Form," later in this lesson for more on formants). By preserving the formant, Monophonic mode retains the intrinsic character of the sound, unlike straightforward Varispeeding, which shifts the pitch and formant of the audio, resulting in the characteristic "chipmunk" effect. See Figure 5.20.

Figure 5.20
The Monophonic Elastic Audio plug-in.

Monophonic mode can be very effective on some kinds of material, but it will sound grainy when used for extreme tempo changes. As the audio is treated in a more linear way than with Rhythmic or Polyphonic mode, any artifacts are spread throughout the program material, instead of being focused in certain areas, such as between transients.

Tip: If you are recording new material and expect to be using extreme Elastic Audio warping, it is best to record in 32-bit float file format to gain the maximum amount of resolution when performing Elastic Audio processing. Elastic Audio works at the file's native resolution, despite what the session bit depth is set for. For example, a 16-bit 44.1kHz file imported into a 96kHz, 32-bit float session will still be processed at 16-bit 44.1kHz with Elastic Audio.

There are no user-editable controls for the Monophonic Elastic Audio plug-in.

Tip: If you find yourself using Monophonic mode, and you are getting close to the results you want but are getting audible artifacts, try switching the track to X-Form and rendering the result.

Varispeed Mode

Varispeed mode simply slows down or speeds up audio without preserving its original pitch. As such, it is not time-stretching in the standard sense of the phrase. See Figure 5.21.

Figure 5.21
The Varispeed Elastic Audio plug-in.

Why Use Varispeed Mode?

- **Sound quality:** Because Varispeed is resampling, rather than using a stretching algorithm, it has little or no impact on the quality of the audio.
- **Preserves continuity of audio:** When pitch preservation is not vital, such as with percussion and some drums with smaller, global tempo changes, you could use Varispeed, as the original continuity of the audio signal is not interrupted.
- **Special effects:** The most common use of Varispeed is for creative effects, such as dramatic slowdowns and turntable-style effects.

Polyphonic Mode

Polyphonic mode is designed for use on complex and mixed source audio tracks. Examples include a polyphonically played piano or a full song mix. Time-stretching this kind of material is very challenging. The program material is likely to contain a mixture of transients and continuous audio.

The Polyphonic plug-in (see Figure 5.22) has two controls that allow the user to fine-tune the algorithm for the best results: Window Length and Follow.

Figure 5.22
The Polyphonic Elastic Audio plug-in.

The Window Length Control

The Polyphonic algorithm treats the audio as small sections. You can hear this if you slow down the audio dramatically—small sections of the audio can be heard to loop. The window length sets the size of the slices into which the audio is divided. (This is often called the Grain Size in granular synthesis, on which this technology is based.) You can set the window length from 6ms to 185ms.

Smaller values produce an even response and more precise transients, but a grainier sound. Higher values improve the sound quality during continuous sounds but can produce audible flamming and repetition of transients. With this in mind, the suggestions listed in Table 5.1 can be used to set the Window Length control for different types of material.

Table 5.1   Elastic Audio Polyphonic Plug-In Window Length Uses

Type of Material	Suggested Window Length
General Purpose	30–40ms
Percussive	20ms or lower
Pads and other legato material	60ms or higher

The Follow Control

This button enables an envelope follower, which causes the original dynamic quality of the sound to be imposed somewhat on the stretched version. This helps transient parts of the sound in particular maintain their original character and sound less stretched.

X-Form

The X-Form plug-in (shown in Figure 5.23) is different from the other algorithms as it cannot be used for real-time warping of audio. Tracks using the X-Form plug-in are always in Rendered Processing mode. This means that when audio is added to the track or any time-related (or X-Form parameter) changes are made, the audio clips must be rendered offline and will not be heard until processing is complete. This can take up to a few minutes for a continuous track of a song.

Figure 5.23
X-Form Elastic Audio plug-in.

Note: You do not have to own the X-Form AudioSuite plug-in to use X-Form processing on an Elastic Audio track.

Why Use X-Form?

Although X-Form warping must be rendered, the payoff is generally excellent results.

Use X-Form under the following conditions:

- When satisfactory results cannot be achieved with the other plug-ins, especially with Polyphonic or complex material.
- When applying an extreme tempo change, especially when slowing the tempo.
- When the very highest sound quality is required.
- When making one-off changes that you can "set and leave."

X-Form has two plug-in controls: Quality and Formant.

The Quality Control

Quality can be set to Maximum or Low (Faster) from a pop-up menu. Unsurprisingly, the Maximum setting produces the highest sound quality. The Low (Faster) setting is much faster and is useful when you need to try out different warping operations. You can always change the track back to Maximum at the end of the production, and all the clips will be reprocessed.

The Formant Control

For audio with clear formants, enable Formant mode to preserve the formant shape of audio when time-stretching.

Tip: Again, if you are recording new material and expect to be using extreme Elastic Audio warping with X-Form, 32-bit float file format will give you the most headroom, accuracy, and resolution to achieve fantastic results, even with extreme changes in time.

More on Formants

Audio with a fundamental pitch has an overtone series, or a set of higher harmonics. The strength of these higher harmonics creates a formant shape, which is apparent if viewed using a spectrum analyzer. The overtones, or harmonics, have the same spacing related to the pitch and have the same general shape regardless of what the fundamental pitch is. It is this formant shape that gives the audio its overall characteristic sound or timbre. When pitch-shifting audio, the formant shape is shifted with the rest of the material, which can result in an unnatural sound. Keeping this shape constant is critical to formant-correct pitch-shifting and achieving a natural-sounding result.

Review/Discussion Questions

1. Why is Split Notes useful? Name a scenario in which you would use it.

2. Why would you use sample-based MIDI tracks?

3. How do you get SysEx data into Pro Tools? How do you send it back out?

4. Can you edit SysEx data in Pro Tools?

5. Explain the benefits of using Collection mode versus Normal mode with Beat Detective.

6. When would you use Beat Detective versus using Elastic Audio? What about vice versa?

7. In the Elastic Properties window, what would you change to hear the music half speed? Twice the speed?

8. Explain when you would use Monophonic versus Polyphonic mode with Elastic Audio. When would you use Polyphonic mode?

Exercise 5

Advanced Beat Detective

This exercise is designed to improve your knowledge of the advanced options for Beat Detective and Elastic Audio. In this exercise, you will follow a real-world music production scenario of matching a live drum performance to a loop. You will use two scenarios: first, using Beat Detective and quantizing the live drums to the loop using Groove Extraction and Conforming, and second using Elastic Audio and Groove Conforming.

Media Used:

310M Exercise 5.PTXT (Pro Tools session file)

Duration:

45–60 minutes

Getting Started

Open the 310M Exercise 5.PTXT session. Take a few moments to look over the session and familiarize yourself with the different drum tracks and the loop you will be trying to match. The drum tracks are already submixed to a stereo auxiliary.

Grouping Tracks for Editing

Before beginning, it is helpful to group all of the drum tracks together. You have grouped tracks together before, but in this exercise you'll be using advanced methods such as group presets to quickly choose attributes as well as marquee dragging in the tracks list to quickly select multiple tracks.

To select multiple tracks for grouping:

1. In the **EDIT** window, hover the mouse over the Track List (either the track type icon or track color icon) until it turns into a marquee selector (crosshairs). See Figure Ex5.1.

Figure Ex5.1
Marquee selector icon.

2. Click and drag from Track 1 to Track 18, as shown in Figure Ex5.2. When you release the mouse, all 18 tracks will be selected.

Tip: To aid in the exercise, it is recommended to turn on Track Numbers by selecting View > Track Number.

Figure Ex5.2
Selecting multiple tracks in tracks list.

3. Select the **NEW GROUP** command under the **GROUP LIST** pop-up menu, or press **COMMAND+G** (Mac) or **CTRL+G** (Windows). The Create Group dialog box will appear.

4. Click on the **ATTRIBUTES** tab (or press **COMMAND+2** [Mac] or **CONTROL+2** [Windows]). See Figure Ex5.3. There are many attributes selected that you will not use and attributes you need that are not clicked.

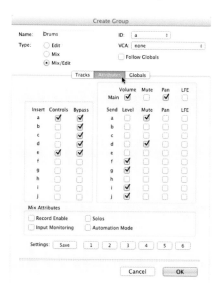

Figure Ex5.3
Attributes tab in the Create Group dialog box.

5. Click on group preset 1 at the bottom of the screen, as shown in Figure Ex5.4. This will select only the attributes you need.

6. Name the group **Drums** and click **OK**; now you are ready to begin editing.

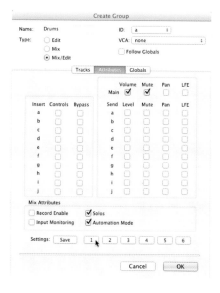

Figure Ex5.4
Selecting group attributes with group preset buttons.

Tip: You can save Group Attribute presets by choosing the attributes you want and then Command-clicking (Mac) or Control-clicking (Windows) a Group Preset button at the bottom to save it, similar to how Zoom Presets are saved in the Edit window.

Best Practices for Editing

This session comes from an original album project. For varying reasons, the song starts at bar 166|1|00. You will notice that the Electric drums track begins exactly at this time, but the live drums begin slightly early. Before using Beat Detective it will help to place the downbeat of the first bar of the drum pattern exactly on the downbeat of where the loop starts.

To line up the downbeat of the drums with the downbeat of the drum loop:

1. Separate the live drums after the drum fill intro but right before the downbeat of the pattern (this will be slightly before bar 166|1|000). See Figure Ex5.5.

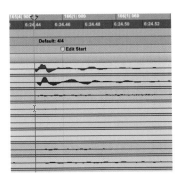

Figure Ex5.5
Creating new clip boundary at downbeat.

Tip: To make selections easy for this exercise, it's best to use Tab to Transients to select your audio on the live drums.

2. After separating the clip, select all audio on the drum tracks until the end of the session by pressing OPTION+SHIFT+RETURN (Mac) or ALT+SHIFT+RETURN (Windows).

3. Switch to SPOT mode. Place the separated drum tracks exactly at bar 166|1|00 by clicking with the Grabber. Next, play the audio and notice how the kick drum flams with the loop. See Figure Ex5.6.

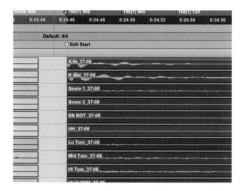

Figure Ex5.6
Moving clip transient to bar downbeat.

4. Before moving on, you'll need to trim the gap created by moving the live drum tracks. To do this, switch to **SLIP MODE** and enable the Trim tool. While holding **CONTROL** (Mac) or **START** (Windows), trim the live drum clips back to the previous clip. See Figure Ex5.7.

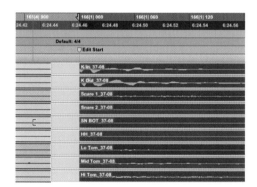

Trimming with constrain

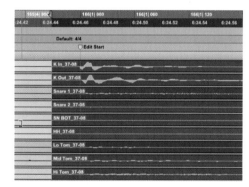

Final result

Figure Ex5.7
Trimming clip back to previous clip using constrain modifier.

5. When you're done, create a small crossfade to smooth the transition.

6. Place the Edit cursor exactly at Bar 166|1|000 and separate the clip. This will allow Beat Detective to use the downbeat without including a crossfade (BD selections cannot contain crossfades).

Using Groove Template Extraction

The goal with this exercise is to match the live drums to the loop on the Electric drums track. The first step is to extract the timing from the loop using Groove Template Extraction in Beat Detective. You'll use only the first four bars for the groove template, which you'll apply to the entire song.

To extract the groove template from the Electric drums track:

1. Select the first four bars of the loop on the Electric drums track (bar 166|1|00 to 170|1|000). Try to use your Start/End/Length key commands to complete the task.

Tip: A useful key command during this exercise is Option+F (Mac) or Alt+F (Windows). This will zoom your selection to fill the edit screen. Another useful key command during this exercise is Control+Command+down arrow (Mac) or Ctrl+Start+down arrow (Windows). This will adjust the track height of the selected track(s) to fill the Edit window.

You will use these key commands often during this exercise.

2. Open Beat Detective (**COMMAND+[8]** [Mac] or **CTRL+[8]** [Windows] on the numeric keypad). Click on **GROOVE TEMPLATE EXTRACTION** in the **OPERATION** pane of Beat Detective. See Figure Ex5.8.

Figure Ex5.8
Choosing Groove Template Extraction in Beat Detective.

3. Capture your selection. Double-check the start and end bar|beat. They should be 166|1|000 and 170|1|000. Also ensure that 1/16th notes are selected for the minimum note value. See Figure Ex5.9.

Figure Ex5.9
Correct start and end beat values in Beat Detective.

4. Since you will be using Elastic Audio later in this exercise, be sure to use Enhanced Resolution for ease of comparision. Click **ANALYZE** to detect the transients.

Note: Enhanced Resolution uses the same transient detection algorithm as Elastic
    Audio.

5. Make sure to select sub-beats and move the sensitivity slider up until you
   see each of the hits you want to quantize, somewhere between 20 and 24%.

6. At this point, you should examine your beat triggers. Some will be off—
   either the beat trigger is inserted in the middle of a hit (166|2|480) or the
   downbeat has been incorrectly identified (168|1|000). At this point, it may
   be helpful to play your selection at half-speed (**SHIFT+SPACEBAR**) to see
   how the triggers match up to the transients of the loop.

7. Scroll through each of the hits to ensure that they are at the start of the
   attack and that none of the triggers are incorrectly identified. Beat triggers
   that are off should be moved to the proper location (168|1|000). Triggers
   inserted in the middle of a hit should be removed (**OPTION-CLICK** [Mac] or
   ALT-CLICK [Windows] with the Grabber tool). See Figure Ex5.10.

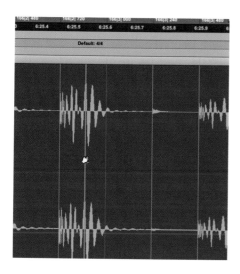

Figure Ex5.10
Example of incorrect detection and deleting
transient with Option/Alt+Grabber tool.

Tip: If you do not identify the transients in this step correctly, the rest of the exer-
    cise will not flow properly. Make sure your triggers are at correct transient
    locations, as you'll use this groove template to quantize the entire song.

8. Once you feel that each hit has been correctly identified at the right location,
   double-check that your Start, End, and Contains fields are correct. Once
   you feel confident the triggers have been properly identified, click **EXTRACT**.
   Type in a comment and choose **SAVE THE GROOVE TO THE CLIPBOARD**.
   You can choose to save to disk as well if you want. See Figure Ex5.11.

Figure Ex5.11

Extract Groove Template dialog box.

Now that you have the groove extracted, you can move on to separating the drum hits and conforming them.

Separating Drum Tracks with Collection Mode

Before you can conform the live drums to the groove you've just extracted, you need to separate the drum tracks into clips. While Beat Detective can usually be applied across the entire grouped drum set, you will be using Collection Mode, Low Emphasis analysis, and High Emphasis analysis to really hone your selections by identifying hits on individual drum parts and then adding them together.

To separate clips using Collection mode:

1. Before beginning, duplicate the current playlist on the drum tracks so you can return to the original take, if needed. You will be reusing the original performance for the Elastic Audio portion of this exercise.

2. Deactivate your Drum group.

3. Select the first four bars of the first kick drum track. Remember that it starts on 166|1|00, but the end of the selection is not exactly at 174|1|000. Use Tab to Transients or your eyes and ears to make the right selection.

Note: Precise selections are essential when working with Beat Detective to separate clips.

4. If Beat Detective is not open, open it and choose **Clip Separation** in the Operation column. See Figure Ex5.12.

Figure Ex5.12

Choosing Clip Separation in Beat Detective.

5. Your Start and End Bar|Beat in Beat Detective should be exactly four bars (166|1|000 to 170|1|000), even though your selection is slightly shorter than that.

Caution: Be careful not to hit Capture as it may put in the wrong value for what the selection should be (a full four bars).

6. Set the Analysis mode to **Low Emphasis**. This will focus on detecting transients with low frequency response. Click on **Analyze**.

Tip: To enable the trigger times, click in the Show Trigger Times box of Beat Detective window.

7. Zoom in on the audio and adjust the sensitivity slider until you see just kick hits (it will be lower than the loop you just analyzed). Try to use the zoom shortcuts you learned earlier in this lesson.

Tip: Another useful shortcut when working with Beat Detective is Shift+S to quickly solo the track you are working with.

8. Switch to **Collection** mode by clicking on the Detection drop-down. You will notice your beat triggers disappear. See Figure Ex5.13.

Figure Ex5.13
Choosing between Normal and Collection mode.

9. Click **Add All**; the triggers will reappear.

10. Next, move your edit selection on the kick track down to the first snare track. It is imperative that you move the same identical selection to the snare track (use the **;** [semicolon] key to move down).

11. Switch back to **Normal Detection** mode, change the Analysis to **High Emphasis**, and click **Analyze** again. Now only the snare hits are seen. You may need to move the sensitivity slider to have triggers at just snare hits.

12. Switch back to **Collection** mode and click **Add Unique**. The snare hits are now added to the detection window.

13. Move the selection to the overhead L track. Switch back to **Normal** mode. Typically, you would not use the overhead tracks, but the drummer is playing a pattern on the ride cymbal. The overhead mics will pick this up. Click **Analyze** and drag the sensitivity slider up until you see the ride cymbal hits. Don't worry that the snare and kick hits are detected.

Tip: Another useful shortcut for Beat Detective work is Restore Last Selection (Option+Command+Z [Mac] Ctrl+Alt+Z [Windows]). This is useful if you inadvertently click somewhere and lose your selection. This shortcut restores the previous selection.

14. Switch to **Collection** mode and click **Add Unique**. The snare and kick hits detected in the overheads will be ignored, and only the kick and snare hits you detected before will remain. At this point we have enough hits detected to separate all the drum tracks. Be sure to leave the detection mode in Collection.

Tip: Using room mics are of little use for detecting triggers and normally always skipped for analysis but always included when separating and conforming.

15. Enable your Drums group. Then press **Shift+P** so that your selection is placed across all drum tracks.

16. Click **Separate**.

Conforming Drum Tracks with Groove Templates

Now that you have the drum tracks precisely separated, you can conform them to the loop using Groove Conform.

To conform the clips to the loop:

1. Your first four bars should still be selected. Click on **Clip Conform** in the Operation column of Beat Detective. Be sure your Start and End Bar|Beat locations are correct in Beat Detective (remember that we are only doing the first four bars). This means the End Bar|Beat should be 170|1|000.

2. Click on the **Conform** drop-down (top right) and choose **Groove**. Underneath this drop-down, click on the **Groove Type** drop-down and choose **Groove Clipboard** (if you saved your groove to disk in the previous section, choose that name instead).

3. Click on **Conform**; you should see the clips on the drum tracks change slightly to match up with the loop. Solo-clear any drum tracks and listen to how tight the performance between the live drums and loop is. You can switch back to the original playlist to compare the two. Before moving on, be sure to set the playlist back to the Beat Detective version you are working on.

4. To finish the process, click on **Edit Smoothing** and choose **Fill and Crossfade** with 5ms crossfades. Play the selection. The live drums should match the loop perfectly with no artifacts or clicks.

5. Continue with the next four bars of the live drums starting at bar 170|1|00. Before beginning, be sure to examine the start of the next four bars you want to quantize. Often, Beat Detective will quantize a clip right on top of the transient of the next four bars. Just trim the start of the next section so the kick drum transient is not clipped as seen here. Once you make your 4-bar selection, check the end as well so that you have selected right up to the down beat of the next four bars (at bar|beat 174|1|000). See Figure Ex5.14.

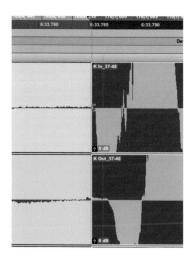

Figure Ex5.14
Trimming a clip to reveal the transient attack.

6. Try using **Collection** mode again by deactivating your drum group and starting with the kick, then snare, then overheads. Later in the song, the drummer switches to the hi-hat for the pattern, so you should use the hi-hat instead of the overheads at that point in the song.

7. Continue quantizing the first 32 bars of the song.

Conforming Drum Tracks with Elastic Audio and Groove Templates

Now that you understand how to use Beat Detective in both Normal and Collection modes, there are times you just don't have the time to be exact. Elastic Audio does a fantastic job of quantizing live drum performances and even has the ability to quantize to a groove template.

To conform live drums with Elastic Audio:

1. Before duplicating the tracks, change the playlist back to the original, before they were quantized with Beat Detective.

2. Start by duplicating your live drum tracks. This will allow you to compare the Beat Detective version to the Elastic Audio version.

3. To select your drum tracks quickly, click on the far left column of your Drums group in the Group List. A solid dot will appear, and all drum tracks will be selected.

4. Duplicate the tracks with **OPTION+SHIFT+D** (Mac) or **ALT+SHIFT+D** (Windows) or choose **DUPLICATE** in the Track menu. The Duplicate Tracks dialog box will appear, as shown in Figure Ex5.15.

5. Be sure to uncheck Group assignments. You'll be grouping the duplicated tracks into a new group.

Figure Ex5.15
Duplicate Tracks dialog box with proper options checked.

6. Click **OK**. The duplicate tracks will appear after the last track in your original Drums group.

7. Drag the new tracks below the Electric Drum stereo loop track. Return your original tracks back to the Beat Detective version.

8. Group all the duplicated drum tracks as you did before with the original drum tracks. Name the new group Drums 2.

9. Enable the Rhythmic Elastic Audio plug-in on any of the duplicated drum tracks. Wait for the analysis to complete.

10. On any Elastic Audio track, select the **ANALYSIS** track view. Zoom in so you see bars 166|1|00 to 168|1|00. You will see the default trigger detection. See Figure Ex5.16.

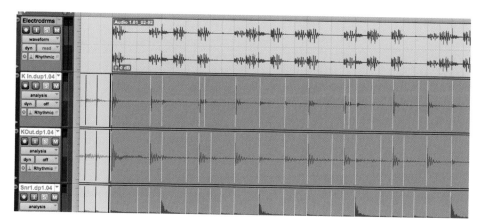

Figure Ex5.16
Analysis view of duplicated Drum tracks.

11. Select all the clips on the duplicated Drum tracks and right-click on a selected clip. Choose **ELASTIC PROPERTIES**. See Figure Ex5.17.

Figure Ex5.17
Elastic Properties window.

12. Click in **EVENT SENSITIVITY** and lower the percentage by clicking and dragging down with the mouse. Adjust the sensitivity such that you are detecting only the start of each hit (about 91%). This will force the Elastic Audio conforming process to focus solely on the start of transients, leading to a more natural-sounding conform result.

13. Next, bring up the **EVENT > EVENT OPERATIONS > QUANTIZE** window by pressing **OPTION+0** (Mac) or **ALT+0** (Windows). See Figure Ex5.18.

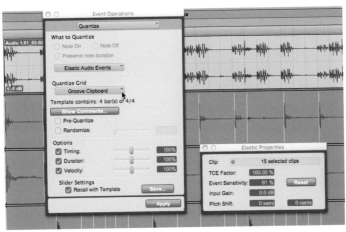

Figure Ex5.18
Quantizing window using a Groove template as the basis for quantizing.

14. Click on the QUANTIZE GRID and choose GROOVE CLIPBOARD.

15. Click APPLY. Now solo the new drum group along with the stereo electric drum track and listen to the result. This method is much easier than the Beat Detective method, but there are subtle differences.

Quantizing with Beat Detective Versus Elastic Audio

Now that you have the drums quantized with both methods, you can compare the sonic differences between the two. With Pro Tools 9 and Pro Tools 10, advancements in Elastic Audio have made the difference between Beat Detective and Elastic Audio negligible, but there is a difference. With Beat Detective, the sonic characteristics of the drum set are not changed when the clips are conformed. Phase coherency and pitch are maintained. Only the timing of the beats is moved.

With Elastic Audio, micro-timing variances may be introduced when time compressing/expanding hits to match a grid or groove. This can lead to tiny changes in the stereo field, as Elastic Audio cannot maintain 100% accuracy of a stereo field across multiple tracks (it can across multichannel tracks). Furthermore, the Elastic Audio processing algorithm must work at the audio file's native resolution. So if you import a 16-bit 44.1kHz sample into a 96kHz/24-bit session, Elastic Audio will process at 16-bits rather than 24 and use 44.1kHz versus 96kHz sampling rate. When doing extreme tempo matching, artifacts may be introduced. To alleviate this, you can use X-Form rendered processing after the timing is matched or use 32-bit floating-point audio files with Elastic Audio to gain as much processing precision as possible.

To audition the differences between Beat Detective quantizing and Elastic Audio quantizing:

1. Solo-safe the Stereo Electric drums track by COMMAND-CLICKING (Mac) or CONTROL-CLICKING (Windows) the track Solo button.

2. Switch your solo mode to X-OR in OPTIONS > SOLO MODE. In this mode, when you solo one set of drums, it cancels the solo on the other set.

3. Solo the Beat Detective drum tracks. Listen to the result. Now solo the Elastic Audio tracks. Notice a subtle change in the stereo field and pitch of the drums (especially the kick drum).

Synchronization

This lesson discusses the common aspects of synchronization that you are likely to encounter as a Pro Tools music expert.

Media Used: None

Duration: 60 minutes

GOALS

- Configure an Avid SYNC Peripheral
- Understand the various forms of clock reference, including Avid Loop Sync
- Understand the various forms of timecode/positional reference, including LTC (SMTPE) and MTC
- Configure and enable 9-pin serial Machine Control
- Configure the Avid Satellite Link option

Introduction

Basic synchronization concepts were introduced in other Avid Learning series courses for synchronizing playback of Pro Tools with other audio and video equipment. This lesson takes the subject much further, covering all the topics you are likely to need to handle the majority of music production scenarios. Having a solid understanding of sync is a highly valuable commodity to a Pro Tools expert. The trend is toward projects (and engineers) crossing the boundaries between the music and post-production fields (DVD releases, for example), and synchronization skills are essential in such situations.

Synchronizing playback with external machines is not the only issue. It is also important that when you connect digital audio signals between Pro Tools and other devices (such as digital tape machines, digital mixers, and even other Pro Tools systems), all the devices share a common clock reference. Otherwise there will be errors in the digital transfers, resulting in clicks and glitches in the audio.

Avid SYNC Peripheral

The Avid SYNC Peripheral (see Figures 6.1 and 6.2) provides all the connectivity and signal reading/generating capabilities for Pro Tools HD systems to synchronize with practically any other professional audio or video system.

Figure 6.1
SYNC HD front panel.

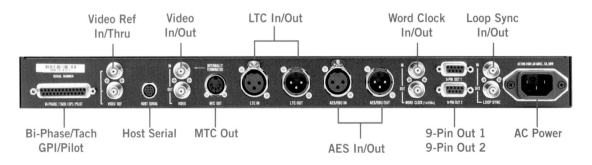

Figure 6.2
SYNC HD rear panel.

Avid SYNC Peripheral Services

An Avid SYNC Peripheral provides the following services:

- **Common Clock Reference**—When a Pro Tools HD system contains an Avid SYNC Peripheral, the SYNC Peripheral can act as a master clock reference for your whole studio. With its word clock output (as well as AES/EBU clock and even LTC as a clock source when working with tape machines), the SYNC Peripheral can send the same clock source to multiple units as well as all the audio interfaces in your Pro Tools HD configuration.

- **"Resolving" to various external clocks**—An external clock reference (covered in detail later in this lesson) can be fed to the SYNC Peripheral. The SYNC Peripheral will then lock to this signal, causing Pro Tools' playback speed (sample rate) to stay in sync with the external reference. While each Avid audio interface has the ability to lock to external word clock, the Avid SYNC Peripheral provides more clock reference choices to lock to, including tri-level sync (SYNC HD only), house black burst (aka "black"), AES/EBU word clock, bi-phase, pilot tone, and video reference.

- **Outputting clock**—The SYNC Peripheral has various clock reference outputs, allowing Pro Tools to control the playback speed of other devices.

- **Reading timecode**—Commonly used to synchronize tape machines with timecode tracks, the SYNC Peripheral reads the signal and passes a timecode location to Pro Tools.

- **Generating timecode**—The Avid SYNC Peripheral can output timecode based on the playback position of Pro Tools in the timeline. This allows other machines to follow Pro Tools or record a timecode reference along with audio.

- **9-pin Machine Control**—The Avid SYNC Peripheral has two ports for industry standard Sony 9-pin (RS-422) connections, allowing Pro Tools to control the transport of an external device (Avid Machine Control option for Pro Tools requires a separate iLok authorization to run).

Configuring the Avid SYNC Peripheral

When configuring an Avid SYNC Peripheral with a Pro Tools HD system, you must be aware of both software settings and hardware connections. Having a thorough understanding of both will make setup easy and aid in troubleshooting sync issues in the future.

Connecting to Pro Tools

Two sets of connections are required to use an Avid SYNC Peripheral with Pro Tools HD:

- A host serial cable (supplied with each Avid SYNC Peripheral) between your Pro Tools HD PCIe hardware and the SYNC Peripheral.

- Loop Sync (clock) cables between the Avid SYNC Peripheral and Pro Tools audio interfaces (supplied with each SYNC Peripheral).

Avid SYNC Peripherals include a 12-foot (approximately 4-meters) mini-DIN 8 serial cable to connect the SYNC Peripheral directly to the host serial port on a Pro Tools|HDX card, Pro Tools|HD Core card, or Pro Tools|HD Native card.

Note: If you use a third-party serial cable between Pro Tools and the SYNC Peripheral, make sure it supports hardware handshaking.

To connect the SYNC Peripheral to a Pro Tools HD system:

1. Connect one end of the host serial cable to the SYNC Peripheral host serial port.

2. Connect the other end to the host serial port on your HD card. If you have multiple HD cards (Pro Tools|HD or HDX), use the connection on the primary or core card only. For multiple HDX users, this is the card connected to audio interface #1. See Figure 6.3.

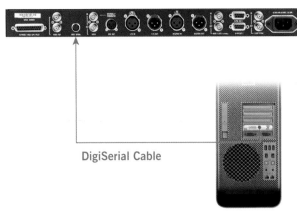

DigiSerial Cable

Figure 6.3
Host serial connection, SYNC HD to Pro Tools|HD Native.

The SYNC Peripheral must be connected to Pro Tools audio interfaces using Loop Sync in order for all interfaces to share a common clock. Furthermore, multiple error messages will appear if the SYNC Peripheral is detected by Pro Tools when the Loop Sync cables are not connected correctly.

To connect the SYNC Peripheral clock to a Pro Tools HD-series audio interface:

1. Connect the LOOP SYNC OUT of the SYNC PERIPHERAL to the LOOP SYNC IN of your first audio interface.

2. Connect the LOOP SYNC OUT of the audio interface (or last audio interface) to the LOOP SYNC IN of your SYNC Peripheral. See Figure 6.4.

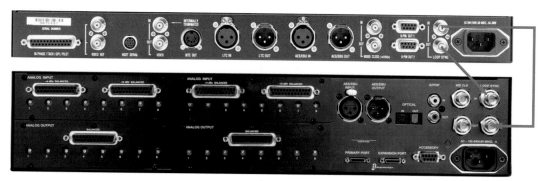

Figure 6.4
SYNC Peripheral connected to a HD I/O using Loop Sync.

3. When using more than one HD-series audio interface, connect all interfaces into the Loop Sync chain. See Figure 6.5.

Figure 6.5
SYNC HD Loop Sync in an expanded Pro Tools HD system.

Controlling an Avid SYNC Peripheral from Pro Tools

Pro Tools HD software automatically recognizes if a SYNC Peripheral is connected to the host serial/DigiSerial port when Pro Tools is launched. When a SYNC Peripheral is recognized, it is automatically enabled in the Setup > Peripherals dialog box.

To view/configure the SYNC Peripheral settings:

1. Choose SETUP > PERIPHERALS and then click the SYNCHRONIZATION tab. See Figure 6.6.

Figure 6.6

The Peripherals > Synchronization dialog box.

Configuring the SYNC Peripheral in the Session Setup Window

Synchronization settings are saved as part of each session, so you should always check the Session Setup window when starting work on a new session to verify the SYNC Peripheral's configuration. In particular, sessions that originate from a Pro Tools system that does not include a SYNC Peripheral will need configuring.

When an Avid SYNC Peripheral has been connected and enabled in the Peripherals window, SYNC Peripheral–specific settings become available in the Session Setup window. If you are locked to any external clock source (such as a house clock or black burst), the SYNC Peripheral must be set as the clock source for your system.

To configure your Pro Tools HD system to use the SYNC Peripheral as a clock source:

1. Choose SETUP > SESSION.

2. In the top section of the window under FORMAT, click on CLOCK SOURCE and choose SYNC from the pop-up menu. See Figure 6.7.

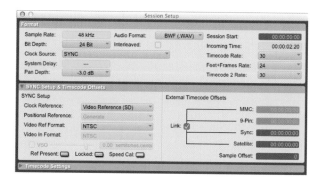

Figure 6.7
Choosing Clock Source in Session Setup.

3. Next, in the SYNC SETUP section, choose the SYNC PERIPHERAL'S master clock reference from the CLOCK REFERENCE pop-up menu. This will be INTERNAL if no external clock signal is being used (see the next section for what external clock source to use). See Figure 6.8.

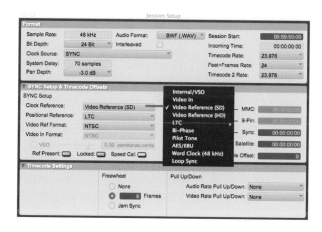

Figure 6.8
Session Setup window with SYNC HD controls.

Selecting Clock Sources

Synchronization within the components of a Pro Tools system is provided by Loop Sync (a specific word clock signal), which is distributed to all audio interfaces.

This is a star topology in which one device is master and the others listen (rather than regenerate the signal). Loop Sync provides the common word clock (or speed) reference for all Pro Tools cards and connected interfaces. The master clock source can be specified from among a number of internal and external sources.

When present, a SYNC Peripheral appears along with your HD-series audio interfaces in the Clock Source menu, located in the Session Setup window. See Figure 6.9.

Clock Source

Figure 6.9
SYNC HD selected as the current clock source.

Choosing a device from the Clock Source pop-up menu makes that device the loop master that all other devices will derive their clock from in the Loop Sync chain. You can set the clock source to the SYNC Peripheral or any digital input on any HD-series peripheral by selecting that device and source from the Clock Source menu.

Clock Reference

When the SYNC Peripheral is the selected clock source in the Session Setup window, a separate Clock Reference pop-up menu is used to select which clock input of the SYNC Peripheral will be used for the clock reference. When syncing with external equipment, the preferable configuration is to have the SYNC Peripheral as the clock source, with an external clock reference feeding the SYNC Peripheral. This external reference should also clock all other synchronized devices in the studio. If this is the case, you don't need to worry about further configuration changes, as all devices will be resolved to the same clock and run at the same speed.

When the Clock Source Is SYNC

When the SYNC Peripheral is the clock source, clock and positional reference selectors become active in the SYNC HD Setup area of the Session Setup window, as shown in Figure 6.10.

Figure 6.10
SYNC HD setup and VSO controls in the Session Setup window.

SYNC Peripheral clock reference choices include Internal/VSO, Video In, Video Reference, LTC, Bi-Phase, Pilot Tone, AES/EBU, and Word Clock. When the SYNC Peripheral is not the selected clock source device, the Clock Reference menu in the SYNC Setup area switches to Loop Sync.

To choose a SYNC Peripheral's clock reference:

1. Select a **SYNC PERIPHERAL CLOCK CHOICE** from the **CLOCK REFERENCE** menu. See Figure 6.11.

Figure 6.11
SYNC HD Clock Reference menu.

The most commonly used dedicated clock references are Video Reference and Word Clock.

Video Reference

Video Reference is actually a video signal (it appears black if you view it), so as well as syncing to the speed inherent in the signal, multiple devices with video playback capability can synchronize frame edge positions. This is the most common clock system in professional studios and is also known as black burst, genlock, and house sync (referring to it being the master clock for the facility). It is distributed from a generator box via BNC video cables and should be plugged into either Video Ref connector on the SYNC Peripheral.

Note: The Video Ref connectors are not labeled input or output, rather, they are both effectively an input and un-buffered loop through.

When working with video reference, you must choose the proper video format, either NTSC or PAL for standard definition (Video Ref SD), or a high-definition setting (Video Ref HD), from the Video Ref Format pop-up menu.

Word Clock

In the same way that video reference is a video signal with no picture content (other than black), word clock is a digital audio signal with no audio content. Digital audio signals such as AES/EBU have clock information embedded in them that is the same as word clock. Word clock can also be used as a "house sync," feeding more than one device, but it is also commonly used between two devices, with one feeding the other. If another device is feeding word clock to the SYNC

Peripheral (again via BNC), you should choose Word Clock in the SYNC Setup section of the Session Setup window. Word clock must run at the same sample rate as the session and other connected devices.

Internal/VSO

Syncing to other common clock sources is the typical operating mode when using SYNC. However, the SYNC Peripheral also includes a VSO mode. Available only when the SYNC Peripheral is set for internal clock, this mode allows you to alter the speed of playback by slowing down the sample rate reference or speeding it up. This is useful for remix or creating dance mix versions of songs where the entire mix needs to be sped up (or slowed down).

To enable VSO mode with a SYNC Peripheral:

1. Set the CLOCK REFERENCE drop-down menu for INTERNAL/VSO.

2. At the bottom of the SYNC Setup section, enable VSO.

3. While playing back audio, move the VSO SLIDER left and right to slow down or speed up the playback speed. See Figure 6.12.

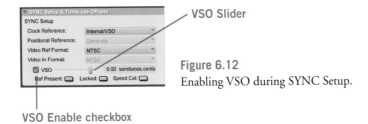

VSO Slider

VSO Enable checkbox

Figure 6.12
Enabling VSO during SYNC Setup.

When the Clock Source Is an HD-series Audio Interface

Because digital audio signals contain word clock, you can use any digital input connected to Pro Tools as the master clock reference for the system. This is useful when you connect a digital audio device that is not connected to a clock reference signal. The typical example would be if you temporarily connected a DAT recorder or other digital device to transfer material in via AES/EBU, S/PDIF, or Optical. It's essential that there be a common clock between the tape machine and Pro Tools (otherwise you will hear clicks in the recording), so you can choose to use the digital input as your master clock temporarily.

When an audio interface (such as an HD I/O or 192) is providing the clock source, it will be the Loop Master. Clock source options are available directly from the Clock Source menu, based on the configuration of that interface in the Hardware Setup dialog box. Choices may include AES/EBU, S/PDIF, Optical, or Word Clock.

To choose a different Loop Sync device as clock source:

■ Select a different Loop Sync device and Clock Source from the hierarchical CLOCK SOURCE menu.

Valid and Invalid Clock Sources

Three lights in the SYNC Setup section of the Session Setup window indicate clock status (see Figure 6.13). If all three lights are lit, then your chosen clock reference is present and is valid.

Figure 6.13
Clock reference and sync indicators in Session Setup.

If you choose a clock source that is currently invalid or unavailable, the Locked and Speed Cal lights will be unlit. You will also receive the warning shown in Figure 6.14.

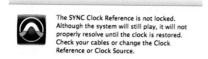

The SYNC Clock Reference is not locked. Although the system will still play, it will not properly resolve until the clock is restored. Check your cables or change the Clock Reference or Clock Source.

OK

Figure 6.14
Hardware clock sync warning.

Under normal conditions, all three status lights will be solid. But sometimes you may find that the Ref Present and Locked status indicators are solid, but the Speed Cal indicator is flashing. Table 6.1 illustrates these conditions.

Table 6.1   SYNC HD Speed Cal Indicator States

Speed Cal	Status	Meaning
Solid	Locked	External Reference is present and locked to chosen session rate
Blinking Slowly	Slewing	Incoming Sample Rate is slower/lower than expected as set by session sample rate
Blinking Fast	Slewing	Incoming Sample Rate is faster/higher than expected as set by session sample rate

There are times where a blinking Speed Cal light is normal operation, such as running in pull-up/pull-down situations in video post-production. There are also times a Speed Cal light indicates an error condition, such as receiving 48kHz word clock when the session is set for 44.1kHz. Whenever you see a blinking sync indicator, be sure to review all your settings to ensure you are not seeing an error indication.

Note: When working at 23.976 frame rate, the 24 Frame Rate LED on the front of the Sync HD will flash. This is normal operation indicating that the system is not running at 24, rather 23.976. This is typical operating mode where a flashing LED is normal and not indicating an error state.

Timecode Formats in Music Production

Properly configuring a clock master is essential when transferring or routing audio digitally between devices. However, in order to have Pro Tools synchronize its positional, or playback, location with another recorder, you also need timecode (SMPTE/LTC/MTC) or MIDI beat clock. In professional settings, LTC and MTC are preferred because they provide higher resolution than MIDI beat clock. When Pro Tools is chasing (syncing to) another machine, it reads incoming timecode, locates to the same point in time, and begins playing back.

Timecode measures time in the standard video scale of hours:minutes:seconds:frames. Several different formats of timecode measure time in slightly different ways, using different frame rates. For music projects, this frame rate typically is 30 frames per second (30FPS) or 25 in Europe and other territories. You can run a music session at any sample rate; however, the frame rate for your session must be set to match that of the timecode used by other machines during the project; otherwise start times will not match.

To set the session frame rate:

■ From the Timecode Rate pop-up menu, choose from the standard frame rates (shown in Figure 6.15).

Figure 6.15
Timecode Rate menu in Session Setup window.

The format of timecode used is determined by the type of project you are working on, as discussed in the following sections.

Music Only

In scenarios where you are working only with music, and the project is not likely to involve video or film (such as syncing Pro Tools to a multitrack tape recorder), it is customary to use 30FPS timecode in North America/Japan and 25FPS in Europe and other territories. However, it doesn't matter which format you use as long as it's the same for all machines that you intend to sync together.

NTSC TV Territories

When video is involved, such as when syncing Pro Tools to a video tape recorder, the standard definition video/television frame rate for your part of the world will be used. In North America, Japan, and parts of South America, this format is NTSC, which has a frame rate of 29.97FPS.

Tip: Obviously, you can't have 0.97 of a frame of video: NTSC video has 30 frames in each timecode second but is played back slightly slower (0.1% slower), resulting in 29.97 frames per second.

There are two flavors of NTSC: drop frame and non-drop frame. Drop frame is a scheme invented to compensate for the 0.1% slower playback used for broadcast color video. In order to align one hour of "slower" video material to one hour of real time (wall clock), a system was invented to skip specific frame addresses at regular intervals over time to account for the 0.1% difference. By skipping two frame addresses at the top of each minute (except for each "tenth" minute,) you eliminate the extra time build-up over an hour.

Tip: When using 29.97 drop frame, location 01:01:00:00 does not exist. If you were to put the cursor at 01:00:59;29 frames and nudge later by one frame, the readout would jump to 01:01:00;02 (thus frame addresses 0 and 1 are dropped or skipped). Even though the frame numbers are dropped, no video information is dropped, rather, just the labels are dropped or skipped. At each tenth minute (01:10:00;00), no frames are dropped.

Drop-frame rates are only used on long-format broadcast applications (TV shows, films for TV, and so forth) or other video material that requires wall-clock lengths. Projects less than a few minutes in length, such as TV commercials and short promos, are not affected by drop frame.

PAL TV Territories

The PAL television and video format is used in most of the rest of the world, including Europe, Africa, Asia, and Australia. PAL video has 25 frames per second, so it uses 25FPS timecode.

Film

Film runs at 24 frames per second. However, as most audio and music work for films is done with pictures that have been transferred to video, it is less common to use 24FPS timecode with Pro Tools. Newer HD handheld video cameras (typically used for reality TV and documentaries) use 23.976 (23.98), which is very close to film speed of 24FPS. As always, check with the other Pro Tools systems you plan to collaborate with and choose the same frame rate for your session.

Using Longitudinal Time Code (LTC)

Longitudinal Time Code (LTC), or SMPTE timecode, is the most common timecode signal used in music production. LTC is encoded as an audio signal. This means that as well as being transmitted using standard audio cables, it can be recorded in the same way as audio. Many audio and video recorders have a dedicated LTC track in addition to normal audio tracks. However, it is possible to record LTC to any device that records audio, and LTC is often recorded (striped) to a track on a multitrack tape. When timecode is striped to a tape, it's important to make sure that the generator and recorder are locked to clock, ensuring the recorded timecode is accurate.

Syncing with LTC and Word/Video Clock

A common sync scenario encountered in music production is to have Pro Tools chasing LTC from a tape machine. The basic outline for making this happen is described in the following sections.

Make Connections

For clock reference, do one of the following:

- Connect video reference or word clock to both the SYNC Peripheral and the tape machine.

- For digital multitrack tape machines or tape machines with digital synchronizers, connect word clock from the tape machine to the SYNC Peripheral.

Tip: Even if a clock reference is unavailable, you can set your SYNC HD to track the speed of the external machine based on the LTC signal itself.

■ For positional reference, connect LTC from the tape machine to the LTC In port on SYNC Peripheral.

Configure Session Setup Window

1. Set the session frame rate to the same as the timecode on the tape (such as 30FPS).

2. Set the CLOCK SOURCE to SYNC.

3. In the SYNC SETUP section, set the CLOCK REFERENCE to VIDEO REFERENCE or WORD CLOCK, depending on which reference you are using. If there is no dedicated clock source connection, set it to LTC.

Tip: When the Clock Reference menu is set for LTC, five choices appear to set the LTC Servo Gain. These settings allow you to choose between faster lockup (lower) and removing jitter (higher). A setting of 0 (zero) offers the fastest lockup time when resolving to LTC but may include more timing jitter in the signal. A setting of 5 removes most of the timing jitter but may prevent the system from locking up to incoming timecode for 6–10 seconds. The default setting of 2 offers a compromise between lockup time and jitter.

4. In the SYNC SETUP section, set the POSITIONAL REFERENCE to LTC. See Figure 6.16.

Figure 6.16
Positional Reference pop-up menu.

Put Pro Tools Online

To trigger playback or recording of Pro Tools from an external source, the system must be online. In this state, Pro Tools waits for timecode and begins synchronous playback or recording as soon as timecode lock is achieved.

To put Pro Tools online, do any one of the following:

■ Click the ONLINE button in the Transport window or at the top of the Edit window. See Figure 6.17.

— Online Button

Figure 6.17
Online button in the Transport window.

■ Press **COMMAND+J** (Mac) or **CTRL+J** (Windows). Alternatively, you can press **OPTION+SPACEBAR** (Mac) or **ALT+SPACEBAR** (Windows).

Play the Tape Machine

When you cue up and play the tape machine, Pro Tools will jump to the incoming timecode location and begin playback in sync.

Recording Slaves to an External Timecode Source

Three options are available for recording while Pro Tools is chasing timecode:

■ Have Pro Tools go into record as soon as it locks to the timecode.

■ Have Pro Tools go into record at the edit cursor or selection when used in conjunction with Machine Control.

■ Manually punch in while playing in sync, using QuickPunch, TrackPunch, or DestructivePunch mode.

To set online recording options:

1. Choose **SETUP > PREFERENCES** and then choose the **OPERATION** tab. The options shown in Figure 6.18 will appear.

Figure 6.18
Online record options in Preferences > Operation.

- **Record Online at Time Code (or ADAT) Lock:** Choosing this option makes Pro Tools start recording on any tracks that are record-enabled as soon as timecode is received.

- **Record Online at Insertion/Selection:** Choosing this option makes Pro Tools record online only at the current cursor position or later when used in conjunction with Machine Control and Pro Tools is declared as a slave machine (not the master).

Refer to the section "Choosing the Transport Mode" later in the lesson for more information on master versus slave deck control.

2. For online recording without QuickPunch, you need to click the Record button in Pro Tools as well as the Online button before playing the external machine. Pro Tools will then drop into record when it locks or reaches the edit selection.

Synchronizing to Analog Multitrack Tape Machines

It is common practice to record LTC onto the highest numbered track on a multi-track tape machine (for example, track 24 of a 24-track tape machine). It's possible to route this LTC directly from the analog machine to the SYNC Peripheral. Pro Tools can then take its speed and positional reference from the incoming LTC, as described previously. However, because analog tape machines are subject to subtle variations in playback speed, Pro Tools will have to adjust its speed constantly to compensate, which is not an ideal scenario. It is preferable for the tape machine to resolve its playback speed to the house sync that is being used, whether that is word clock or video reference. Because professional analog tape machines do not generally have a built-in synchronizer, an external synchronizer will be required. Two common external synchronizers found in professional studios throughout the world are Timeline Lynx and Motionworker. Both of these have the capability to read incoming video or word clock and resolve the tape machine's playback speed to the clock. If multiple tape machines are involved, each machine will require its own synchronizer.

As one example, you may have a 48-track analog recording session (played back on two 24-track tape machines) that needs to be transferred into Pro Tools. The first step is to connect the clocks. Each of the two tape machines will need to be connected to an external synchronizer (the two synchronizers are then connected to each other, often using a proprietary connector), and the house video reference is sent to each synchronizer and the SYNC Peripheral. Once the clock connections have been made, positional reference must be sent from a tape machine to Pro Tools or from Pro Tools to a synchronizer that is controlling the tape machine.

The next step is to have the two analog machines synchronized to each other by feeding LTC from track 24 of each machine to its respective external synchronizer. One machine is designated as master and one as slave. The slave synchronizer will compare the timecode coming from the master and slave tape machines and make small adjustments to the playback speed to keep them locked. Once the two analog machines are correctly synchronized, a reshaped (or regenerated) copy of the master LTC is fed from the synchronizer to the LTC input of SYNC Peripheral. Pro Tools can then use the incoming LTC for positional reference while using the house video reference for clock/speed reference.

Using MTC (MIDI Timecode)

MIDI timecode uses the same SMPTE time format as LTC (hours, minutes, seconds, frames) but is encoded as a stream of MIDI messages. MTC allows software to sync to timecode via a MIDI interface, but it is also used by some hardware devices (mixing consoles, for example) instead of LTC. Although messages are sent every quarter of a frame, MTC is less stable than LTC due to the fact that two TC frames are required to transmit a single TC frame address resulting in a slightly less stable timing reference.

Uses for MTC

Pro Tools can chase MTC, although in most professional situations it is preferable to use a SYNC Peripheral and LTC (or Machine Control) to slave Pro Tools. It is generally more common to generate MTC from Pro Tools. Pro Tools can generate MTC directly to any MIDI port or via the MTC output on a SYNC Peripheral. An Avid SYNC Peripheral is useful in that it constantly transmits MTC, whether you are generating or chasing incoming timecode. It can therefore be used to redistribute incoming timecode to MTC-compatible devices. When syncing Pro Tools systems with Avid VENUE consoles, MTC is required to be generated from Pro Tools to the MTC input of the VENUE console.

MTC Versus MIDI Beat Clock

MTC offers an absolute time alternative to MIDI beat clock (a tempo-based clock that uses song position pointers [SPP] information in bar and beat time values). Beat clock/SPP is useful when syncing two music devices together, such as a sequencer and a drum machine, but when syncing with external recorders or mixing consoles, MTC is preferable as it provides greater resolution.

Using 9-Pin Machine Control (Deck Control)

With the Machine Control option installed, Pro Tools can control the transport functions of another machine that is Sony 9-pin–compatible (also known as RS-422). This option requires a 9-pin serial cable from the machine to the SYNC Peripheral 9-pin port, a COM/serial port on your Windows computer (which may require a Rosetta Stone on Windows to convert RS-232 to RS-422), or a third-party Keyspan USA-28X USB to serial converter on the Mac. The Machine Control port on external machines will be labeled Remote, 9-Pin, Machine Control, or RS-422. Assuming that your SYNC Peripheral is connected and configured properly and your external machine is on and in remote mode, you are ready to enable Machine Control. See Table 6.2.

To enable Machine Control:

1. Choose SETUP > PERIPHERALS and click the MACHINE CONTROL tab. The options shown in Figure 6.19 appear.

Table 6.2   Machine Control Supported Connections

Connection Type	Mac	Windows
COM1 Port	N/A	Yes
COM2 Port	N/A	Yes
Keyspan USA-28X USB-Serial Converter	Yes	No
SYNC 9-Pin Out 1	Yes	Yes
SYNC 9-Pin Out 2	Yes	Yes

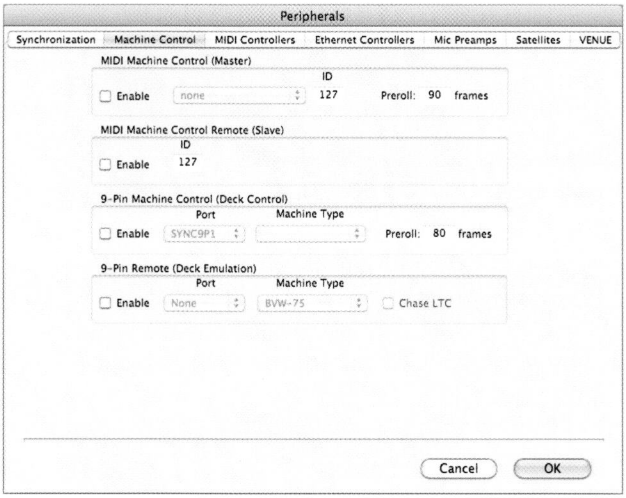

Figure 6.19
Enabling Machine Control
in the Peripherals dialog box.

2. In the **9-PIN MACHINE CONTROL (DECK CONTROL)** section, click the **ENABLE** box.

3. From the **PORT** pop-up menu, choose the serial port that you will be using for Machine Control. When using a SYNC Peripheral, you will be able to access either of the two 9-pin remote ports for Machine Control. (In Figure 6.20, the SYNC 9-Pin Out 1 port is selected.)

Figure 6.20
Choosing the correct 9-pin port on the SYNC HD.

4. From the MACHINE TYPE pop-up menu, click and hold to choose the Machine Control type you will be using. Clicking and holding on the MACHINE TYPE menu will usually automatically detect and select the attached machine. If your machine is not a standard machine from the list, the drop-down will usually default to GENERIC. You can make a selection to override this setting.

5. Click OK.

6. If you're using a SYNC Peripheral with video reference, you may open the Session Setup window, click the POSITIONAL REFERENCE pop-up menu, and select SERIAL TIMECODE. See Figure 6.21.

Figure 6.21
Select Serial Timecode from the Positional Reference pop-up menu.

This is an extremely useful feature, as it removes the need for a separate LTC timecode connection. Instead, timecode is read directly via the 9-pin interface.

Set your 9-pin controllable VTR or ATR to Remote or External mode to receive the 9-pin Machine Control commands from Pro Tools.

7. Click OK to close the window and begin using Machine Control.

Choosing the Transport Mode

When 9-pin deck control is active, Pro Tool's transport controls (on-screen buttons and keyboard shortcuts, such as the spacebar) can either be directed toward controlling Pro Tools directly or toward the remote machine. The Transport Master is chosen from a pop-up menu at the bottom of the Transport controls (in both the Transport window and the Edit window toolbar). See Figure 6.22.

Figure 6.22
Transport Master mode pop-up arrow.

Transport Master Selector

To set the Transport master:

1. Open the Transport window.

2. Click the Transport Master selector; then choose a master from the **Transport** submenu. Alternatively, you can use **Command+** (Mac) or **Control+** (Windows). See Figure 6.23.

Figure 6.23
Choosing a Transport Master.

- **Pressing Play when Transport is set to Pro Tools and Pro Tools is Online**—Cues the remote machine to Pro Tools' timeline position. The machine will begin playback at this position, and Pro Tools will sync to the machine.

- **Pressing Play when Transport is set to Machine**—Causes the machine to start playing at its current position. If you want Pro Tools to slave to the external deck, put Pro Tools Online, and it will cue to the machine and play back in sync.

Machine Control Preferences

The Machine Control section of the Preferences dialog box, shown in Figure 6.24 (choose Setup > Preferences > Synchronization to view it), provides options that enable you to specify the following aspects of Machine Control behavior.

Figure 6.24
Machine Control settings in Synchronization preferences.

■ **Machine Chases Memory Location**—With this option enabled, navigating to a specific location in a session with a Memory Location causes a connected transport to chase to that location.

■ **Machine Follows Edit Insertion/Scrub**—With this option enabled, navigating to a specific location in a session by moving the selection point or by scrubbing a track causes a connected transport to chase to that location. When choosing this option, use the pop-up menu to state whether the remote device is a tape-based machine (sends jog commands) or non-linear device (sends cue commands). This setting is typically unchecked as it causes excessive wear on linear tape machines.

- **Machine Cues Intelligently**—With this option enabled, if you navigate to a cue point more than 10 seconds from the current location, Pro Tools will command a connected transport to fast wind to the desired location at full speed to within 10 seconds of the cue point. Cueing will then slow to normal speed until the point is reached. This significantly speeds up tape cueing over long winds.

- **Stops at Shuttle Speed Zero**—With this option enabled, Pro Tools sends a Stop command when shuttle speed equals zero. While most machines automatically stop when shuttle speed is equal to zero (in other words, whenever you stop shuttling), some machines require an explicit stop command to park correctly. Consult the manufacturer of your machine if you need to determine its shuttle stop capability.

- **Non-Linear Transport Error Suppression**—With this option enabled, Pro Tools will ignore any 9-pin errors received from non-linear audio and video devices.

Machine Control Shortcuts

In addition to the standard transport buttons, you can use the Machine Control shortcuts commands listed in Table 6.3 for playing and cueing.

Table 6.3 Common Machine Control Shortcuts

Command	Macintosh	Windows
Rewind	Shift+<	Shift+<
Fast Forward	Shift+>	Shift+>
Shuttle Backward (Transport=Machine ONLY)	Option+comma	Alt+comma
Shuttle Forward (Transport=Machine ONLY)	Option+period	Alt+period
Toggle Transport Master	Command+\	Ctrl+\
All Transport Buttons Off	Command+period	Ctrl+period
Locate to Selection	Command+Left Arrow	Start Ctrl+Left Arrow
Locate to Selection End	Command+Right Arrow	Ctrl+Right Arrow
Frame Bump Backward	Option+Command+comma	Ctrl+Alt+comma
Frame Bump Forward	Option+Command+period	Ctrl+Alt+period

Machine Control Error Messages

You might see an error message when trying to initialize or use Machine Control.

If you see the message shown in Figure 6.25, verify the following:

- The 9-pin cable is properly connected to the deck (typically RS-422 or remote port).

- The 9-pin cable is connected to the serial port you specified in the Machine Control section of the Peripherals dialog box (for instance, SYNC 9-Pin Out 1 versus SYNC 9-Pin Out 2).

- The deck is turned on and set for remote, or external control.

Figure 6.25
Machine Control initialization error.

Understanding Satellite Link

The Avid Satellite Link option is similar to 9-pin control in that it lets you link multiple Pro Tools systems together. However, unlike 9-pin control, Satellite Link is significantly easier to set up and requires an active Ethernet connection between computers and a common clock reference for both systems. Satellite Link was created for film mixing dub stages that typically use two or more Pro Tools|HD-series hardware systems to play back hundreds or even thousands of tracks. Satellite Link supports up to 12 Pro Tools|HD 10 systems (or up to 11 Pro Tools|HD 10 systems and an Avid Media Composer Video Satellite or Pro Tools Video Satellite LE system) over an Ethernet network so that you can cue and play transports, make selections, and solo tracks across any of the systems from any linked workstation.

Satellite Link in Music Production

In most music scenarios, it is unlikely that more than two Pro Tools systems would be linked together. Some typical reasons for using Satellite Link are as follows:

- **Increased track count**—You may require more track count or storage bandwidth because the project is unusually large, or because you have a number of record tracks used for "stems" (see Lesson 7, "Pro Tools HD/HDX Mixing Concepts").

- **High sample rate production**—With higher sample rates, track counts decrease. By linking multiple systems together you can achieve typical production track counts while running 88.2/96kHz or even 176.4/192kHz sessions.

- **Dedicated mixing platform**—In large projects using many plug-ins, it can be useful to divide mixing and playback duties between two Pro Tools systems.

- **Composing to video**—Running a guide video on an Avid Media Composer Video Satellite or Pro Tools Video Satellite LE system can be useful to free up resources on your main composing system, especially if the video is HD.

Installation and Authorization

In Satellite Link configurations, one Pro Tools system is designated the administrator, and other linked systems are satellites. While satellite functionality is included in Pro Tools 10, an iLok authorization for Satellite Link is a separate option that must be purchased, and the iLok asset must be present on any Satellite systems.

Tip: The administrator system does not need to have a Satellite Link option iLok authorization.

Configuring Satellite Link Settings

The following steps describe how to set up Satellite Link between two Pro Tools systems that are connected to the same Ethernet network. Please be aware that you must setup the Satellite system before setting up the Administrator system.

To configure Satellite Link on the Satellite system:

1. Choose SETUP > PERIPHERALS and click the SATELLITES tab. See Figure 6.26.

Figure 6.26
Satellite Link configuration page.

2. Choose the SYSTEM NAME that the satellite system will use on the network.

3. In the MODE section, choose SATELLITE.

4. In the ADVANCED NETWORK SETTINGS, choose an INTERFACE (network) if the system has more than one Ethernet connection (on Apple MacPros, there are two Ethernet ports—Ethernet0 and Ethernet1). Ensure that the Ethernet port chosen has a valid IP address. Leave the TCP/UDP PORT set to the default setting. Although a DHCP-based IP address will work, setting a static or manual address will ensure that your system always has the same IP address.

Tip: The TCP port needs to change only if there is another Satellite Link network on the same Ethernet network or if the port is blocked on larger WAN with managed routers and blocked ports.

To configure Satellite Link on the Administrator system:

1. Choose SETUP > PERIPHERALS and click the SATELLITES tab.

2. Choose the SYSTEM NAME that the administrator system will use on the network.

3. In the MODE section, choose ADMINISTRATOR.

4. Select the administrator system in the SYSTEM 1 pop-up menu.

5. Select the satellite system in the SYSTEM 2 pop-up menu.

6. In ADVANCED NETWORK SETTINGS, choose an INTERFACE (network) if the system has more than one Ethernet connection (on Apple MacPros, there are two Ethernet ports—Ethernet0 and Ethernet1). Ensure that the Ethernet port chosen has a valid IP address. Leave the TCP/UDP PORT set to the default setting unless a new port address was used in the prior steps.

Using Satellite Link

Once the systems are linked, additional link indicators will display in the Transport window as well as in the transport section in the Edit window toolbar of both systems. See Figure 6.27.

Link Button   Individual Satellite Link Enable Buttons

Figure 6.27
Satellite Link controls in the Transport window.

These link indicators function as online buttons, enabling you to take machines online/offline from either the master or the slave. Machines can be taken online/offline while stopped or during playback by clicking the online buttons or by pressing Option+Shift+L (Mac) or Alt+Shift+L (Windows) to link/unlink systems. You can also use Option-click (Mac) or Alt-click (Windows) on the icons to link/unlink all systems at once.

Link-enabled systems always play back in sync. All other linked behavior is configured in the Satellite section of the Synchronization page of Pro Tools Preferences on each system.

Linking Play Selections

If all the linked systems are set to Transmit and Receive Play selections, you can make Edit window selections on any system, and they will be reflected on all others. By selectively changing the Play Selection preferences, you can limit which machines are allowed to make global Edit window selections.

Solo Linking

By linking solos across satellite-linked Pro Tools systems, soloing a track will affect all the mixer channels on all linked systems as though they were part of one mixer. In other words, if you solo a single track on one Pro Tools system, all tracks on the other systems will be muted when using Solo In Place (SIP) mode. Other solo modes (such as X-Or, Latch, and Momentary), as well as AFL/PFL and SIP, also interact with Satellite Mode.

Tip: For more information about how solos work across Satellite linked systems, please consult the *Solo Linking* section of the *Satellite Link Guide* included in your Pro Tools documentation folder.

Review/Discussion Questions

1. Name at least three different services the SYNC Peripheral provides for music-based Pro Tools|HD systems.

2. Which two cable connections are required in order for an Avid SYNC Peripheral to function properly with your Pro Tools|HD system?

3. Explain the difference between clock reference and positional reference.

4. What does it mean when the Speed Cal LED in the Session Setup window is flashing slowly? What about when it is blinking quickly?

5. What are the typical frame rate settings used for film? NTSC video? PAL video?

6. When using LTC as clock source, what are the differences among the five choices (0–5)?

7. Explain the differences between LTC and MTC timecode.

8. What is required to use 9-pin serial control from Pro Tools to an external machine?

9. What is required in order to link two or more Pro Tools|HD systems together with Satellite Link?

10. When soloing a track, what Satellite Link setting effectively mutes all other channels on all other "linked" systems (when using Solo In Place mode)?

Synchronization

This exercise tests your knowledge of synchronization configurations. This exercise offers several synchronization examples. If you do not have access to multiple Pro Tools|HD-hardware systems, please look over the exercise as a refresher on what steps are necessary for advanced synchronization of multiple systems.

Media Used:

310M Exercise 06-Admin.PTXT and 310M Exercise 06-Satellite.PTXT (Pro Tools session files)

Duration:

45–60 minutes (varies depending upon equipment access)

GOALS

- Diagram the steps necessary to lock a multitrack tape recording to Pro Tools using Machine Control and LTC

- Lock multiple Pro Tools|HD-hardware systems together with Avid SYNC Peripherals and LTC

- Lock multiple Pro Tools|HD-hardware systems together using Satellite Link

Introduction

Synchronization is often considered a difficult topic, mainly because there are so many different combinations of equipment to deal with. However, with a good understanding of synchronization theory and some hands-on experience, you should be able to understand and handle most situations.

In the first part of this exercise you will consider two different synchronization scenarios and decide how to connect the various pieces of equipment together. In part two, you will synchronize two Pro Tools|HD systems together using Avid SYNC Peripherals. In part three, you will lock two Pro Tools|HD systems together with Satellite mode, using just an Ethernet connection and a word clock connection between your systems.

Part One: Sync Configuration Diagrams

In this part of the exercise you are given two scenarios with different cabling requirements and goals. Use what you have learned in the lesson to draw the diagrams.

Tip: Feel free to write on a separate piece of paper instead of writing in your book.

Complete the following diagrams:

1. Draw cable connections between the equipment.

2. Label the types of cables, such as 9-pin Machine Control, LTC, and so on.

3. Label the ports/connections in use, such as Vid Ref In.

Note: You do not need to draw audio or video connections.

These exercises are intended as discussion points and can be completed as a group with assistance from your instructor where necessary.

Scenario 1: Transferring from Multitrack Analog Tape to Pro Tools

Draw the connections required to control the transport and synchronize the analog tape decks with Pro Tools. Assume the audio connections are already made. See Figure Ex6.1.

SYNC HD I/O

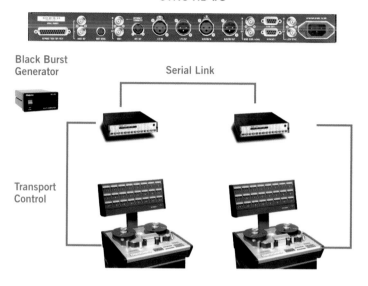

Black Burst
Generator

Serial Link

Transport
Control

Analog Tape Recorders

Figure Ex6.1
Synchronizing analog tape deck(s) to
Pro Tools|HD with SYNC HD.

Scenario 2: Synchronizing Playback
with a Video Tape Recorder

Draw the connections required for Pro Tools to synchronize and control the transport of a professional video deck, such as an HDCAM-SR. Assume the audio connections are already made. See Figure Ex6.2.

SYNC HD I/O

Black Burst
Generator

Professional
Video Deck

Figure Ex6.2
Synchronizing a professional
video deck to Pro Tools|HD
with SYNC HD.

Part Two: Syncing Two Pro Tools Systems

This part of the exercise gives you the opportunity to try different synchronization settings with Pro Tools and an Avid SYNC Peripheral, and to experience how these affect the stability of sync. If you do not have access to Avid SYNC Peripherals, go through the exercise as best you can and familiarize yourself with the steps involved.

Opening the Sessions and Making Connections

We'll start by opening the same session on each Pro Tools|HD system and making a simple audio LTC connection from one SYNC Peripheral to the other.

To open the sync test session on each Pro Tools|HD system:

1. On each Pro Tools|HD system, open **310M EXERCISE 6-SYNC TEST.PTXT**. Save the session on an appropriate drive.

2. The session contains only a single **AUX INPUT** track with the **CLICK** plug-in inserted on it. The timecode ruler is shown and has been designated the main ruler.

To send timecode (LTC) from one SYNC Peripheral to the other:

■ Using an XLR audio cable, connect the **LTC OUT** of the **SYNC PERIPHERAL** attached to the master Pro Tools|HD system to the **LTC IN** on the **SYNC PERIPHERAL** connected to the slave Pro Tools|HD system.

Setting Up Proper Session Settings

Now that you have timecode routed from one system to the other, the rest is simply software configurations in the Session Setup window in Pro Tools. We'll start by simulating timecode sync between an analog tape deck and Pro Tools with LTC only. In this configuration, LTC is used for clock reference as well as start and stop. The timecode master Pro Tools|HD system will be emulating the tape machine.

To set up Pro Tools for sync with LTC only:

1. On the timecode master system, open the Session Setup window. See Figure Ex6.3.

Figure Ex6.3
Session Setup window of the timecode master system.

2. Verify that the session start time is 00:59:58:00.

3. Set the **TIMECODE RATE** to **30FPS**.

4. In the **SYNC SETUP** section, set the **CLOCK REFERENCE** to **INTERNAL/VSO**.

5. On the **SLAVE** system, open the Session Setup window. See Figure Ex6.4.

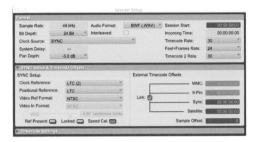

Figure Ex6.4
Session Setup window of the timecode slave system.

6. Verify that the **SESSION START TIME** and **TIMECODE RATE SETTINGS** match the master system.

7. Set **CLOCK REFERENCE** to **LTC** (**LTC 2—AVERAGE**). See Figure Ex6.5.

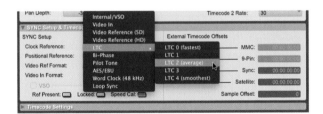

Figure Ex6.5
Setting LTC as Clock Reference in Session Setup window.

8. Set the **POSITIONAL REFERENCE** to **LTC**.

This scenario uses timecode for both positional reference as well as clock rate. With the latter, Pro Tools adjusts its playback speed by tracking the incoming timecode with near-sample accuracy, slewing playback speed as the tape speed slews.

To play back both systems together:

1. Put the slave system online. To do this, click the blue **ONLINE** button in either the Edit window toolbar or the Transport window, or press **COMMAND+J** (Mac) or **CTRL+J** (Windows) or **OPTION+SPACEBAR** (Mac) or **ALT+SPACEBAR** (Windows). See Figures Ex6.6. and Ex6.7.

Figure Ex6.6
Online button in the Pro Tools Transport window.

Figure Ex6.7
Online button in the Edit window toolbar.

2. In the master system's Transport window, click the GEN LTC button. See Figure Ex6.8.

Figure Ex6.8
Enabling Generate Timecode on the Pro Tools transport.

Note: You must have the Synchronization view options enabled from the Transport pull-down menu in order to see the Generate buttons.

3. Press **PLAY** on the master system. The slave system should lock up and play back in sync with the master. The metronome clicks should verify that playback is in sync. If the slave does not respond, check your connection and settings.

4. On the master system, check the VSO box in the **SYNC SETUP** section of the Session Setup window. This enables **VARIABLE SPEED OVERRIDE**, which allows you to adjust the playback speed (sample rate) of Pro Tools manually. See Figure Ex6.9.

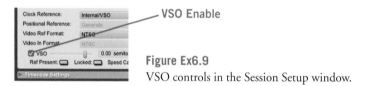

Figure Ex6.9
VSO controls in the Session Setup window.

5. Slowly move the VSO slider in either direction and listen to the results. How far can you move the slider in either direction before it causes a problem?

Part Three: Syncing 2 Pro Tools Systems with Satellite Link

This part of the exercise allows you to synchronize two Pro Tools systems using only an Ethernet connection for transport control and positional reference using Pro Tools|HD Satellite mode. You will also connect word clock from your Administrator Pro Tools|HD system to the Satellite Pro Tools|HD system to resolve their clocks as well.

Enabling the Satellite Machine

Before syncing the two Pro Tools machines, you need to confirm the Ethernet settings on the Satellite machine match the Administrator machine. Also, you need to enable Satellite mode on the Satellite Pro Tools machine for the Administrator to see it.

To verify proper Ethernet configuration:

1. On the Satellite system, open **SETUP > PERIPHERALS** and click on the **SATELLITES** tab. Enter a **SYSTEM NAME** for the Satellite machine (such as **PT SATELLITE**).

2. In the Advanced Network Settings section you will see your current computer's IP address. It doesn't matter what address it is, but it must be a valid IP address (an address ending in .0 or .192 will not work).

Tip: If your computers are not on an existing network, you can simply connect an Ethernet cable between the two computers (MacPros) or on some windows machines, an Ethernet cross-over cable is required. Manually set the Ethernet addresses in each computer's Network Control Panel settings to a similar range—192.168.1.5 on one system and 192.168.1.6 on the other, for example. Also, the subnet mask and router (or gateway) will be identical on each system (255.255.255.0 for the subnet mask and 192.168.1.1 for the router are typical settings).

3. Note the TCP/UDP port number (see Figure Ex6.10). It must be the same on the Administrator system. The default TCP/UDP port is 28282.

Figure Ex6.10
Verifying the TCP/UDP port.

Tip: On some larger network configurations, port 28282 may be blocked at the router. If you find that to be the case, port 10000 is a common alternative that works.

4. While still on the Satellite system, ensure that **SATELLITE** mode is enabled. See Figure Ex6.11.

5. After verifying all settings, click **OK** and switch to the Administrator machine.

Figure Ex6.11
Selecting Satellite mode.

Enabling the Administrator Machine

Configuring the Administrator settings will be similar to Satellite mode with regard to Ethernet and port settings. Once those are confirmed, the Administrator machine configures or declares Satellite machines for use with the Administrator machine.

To verify you have a proper IP address:

1. On the Administrator system, open Setup > Peripherals and click on the Satellites tab.

2. Under System Name, type a name for the Administrator machine (such as PTAdmin). See Figure Ex6.12.

Figure Ex6.12
Entering a name for the Administrator machine.

3. In the Advanced Network Settings section, you will see your current computer's IP address. It doesn't matter what address it is, but it must be a valid IP address in the same range as the Satellite machine. For example, if you used 192.168.1.6 for the Satellite system, use 192.168.1.5 for the Administrator machine.

Tip: If you have a computer with multiple Ethernet ports (such as a MacPro), be sure you are looking at the IP address of the Ethernet port you are using for Satellite Link. If you are not sure, click on the IP address, and the port number will precede the IP address.

Declaring Administrator and Satellite Machines on the Administrator Computer

After Ethernet connections are made and addresses and ports confirmed, you can declare administrator and satellite machines. This is done only on the Administrator system.

1. On the Administrator machine, click on the **SYSTEM 1** drop-down and choose the **ADMINISTRATOR PRO TOOLS SYSTEM** on the network. See Figure Ex6.13.

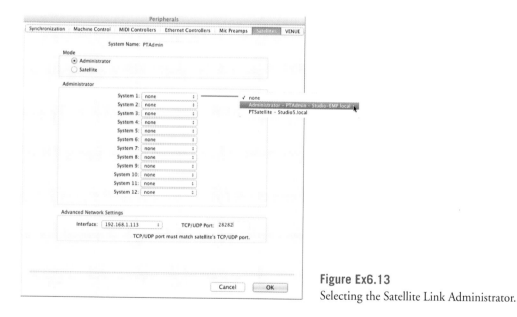

Figure Ex6.13
Selecting the Satellite Link Administrator.

2. Next, click and hold on the **SYSTEM 2** drop-down and wait until the Satellite machine name appears (it may take a few moments). Choose your Satellite machine and click **OK** to confirm the dialog box. When complete, it should look like Figure Ex6.14.

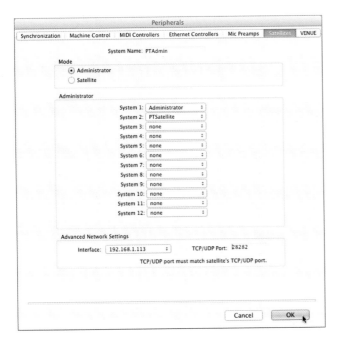

Figure Ex6.14
The Peripherals > Satellites dialog box
with multiple machines configured.

Verifying Link Operation

Once the Satellite Link is made, additional icons will appear in the Transport window as well as in the transport controls in the Edit window.

To see these icons, Synchronization must be checked in the Transport window pop-up menu or Edit window Toolbar pop-up menu.

To view the Satellite Link icons in the Transport:

■ In the Transport window, click on the Transport window pop-up menu and choose **SYNCHRONIZATION.** See Figure Ex6.15.

Figure Ex6.15
Transport window pop-up menu.

or

■ In the Edit toolbar, click on the Edit window pop-up menu and choose **TRANSPORT** and **SYNCHRONIZATION.** See Figure Ex6.16.

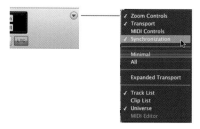

Figure Ex6.16
Edit window pop-up menu.

When shown in either the Transport window or the Edit window, the name of each of your systems and their associated Satellite Link buttons will appear. A satellite machine can be brought online or taken offline from the Administrator or from a Satellite machine.

Above the Satellite Link buttons is the Link button. This button controls the link status of an individual machine. This is similar to the Online button on the Transport. See Figure Ex6.17.

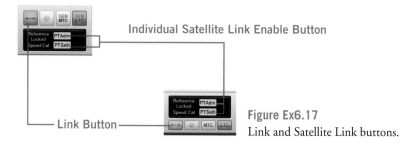

Figure Ex6.17
Link and Satellite Link buttons.

To have both Pro Tools|HD systems play back in sync:

1. Ensure that the **Satellite Link** buttons are enabled for both systems.

2. Ensure that the **Link** button is active on both systems.

3. Press **Play**, and both systems will play back in sync.

4. While playing back, disable the **Link** button on the satellite machine. Both Pro Tools systems will continue to play. But now press **Stop** on the satellite machine. Notice that the Administrator machine continues to play.

5. While keeping the administrator machine playing, re-engage the **Link** button on the satellite machine and notice how it locks up right away and matches the time of the administrator machine.

When syncing multiple Pro Tools|HD systems, you should provide word clock from one system to another to ensure sample-accurate playback. Discuss the best way to accomplish this with your particular setup. Remember, the SYNC Peripheral and all Pro Tools HD-series interfaces have word clock ports.

Pro Tools HD/HDX Mixing Concepts

This lesson explores the technology behind the different Pro Tools mixers available for Pro Tools. You will learn how to optimize your use of each system, see how to preserve the highest possible audio quality, and gain an understanding of the differences between systems and the ramifications of moving projects back and forth between systems.

Media Used: 310M Exercise 07.PTXT

Duration: 75 minutes

GOALS

- Understand the relationship between bit depth, dynamic range, and dither

- Understand the differences between the different Pro Tools mixers (Pro Tools HD|Native versus Pro Tools|HD versus Pro Tools|HDX)

- Understand the differences between Pro Tools|HD TDM architecture and Pro Tools|HDX architecture

- Understand the differences between 48-bit fixed-point mixing and 64-bit floating-point mixing

- Understand the factors that affect DSP usage

- Recognize the differences between DSP plug-ins and Native plug-ins

- Recognize appropriate use of Native plug-ins with Pro Tools|HD and Pro Tools|HDX

- Understand jitter

Introduction

Having a solid understanding of digital audio and the theories behind the Pro Tools mixer will give you the foundation upon which to build best practices to optimize your recordings and mixes. This lesson begins by re-acquainting you with some vital digital audio concepts that will help you appreciate the differences between the various Pro Tools platforms. You will also learn about the DSP-accelerated hardware architecture of both Pro Tools|HD and Pro Tools|HDX, as well as how DSP resources are managed. The heart of this discussion will delve into the differences between double-precision 24-bit environments (48-bit fixed-point processing) and dual-precision 32-bit environments (64-bit floating-point processing). This lesson also discusses how to optimize voice usage with Native plug-ins on DSP-accelerated systems. The lesson concludes with a short discussion of jitter and how it affects the sample rate clock.

Bit Depth, Dynamic Range, and Dither

Before comparing the different Pro Tools systems, it will help to review the principles of digital audio. By doing so you will come to understand the practical reasons behind using high resolution audio processing and maximizing headroom, footroom, and dynamic range.

Quantization and Quantization Errors

When an analog audio signal is digitized into Pro Tools, the analog-to-digital convertor (ADC) chip in the audio interface takes a rapid series of measurements of the amplitude (level) and interval (frequency) of the signal. When enough measurements are taken over a small window of time (i.e., when using a sufficient sample rate), a precise reproduction of the original signal can be stored within the human hearing range as a digital file.

Each measurement (sample) is recorded as a quantized or digitized number. The larger the range of numbers available to record measurements, the more accurately the original signal will be represented (for example, 24-bit/192kHz sampling will always record a more precise signal than 16-bit/44.1kHz). But the measurements always reference a finite scale—with common audio interface converters (delta sigma)—these are called *quantization units*. Each sample's amplitude must be rounded to the nearest step along this finite, or quant, scale, so there will always be a minute difference between the original signal and the signal described by the measurement scale. This difference is known as "quantization error."

In Figure 7.1, the actual audio signal is superimposed on a quantization grid. Notice that the grid does not have the resolution required to capture the sound at the precise amplitude at the precise time.

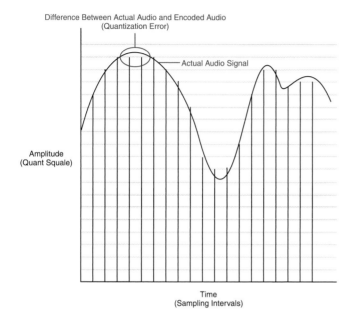

Figure 7.1
Quantization errors between actual audio signal and sampling resolution.

However, the finer the resolution of the measuring system (higher sample rates, larger bit depths), the smaller the quantization error will be.

Bit Depth and Dynamic Range

Computers use a binary number system to represent values as a series of 0s and 1s, with each 0 or 1 represented by a single binary digit, or bit. When recording digital audio, the number of bits that will be used to store each sample is determined when you create a session in Pro Tools (or later if you change the bit depth in the Session Setup window). You have your choice of 16-bit, 24-bit, or 32-bit float. More bits means more steps on the measurement scale, and therefore finer resolution. However, larger bit depths and higher sampling frequencies require significantly more storage space and processing power.

To clearly illustrate how bit depth affects resolution, consider a 3-bit system, which has 8 steps of measurement. Figure 7.2 shows a sine wave at progressively quieter levels and how it is measured by a 3-bit system. The first waveform is the loudest the system can represent. The second is quieter and is only crossing over one step either side of the center point. The final waveform is too quiet to be represented at all by the system.

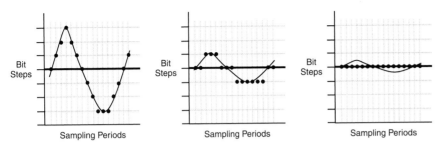

Figure 7.2
A very loud, very quiet, and undetectable signal in a 3-bit (8-step) digital audio system.

This figure shows how dynamic range (the difference between the quietest signal and the loudest signal a system can reproduce) is related to the bit depth. In this 3-bit example, you could only pull down the fader for a signal recorded at maximum level by –18dB before the signal would become too quiet for the system to reproduce. In fact it works out that for every bit you add, the dynamic range of the system is increased by approximately 6dB (6.02dB to be exact). See Table 7.1.

Table 7.1	Theoretical Versus Usable Dynamic Range with Common Bit Depths	
Bit Depth	**Theoretical Dynamic Range**	**Practical Dynamic Range Limit**
1	6.02dB	N/A
16	96dB	84dB
24	144dB	132dB
32	192dB	180dB

As you can see from Table 7.1, using higher bit depths will increase dynamic range. But modern converter technology is limited to roughly 128dB of dynamic range. This is because the two least-significant bits of the sampling word (or bit depth) are reserved for noise floor. A signal cannot go from program material to nothing —it must pass through a noise floor. For example, even though 16-bit audio files have a theoretical dynamic range of 96dB, their usable dynamic range is 84dB. This explains why most CD players quote a dynamic range of 84dB when the theoretical dynamic range is 96dB for a 16-bit audio file.

With 24-bit files, the usable dynamic range matches closely to human hearing. But with floating-point, your audio files and the mixer have more dynamic range than human perceptibility, resulting in a digital file that can retain more of its original signal, even with extreme gain changes during mixing and processing.

Comparing Different Pro Tools Mix Engines (PT Native, PT|HD, and PT|HDX)

With a fundamental understanding of bit depth and quantization, we can move on to the mixing differences between Pro Tools host-based (or *Native*) systems, Pro Tools|HD systems, and Pro Tools|HDX systems.

Pro Tools Native Mixers

Developed and released originally with Pro Tools LE in 1998, the Pro Tools Native mixer employed floating-point processing for mixing and plug-in processing. Floating-point mixing, rather than fixed-point mixing (discussed next), was deployed because it lends itself to modern computer platforms such as Intel-based processors (x86 architecture) and previous Apple/IBM G4/G5 processing architecture. In fact, nearly all host-based digital audio mixing platforms use 32-bit floating-point calculations (and some even 64-bit architecture) at their core. How well the mixer is implemented on the host is the subject of fierce debate. However one thing is certain: Programming 32-bit floating-point mixing well on a host processor (especially when considering summing errors, dithering, and precision) takes a fair bit of processing power and digital audio knowledge. To do 64-bit mixing requires even more of both.

Pro Tools|HD Mixer

Released in 1994 and developed entirely on the Motorola 56k DSP platform, the Pro Tools TDM mixer evolved over the subsequent 17 years using purpose-built DSP chips linked together with a patented real-time audio system known as TDM (time division multiplexing). While the Motorola DSPs provided the raw processing power required for recording, processing, and mixing, Digidesign's custom-designed TDM chips allowed the audio to move between DSPs and audio interfaces in real time—similar to how audio passes through a digital console. The primary advantages of a TDM-based system versus a host-based system are as follows:

■ Mixing and processing tasks are offloaded to dedicated DSP processing cards rather than using the host computer CPU.

■ Additional DSP cards can be installed into the same computer to increase computing power rather than buying a new computer to get more power.

■ Input-to-output throughput latency is reduced to undetectable levels rather than having to wait through a buffer cycle on a host-based system to hear your live input.

During the past 19 years, the TDM mixer evolved from 16-bit to 24-bit to 48-bit mixing. Moving to a double-precision 24-bit environment (48-bit fixed-point processing) improved headroom, footroom, processing accuracy, and audio detail, resulting in a much improved mixer. With the addition of automatic delay compensation in the Pro Tools|HD platform, Pro Tools quickly became a de facto mixing platform for the entire audio industry. Yet this powerful, scalable, expandable system uses standard consumer-grade computers as a host rather than costly fixed-architecture mixing consoles or purpose-built audio processing platforms that quickly become obsolete. In fact, mixes created on Pro Tools III TDM systems (version 3.3 or higher) can still be opened 16 years later on today's Pro Tools|HD or HDX systems (plug-in availability may vary).

Pro Tools|HDX Mixer

The Pro Tools|HDX platform combines the best of both worlds—dedicated DSP processing, expandability, and the predictability of the Pro Tools|HD platform paired with an expanded 64-bit floating-point mixer, increased delay compensation times, contemporary 32-bit floating-point DSPs, and an improved interchange capability with host-based Pro Tools systems. Built upon 32-bit floating-point DSPs from Texas Instruments and large FPGAs to handle inter-DSP communication at full 32-bit word lengths, the HDX card increases power and performance to roughly four times that of the previous Pro Tools|HD Accel cards. To summarize, HDX increases the capability of a Pro Tools HD system by doing the following:

■ Using a 64-bit floating-point mixer that offers increased headroom, dynamic range, resolution, and accuracy.

■ Retaining 64-bit mixing values when mixers span DSP chips.

■ Employing the same mixer as host-based Pro Tools systems, ensuring common-sounding mixes when moving projects to different Pro Tools 9/10 systems.*

■ Using a full 32-bit data path from audio file to final mix bus, removing many truncation and dithering points in the Pro Tools|HD mixer.

■ Expanding automatic delay compensation buffers up to 16,383 samples.

■ Providing twice as many DSPs as Pro Tools|HD (HDX = 18 versus Pro Tools|HD = 9) per card, running at faster clock speeds (HDX = 350+MHz versus Pro Tools|HD Accel PCIe = 220MHz).

* When using AAX plug-ins.

Having reviewed the general differences between the Pro Tools mix engines, let's look further into floating-point processing versus fixed-point processing.

Fixed-Point Versus Floating-Point Processing Overview

As mentioned previously, Pro Tools|HD hardware uses 48-bit fixed-point processing, while host-based Pro Tools systems and HDX hardware use a different mathematical system—dual-precision 32-bit floating-point, also known as 64-bit floating-point processing. While at first glance 64-bit floating-point processing offers more bits than 48-bit fixed-point processing, how the bits are used, how numbers are represented, and what types of calculations are used affect rounding errors, resolution, and accuracy. This section briefly explains the two approaches as well as their benefits and challenges. Later in this lesson, we will revisit these topics, after gaining a more thorough understanding of how the entire mixer works.

Fixed-Point Processing

In fixed-point coding, numbers are represented linearly in binary and constrained by the number of available bits—24 in the case of a digitized signal from an HD I/O interface, through the TDM connection to the DSPs on the Pro Tools|HD cards. In contrast to floating-point systems, fixed-point systems have a consistent noise floor that is roughly –144dB below 0dBFS (for 24-bit sessions), resulting in good low-level detail, predictable summing characteristics, and predicable dithering results due to a fixed bit for noise floor (least significant bit, or LSB). Pro Tools|HD uses a 48-bit mixer to combine signals together. The increased bit depth offers increased detail and resolution. In addition, the Pro Tools|HD mixer uses a 56-bit accumulator for extra computational headroom when inputting values into a mixer before calculating results and rounding down to a final 48-bit result.

To demonstrate how increased resolution works, imagine applying an audio process to a signal (such as gain or EQ). Take two numbers: the amplitude of a signal and some amount of gain change being applied to the signal (using the more familiar decimal system here):

0.96 (original signal amplitude) × 0.612 (negative gain) = 0.58752 (resulting signal amplitude after gain change)

You can see that multiplying the numbers produces a new number with more digits than the original number. If you were limited to our initial resolution (two decimal places), the result would be rounded to 0.59.

With a 24-bit signal, this rounding error may be small, but it could become significant over successive processes. Pro Tools|HD uses a 48-bit fixed-point scheme, which doubles the digital word length to 48 bits by using two 24-bit words to represent 48 bits. This reduces the amount of rounding required and adds a tremendous amount of resolution after the decimal point. When binary numbers are used, the 48-bit scheme provides 281,474,976,710,656 discrete values.

You might think about bit depth like this: Each added bit represents 6.02dB of added dynamic range, so a 24-bit system has a theoretical dynamic range of 144dB, while a 48-bit system has a theoretical dynamic range of 288dB. While increasing bit depth increases dynamic range, it also provides more decimal points to store the digital audio. That means increasing audio bit depth not only provides increased dynamic range, but it also provides the added benefit of higher resolution or accuracy when storing the amplitude values of the audio samples.

Floating-Point Processing

In floating-point coding, numbers are represented using the scientific notation of mantissa/significand (base number) and exponent (multiplier). For example, the number 256,000,000 is illustrated in Figure 7.3.

Figure 7.3
Floating-point equivalent
of a decimal number.

With floating-point notation, the value 256,000,000 requires only four numbers to represent (2, 5, 6, and 6). This allows the floating-point system to store very wide ranging values by changing the exponent as compared to fixed-point processing, where the scale is fixed and cannot be adjusted (except by widening the bit depth). With audio, wide range translates to very large dynamic ranges and higher audio quality.

With 32-bit floating-point systems, 1 bit is reserved for the sign, 23 bits are reserved for the mantissa, and 8 bits are reserved for the exponent. With 64-bit floating-point systems, 1 bit is reserved for the sign, 52 bits are used for the mantissa, with 11 bits used for the exponent. In the simplified decimal example in Figure 7.3, which has three digits for the mantissa and one for the exponent, you can store all the numbers from 0 to 999 with the exponent set to 0. To go above 999, you would need to increment the exponent by 1 (which multiplies the mantissa by 10). The number series would then span from 10 to 9990 in steps of 10.

With a system that can represent very wide ranges, yet has a word depth larger than 24-bit, 64-bit floating-point mixers have the ability to retain and process more mathematical resolution because of their expanded word length and reliance on the exponent to provide increased dynamic range. This is commonly referred to as moving the window around the bit tree. The practical translation is that 64-bit floating-point provides much more headroom and dynamic range without losing any low-level detail when mixing or processing audio.

Comparing Pro Tools|HD Versus HDX Versus Native Mixers

Moving projects between Pro Tools|HD using dual 24-bit (48-bit) DSP architecture and host-based Pro Tools systems using 64-bit floating-point processing appears identical. But underneath, they have slight variances (such as pan depths, headroom, and clipping characteristics) that may lead to slightly different-sounding mixes. Much of that difference depends upon what version of Pro Tools you are using.

Pro Tools|HDX with Pro Tools 10.x software fundamentally changes this paradigm. While retaining the on-demand power, scalability, and stability of Pro Tools|HD, Pro Tools|HDX uses 32-bit floating-point DSPs to re-create the same 64-bit floating-point mixer used on host-based Pro Tools systems 10.x or later. This allows a mix created on a Native Pro Tools system to run on the dedicated DSPs of Pro Tools HDX and sound identical, while completely off-loading the host-based processor for other tasks (such as processor-intensive virtual instruments). When using AAX-based plug-ins, sessions automatically switch between Native and DSP versions of the plug-ins.

However, if you find yourself faced with moving projects between Native and DSP-accelerated systems, it's good to understand the differences.

Common Mixing Errors When Moving from Pro Tools Host-Based to Pro Tools|HD

As noted, Pro Tools host-based systems (or Pro Tools LE) have always used floating-point mixing. This was done to take advantage of modern computing processors to mix and process signals efficiently. However, the product was aimed at consumers who were not necessarily professional audio engineers. It would be quite easy to clip a sum point in the LE mixer or the internal plug-in process. Therefore, the following measures were put into place to alleviate common mixing problems:

- Signals summed at a bus point, if clipped, would be rounded to just below clip on Pro Tools LE. The same bus point, if shown on Pro Tools|HD, would show clip. This would typically result in a mix that looked and sounded fine on a Pro Tools LE system but might clip on a Pro Tools|HD system.

- If a plug-in was inserted on the bus point, as is often the case with Aux Submasters, the Pro Tools LE mixer would not allow a clipped signal to pass to the first instance of a plug-in on that summed track. To alleviate the problem, the signal was rounded down using floating-point mixing to reduce the level below clip before passing it to the first plug-in on the Aux Submaster. Again, if the mix was moved to a Pro Tools|HD mixer, you could see clipping at the input of the plug-in, requiring you to rebalance the mix to alleviate the problem.

- Pro Tools LE had 36dB of headroom in the mixer, while Pro Tools|HD has 56dB of headroom in the mixer. But people could not understand how Pro Tools|HD could clip while Pro Tools LE would not. In actuality, Pro Tools was modifying gain stages in the Pro Tools LE mixer without it being very obvious.

- Pro Tools LE used 32-bit floating-point calculations for processing with RTAS (Real-Time AudioSuite) plug-ins, whereas Pro Tools|HD uses 24/48-bit DSP (or TDM) plug-ins. While the sound and algorithms were meticulously programmed by the manufacturers to yield similar sound, some DSP plug-ins are not available in Native versions, and vice versa. However, when moving mixes from LE to TDM, a TDM system can still run plug-ins as Native versions.

- Pro Tools|HD has had automatic delay compensation running for years. But automatic delay compensation was not introduced to host-based Pro Tools systems until Pro Tools 9, although host-based plug-ins could always auto-compensate on audio/disk tracks, assuming there was no look-ahead functionality built into the plug-in.

- Pro Tools LE used −3dB pan laws, whereas Pro Tools|HD used −2.5. This meant that additional time would be required to rebalance a mix when moving from Pro Tools LE to Pro Tools|HD for tracks that were panned to the center position or dynamically panned across center. Prior to Pro Tools 9, TDM systems could be forced to use a 3dB pan law by removing the stereo mixer plug-in, and using the surround mixer plug-in for both stereo and surround-sound mixes. With Pro Tools 9 and later software, pan laws are adjustable on a session by session basis from within the Session Setup window.

All of these issues are resolved when moving host-based Pro Tools 9 or later sessions to HDX because of the common 64-bit mixer and the introduction of AAX plug-ins, which can run either on the host or on the HDX 32-bit DSPs.

DSP-Based Mixers and DSP Usage

Now that you have a better understanding of fixed-point versus floating-point processing and how the mixer architecture applies to dynamic range and resolution, it's time to review the hardware components of Pro Tools|HD and Pro Tools|HDX. Understanding these differences can help you to create better sounding mixes and point you in the right direction when troubleshooting issues.

Pro Tools|HD and TDM

As mentioned earlier, the Pro Tools|HD platform is composed of DSP chips mounted on a PCIe card that interconnect using a data highway called time division multiplexing (TDM). Figure 7.4 shows a Pro Tools|HD Accel card.

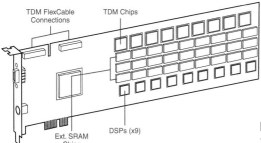

Figure 7.4
Pro Tools|HD Accel card.

TDM is a widely used technology in which multiple digital channels or streams of data are sent via a single bus. Instead of using individual physical connections for each stream (connecting one DSP to another DSP), a very high data transmission speed is used, with each stream allocated a "timeslot" to go from DSP to DSP (or interface). This means that connections between points connected to a TDM bus can be made and changed simply by changing which timeslot a point is listening to.

Pro Tools|HD-series cards feature Avid's TDM II architecture. Channels from sources such as disk tracks, sends, or buses can be combined together or *multiplexed* onto a data highway (TDM bus) so that all signals can propagate throughout the system simultaneously and be accessed within a single sample period.

TDM II runs fast enough to accommodate many audio signals at the same time. Each separate audio signal, or *stream*, takes up a single timeslot on this multiplexed bus. One of most powerful features of the TDM II architecture is that a single timeslot can be used to broadcast data to many destinations simultaneously. Data can also be sent bi-directionally and privately between DSP chips, which effectively provides a very large number of available timeslots. This provides a huge number of potential connections for routing, processing, and mixing audio signals within Pro Tools.

On Pro Tools|HD cards, the DSP chips are arranged serially, with 512 connections, or timeslots, between each chip. Many more than 512 connections are technically possible, as signals only need to use slots on the bus between the chips at their source and destination. (See Figure 7.5.)

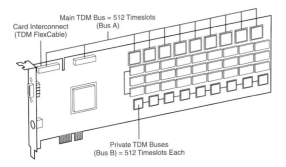

Figure 7.5
Main TDM bus and private buses between chips.

HDX Architecture

The Pro Tools|HDX platform is similar to Pro Tools|HD in that it has dedicated DSP chips mounted on a PCIe card. However, that is where the similarity ends.

The first thing to note is the HDX card has twice as many DSPs as the previous generation (as shown in Figure 7.6), providing roughly 1.5 times the processing power of Pro Tools|HD.

Another substantial difference between Pro Tools|HDX and Pro Tools|HD is that Pro Tools|HDX does not have TDM chips—rather, all DSPs are connected to a central FPGA (Field Programmable Gate Array). This star configuration of DSPs connected to a single FPGA allows the FPGA to control what signals go to which DSPs in a timely and efficient manner, yielding the following benefits:

- By having one FPGA chip connected to each DSP, expert programming is employed to keep latency between chips to a minimum.

- By using an FPGA instead of fixed ASIC chips for data communication, new programming changes and firmware updates can be easily applied. This provides the potential for new features and improvements without having to update hardware with costly hardware exchanges.

The DSP chips used on the HDX card are quite different from those used on previous generation Pro Tools|HD hardware. Rather than using fixed-point processing DSP (Motorola 56k family), the HDX card employs Texas Instruments 32-bit floating-point DSPs. This allows Pro Tools to have a common mixing and processing environment that spans both DSP-accelerated systems and host-based Pro Tools systems. Also, these 32-bit floating-point DSPs are much more powerful than their predecessors, allowing you to mix more signals, employ more signal processing, and have higher track counts than previous Pro Tools|HD systems per chip. In fact, at 48kHz, HDX cards are typically four times more powerful than previous generation Pro Tools|HD Accel cards.

HDX cards also utilize uniform DSP cores. This means that any plug-in can run on any DSP core. This was not the case with previous generation Pro Tools Accel cards, which had an assortment of different external RAM components for DSP chips. In rare circumstances, you could seemingly have enough free DSPs for a particular plug-in that used external RAM (such as a reverb), but because the available DSPs did not have external RAM, a DSP shuffle would occur.

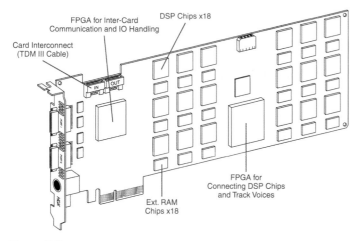

Figure 7.6
Diagram of HDX card architecture.

Pro Tools|HD DSP Shuffle

When a new session is opened, Pro Tools|HD attempts to reload all the plug-ins and mixers onto any DSPs that have already been allocated. But when running low on DSP resources, the software will automatically perform a DSP shuffle to optimize DSP mixing—typically when a new plug-in is inserted that may not necessarily have a free DSP to load on.

HDX (and previous generation Pro Tools|HD) also offers the ability to convert any plug-in that runs on the DSP to a Native version (assuming an equivalent plug-in is available on the system). This means that if you need more processing power, you can always use the power of the host computer to complement your dedicated DSP processes.

Note: When converting between DSP and Native versions of plug-ins, there could be audible sonic differences.

At the time of print, Pro Tools|HDX systems support up to three HDX cards maximum. However, the hardware system is designed to eventually support up to seven total HDX cards installed in a single system.

Mixer Creation

Now that you have a better understanding of the core technology powering the Pro Tools DSP-accelerated hardware, it's time to look at the technology that powers the Pro Tools HD mixer. Each time you open a session, a mixer is created on your DSP chips. You learned in earlier courses that plug-ins use DSP chips. So do mixers, except that mixers can span more than one chip and communicate with each other at full 64-bit word lengths with HDX and 48-bit word lengths with Pro Tools|HD. When you go beyond a certain number of mixer channels (including audio tracks, Aux Input tracks, Instrument tracks, and sends), Pro Tools will use another DSP to expand mixer capacity.

As in the analog world, every auxiliary send (internal mix bus) or output bus that you use demands that a summing mixer exist for that group output. On an analog console, the number of these summing mixers is dictated by the physical layout of the console (for instance, a 24-bus console has 24 buses). In the Pro Tools mix environment, this number is variable (up to 256 internal mix buses and up to 192 mono or 96 stereo output buses) depending on the number of output mixes or sends that you choose to create. Pro Tools allocates DSP power as it is needed, in order to build the mixers for each session as additional buses are used.

Monitoring Mixer Usage with the System Usage Window

Pro Tools HD software provides an easy way to track how much processing powering is being used for mixing on the DSP chips from within the System Usage window, shown in Figure 7.7.

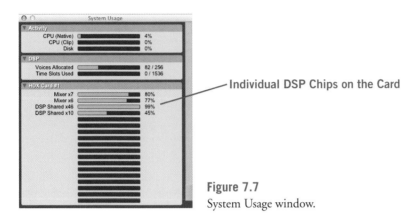

Individual DSP Chips on the Card

Figure 7.7
System Usage window.

Each mixer will use a DSP chip. The number of mixers that share the DSP chip for mixing can vary, depending upon their configuration.

Stereo

Each TDM stereo mixer has the dimensions $N \times 2$, meaning that it mixes a variable number of inputs to an output pair. For example, a session with 48 tracks would require a 48×2 mixer. If one of the tracks is assigned to Output 3–4, however, two mixers are required—one 47×2 mixer routed to Output 1–2, and one 1×2 mixer routed to Output 3–4. Depending upon the number of tracks and the width of the mixer (stereo versus mono), two separate $N \times 2$ mixers typically fit on a single DSP chip. However, as more tracks are added or more discrete buses are used, Pro Tools will be forced to use another DSP for mixing without having used the first DSP 100%.

In Figure 7.8, a single mixer is created for 48 channels to a pair of outputs on a Pro Tools|HDX system. The DSP is only at 49% for all 48 tracks.

In Figure 7.9, a send is used across all channels to a second set of outputs. Notice that the DSP usage gauge has increased to 69% but has successfully created two distinct 48×2 mixers on the same DSP chip. This is the equivalent of a 96×4 mixer. Also notice that the DSP gauge for the DSP chip now says Mixer x2.

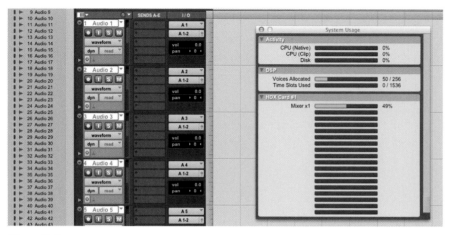

Figure 7.8
System Usage window showing DSP mixing resources.

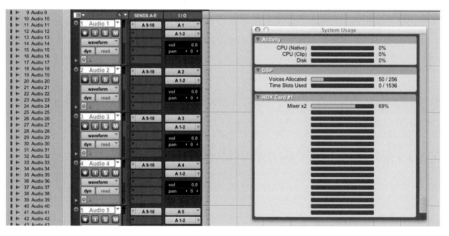

Figure 7.9
System Usage window showing two 48 × 2 mixers on a single chip.

In Figure 7.10, a second send has been used across all tracks to go to a third set of outputs. At this point the mixer cannot run three distinct 48 × 2 mixers on a single DSP chip, so it assigns the third 48 × 2 mixer to a second DSP chip. Notice that the DSP gauge says Mixer x1.

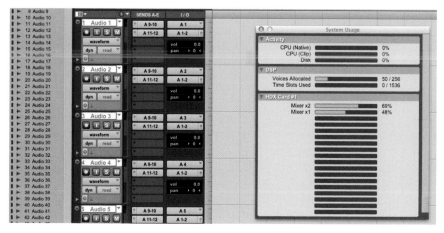

Figure 7.10
System Usage window showing three 48 × 2 mixers on two DSP chips.

Multichannel

When using surround paths, each surround mixer can have a variable number of outputs as well as a variable number of inputs. For example, the 5.1 format requires six outputs. However routing to this output is usually done through various multichannel buses (LCR, 5.0, 5.1). In Figure 7.11, 32 tracks are assigned to four different auxiliary submasters; two are 5.0 mix buses, and two are 5.1 mix buses. These submasters are subsequently bussed to a single 5.1 output bus going to the interface. Notice that two different DSPs are employed for this mix; the first DSP is used for the submixing, and the second DSP is used for the final output bus to the interface.

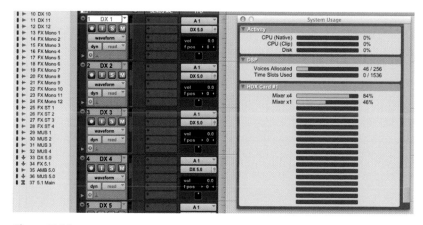

Figure 7.11
System Usage window showing four 32 × 5.0/5.1 mixers on a single DSP.

Adding more internal buses for effects (such as reverb) will also contribute to the number of DSPs required. In Figure 7.12, two mono buses have been added for two different reverb sends across all source tracks. Notice that 75% of a single DSP chip has now been utilized for these sends.

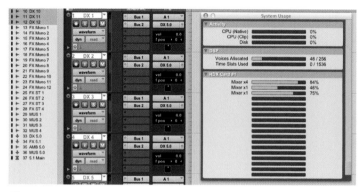

Figure 7.12
System Usage window showing additional DSP mixers for internal effects.

As the track count grows in high-sample rate production (such as 96kHz), more and more of the DSPs will be required for mixing.

Identifying Which Mixers Are Used on What DSPs

With Pro Tools 10.x and HDX, the System Usage window provides detailed information on the number of mixers and their configuration on a single DSP.

To get a listing of what mixers are running on individual DSPs:

1. Open the System Usage window (**WINDOW > SYSTEM USAGE**).

2. Hover the mouse over a DSP gas gauge that has a mixer process running, as shown in Figure 7.13. A pop-up display will appear showing the processes running on that DSP chip.

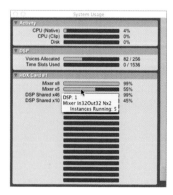

Figure 7.13
System Usage window showing detailed mixer information.

Dither

When you reduce the bit depth of a signal, you run the risk of eliminating, or truncating, program material in the least significant bits. For example, when moving from 24 bits to 16 bits, any low-level audio in the bottom 8 bits gets truncated, which can cause audible quantization errors. In an effort to mask the quantization errors, you have the option of adding dither, which creates an artificial "noise floor" at the least significant bit (LSB), ultimately helping to mask the quantization errors caused by the original truncation of the file. The LSB represents the quietest amplitude level that can be recorded by a digital system. Hence, dither creates a noise floor at the quietest level that can be represented at a given bit depth. Dither is applied in several instances:

■ When a signal in the Pro Tools|HD mixer is sent from the mixer to a physical output (when using the dithered mixer).

■ On Pro Tools|HD, when a signal is processed in a higher bit depth plug-in process (48-bit for Pro Tools|HD) and is sent back to the mixer chips.

■ When choosing Export Clips as Files from the Clips List to a lower bit depth file. In this case dither is automatically applied.

Why Dither Works

Perceptually, the effect of dither is to de-correlate the quantization distortion from the original signal by exaggerating signal activity around the LSB. In other words, instead of hearing a slightly distorted version of the original signal, you hear the original signal plus some very quiet uncorrelated noise, which is preferable.

Figure 7.14 is a recording of dither noise that POW-r Dither uses (discussed in the next section). The dither signal has been amplified by stacking four Trim plug-ins at +12dB on top of each other (thus boosting the signal 48dB).

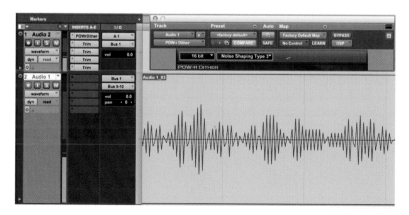

Figure 7.14
Waveform of POW-r Dither Type 3.

This seemingly random waveform again would be introduced near the bottom of a 24- or 32-bit signal, in order to mask the quantization error.

Not all dither is the same. In fact, POW-r Dither gives you three different algorithms to choose from, as discussed in the next section.

When to Apply Dither Plug-ins

Because dither masks low-level quantization errors that occur during file truncation, it should be used after all gain-based processing has occurred, as the final step when converting a high bit depth audio file to a lower bit depth file. Often this is done when creating the final mix of a 24-bit music project going to 16-bit for CD replication. Adding dither allows the low-level signals of a high bit depth audio file to still be perceived to some extent in the reduced-bit version.

Note: When converting 32-bit floating point files to 24-bit fixed-point files, truncation is applied with no dither, although dither is applied if further reducing the bit depth of the fixed-point file.

Dither is added at the least significant bit, which will typically be the noise floor. Once the conversion is completed, the new audio file will have an increased noise floor, but the quietest parts and finest details of the recording will be heard through the dither.

When trying to decide if dither is necessary, consider the following:

- Audio signals with quiet passages will have less distortion if dither is applied.

- Dither should always be applied when converting from a fixed-point file to a lower bit depth, assuming no further processing or summing will be applied.

- Dither is not needed when converting to a higher bit depth.

Caution: Dither should never be applied during a sample rate conversion. The noise added at the least significant bit interacts with the sampling conversion algorithm and may lead to a slightly degraded sound while converting. If you must reduce the bit depth of a file and sample-rate convert it (such as creating a 16-bit/44.1kHz version of a file from a 24-bit/48kHz master file), break the process into two steps—convert the file's sample rate first to the target sample rate but retain the bit depth (in this case 44.1kHz but still a 24-bit file). Open the new file at the new sample rate in a new 44.1kHz session and then reduce the bit depth with dither.

Dithering Down to 16-Bit for CD

Music that has been recorded and mixed at 24-bit must at some point be reduced to 16-bit for CD reproduction. If you are providing a final CD-ready master, this may become your responsibility. Dither should normally be used in this situation to preserve some of the benefit of the 24-bit mix.

In the Avid Learning Series   Dither plug-ins are introduced in the Pro Tools 110 course.

Caution: **If you are supplying a finished mix that will be worked on further by a mastering engineer, you should not reduce the bit depth or apply dither.**

Flavors of Dither

A number of plug-ins provide dither, including the Dither and POW-r Dither plug-ins that are included with all Pro Tools systems. Some dither plug-ins, including POW-r Dither, provide different types of dither that suit various types of program material. Other "mastering" plug-ins, such as Maxim, provide dither at their output stage. One thing they all have in common is that they must be the very last process in the signal chain before going to the outputs or being recorded via Bounce to Disk. Dither must therefore be the last insert on a Master Fader (which is the only track type that supports post-fader inserts). Figure 7.15 shows both the POW-r Dither and Maxim plug-ins.

Figure 7.15
The POW-r Dither plug-in (left) and Maxim plug-in (right) both provide dither.

DigiRack Dither

The DigiRack Dither plug-in shown in Figure 7.16 uses basic dither with a single noise-shaping option. The DigiRack Dither plug-in does not provide any selectable noise-shaping options. Instead, it uses a standard dithering setting to retain a linear frequency response when reducing resolution. This does not always translate into the best stereo mix. Instead, consider using the POW-r Dither plug-in when reducing the resolution of a final stereo mix, since it provides selectable noise-shaping options.

Figure 7.16
DigiRack Dither plug-in.

POW-r Dither

POW-r Dither (*Psycho-Acoustically Optimized Word Length Reduction*) is an algorithm created by the POW-r Dither Consortium, composed of John La Grou (Millenea Media), David McGrath (Lake Audio, now part of Dolby Labs), Daniel Weiss (Weiss Electronics), and Dr. Glenn Zelniker (Z Systems). Their algorithm provides a method to reduce word length (or bit depth) while retaining a high degree of perceived dynamic efficiency and very low noise. This plug-in has three different settings, optimized for different program material. You should listen carefully in a studio-quality monitoring environment to judge which option provides the best results on your mix.

- **Type 1:** Has the flattest frequency spectrum in the audible range of frequencies, modulating and accumulating the dither noise just below the Nyquist frequency. Recommended for less stereophonically complex material such as solo instrument recordings and spoken word.

- **Type 2:** Has a psycho-acoustically optimized low order noise-shaping curve. Recommended for material containing some stereophonic complexity. Also recommended if the final mix is slightly bright or edgy.

- **Type 3:** Has a psycho-acoustically optimized high order noise-shaping curve. Recommended for full-spectrum, wide stereo field material. Also recommended if the final mix is right where you want it and you don't want any imaging or clarity to be lost when reducing the word lengths.

Caution: Applying any further processing, especially gain-based processes after applying Type 2 or 3 dither, can make the dither audible in certain frequency bands.

The Pro Tools HD Mixer

At this point you have a solid understanding of the theories behind the Pro Tools mix environment. In this section you will explore the Pro Tools mixer in more detail to uncover more similarities and differences between the two DSP-accelerated platforms. Understanding exactly what is (and isn't) happening when you mix signals in Pro Tools can be a great asset. It will allow you to proceed with confidence, knowing that your mixing methods are not detrimental to sound quality.

First we'll introduce the main topics; then we'll go back and explore them more deeply while looking at how an audio signal is handled on its way through Pro Tools.

Double-Precision Processing

Pro Tools's audio interfaces can digitize analog signals or receive digital signals at a maximum bit depth of 24 bits (32-bit float files can also be used, but the actual PCM audio resolution of the converter is still 24 bits). We saw earlier that 24 bits equals a theoretical dynamic range of 144dB, which is a much more dynamic range than the human ear can perceive. This is the maximum resolution of audio signals when they come into the system, leave the system digitally, or arrive at the DACs for conversion back to analog signals. However, the Pro Tools mixer uses 48-bit values (Pro Tools|HD) or 64-bit values (Pro Tools Native or HDX) when mixing and processing signals to retain clarity and detail and avoid unnecessary rounding errors. The other advantages to using large bit depth mixers are headroom, footroom, and processing capacity.

Headroom

The 48-bit mixer and the 64-bit mixer both offer a huge amount of headroom for mixing together signals without clipping. In fact, mix buses in Pro Tools|HD have 54dB of headroom above the maximum for any individual channel. This means that you can mix 128 tracks of maximum-level, in-phase audio, with every fader at +12, and still not clip the bus internally. With 64-bit floating-point processing, the mixer headroom provides more than 1,500dB of dynamic range.

Tip: In real-world terms, this means that you will never clip a bus input when mixing signals. Master Faders on buses and outputs can be used to scale the final result to a level that doesn't clip when the signal returns to 24 bits or 32-bit float in the Native/HDX mixer.

Footroom

With the 48-bit mixer, you can pull signals down drastically without losing any of the original resolution. If the mixer worked at 24-bit, pulling a fader down would immediately start reducing the resolution of the signal. In fact, with the 48-bit mixer, faders can be pulled down to nearly –90dB before any of the original resolution is lost. With the 64-bit mixer, the full 32-bit floating point word traveling through the system is also retained, even when pulling a fader down to inaudible levels.

Tip: In practical terms, this means that you don't need to worry too much about where your faders are positioned. Your original recordings will be represented with all their resolution intact in the mix. Also, it makes no difference whether you set your faders low and have the master high or vice versa, but employing proper gain stages throughout your mix will always yield better results.

Eventually, your mix must leave the mixer and be sent across the HD Mixer to the outputs or to analog outputs via the DACs (digital-to-analog converters). This requires going back to a standard 24-bit signal. With the 48-bit mixer, this is either achieved simply by discarding the bottom 24 bits (truncation) and then applying dither. Remember, the difference between these two methods is only slight; although you are discarding half your bits, they represent only extremely fine details of the signal that are below –144dB. Using dither will reduce quantization noise below this level, at the expense of the noise floor at –144dB.

The 64-bit mixer uses two 32-bit words to represent the audio, with the first 23 bits of data in each 32-bit word representing the actual bits of audio. However, throughout the entire mix and summing process, those 32 bits have never been lost. So again, when the signal is converted from 64-bit, to 32-bit, to 24-bit, the entire 24-bit signal is maintained.

Master Faders allow you to choose which 24 bits (or 32 bits on HDx and Native mixers) make up the signal that reaches a bus or output. This will be explained in more detail in the next section.

Looking in More Detail: An Audio Signal's Tale

This section reviews the entire path of the audio signal, how quantization is minimized, how summing characteristics are different between fixed-point and floating-point processing, and where truncation points occur in each system.

Analog to Digital Conversion

A signal that enters the input of an Avid HD I/O is digitized at 24-bit resolution. The 24-bit signal has a theoretical dynamic range of 144dB. The ADCs on the HD I/O have an incredible dynamic range of 122dB on the ADC side, so there is plenty of resolution in the 24-bit signal.

On a Pro Tools|HD system, once the signal is digitized, it is transferred over the TDM bus at 24-bit resolution to the DSP chips for plug-in processing. With Pro Tools|HDX, the signal is converted on the HDX card to 32-bit floating point and transferred to the DSPs.

Tip: To take full advantage of the 64-bit mixer resolution, it is recommended to create your session using the 32-Bit Float Bit Depth setting. This will allow you to use Elastic Audio at full resolution and offer a way to print your final mix to disk at a 32-bit float file.

Plug-in Processing

Audio signals in the Pro Tools mixer are often processed with plug-ins. However, the data pathway used to get to the plug-ins is different, depending upon which mixer you use.

Pro Tools|HD

DSP plug-in processing is carried out at 24-bit or 48-bit resolution, depending on how the plug-in is coded. Plug-ins that process at 48-bit resolution take advantage of the ability of 24-bit DSP chips to perform double-precision processing (using two 24-bit words). The 48-bit result of such calculations is converted back down to 24-bit resolution in order to be passed on to the next plug-in or back to the mixer. Figure 7.17 shows an overview of the signal path in the Pro Tools mixer.

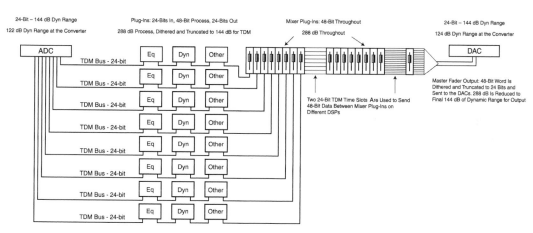

Figure 7.17
Pro Tools|HD system diagram.

48-Bit Mixing

Once the signal has left the inserts, it is added to the Pro Tools mixer. At this stage the 24-bit word is multiplied by another 24-bit word that represents the fader and pan positions, producing a 48-bit word that stays at 48-bit resolution throughout the mixer. Although connections in the TDM bus are 24-bit, two 24-bit timeslots are used to pass the two 24-bit words of mixer data between DSPs, maintaining an internal dynamic range of 288dB. As already stated, the additional 24 bits provide the mixer with a larger amount of headroom and footroom above and below the original 24-bit word, making the mixer very difficult to clip as you add more inputs to the mix bus. Specifically, nine bits are reserved for levels above 0dBFS, providing 54dB of headroom. Fifteen bits are added to the other end of the 24-bit word. The practical implications of this are that you can do the following:

■ Sum 128 tracks of correlated, full-code audio with all the faders at +12dB without clipping the input of the bus.

■ Pull down any channel fader to around −90dB without losing any of the original 24 bits.

The DSP chips on a Pro Tools|HD card use a 56-bit register, meaning that 56 bits are available on the chip to store the results of any calculations. Let's consider in more detail why reserving extra bits maintains resolution when processing digital audio. The diagram shown in Figure 7.18 represents four points in time in a 24-bit mixer.

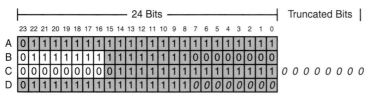

A   A Single 24-Bit Full Code Input in a 24-Bit Mixer.
B   128 Full Code Inputs Summed at Unity Gain with a Master Fader Used to Pull the Result out of Clipping. 8 Bits Are Lost and Result in 16 Bits of Data.
C   One Full Code Channel with its Channel Fader Set at −42 dB. Again, 8 Bits Are Lost to Truncation and Result in 16 Bits of Data.
D   The Truncated Word with its Fader Pushed Back up to 0 dB. The Truncated Bits Are Lost and the Result is Much Different from Example A.

Figure 7.18
24-bit mixer truncation points.

■ **Row A:** Shows the original, full-code input channel as it appears at the mixer. There is no initial multiplication performed, so it is at full level at both the DAC and the mixer.

■ **Row B**: Shows 128 summed channels of full code 24-bit audio. A master fader would have to be used to pull the output level down by −42.1dB to pull it out of clipping, but the penalty in this system is a loss of eight bits.

■ **Row C**: Shows an individual channel reduced by 42dB. Since there are no footroom bits available, the lowest bits are simply cut off, and the result is a 16-bit word.

■ **Row D**: Shows the truncated word with its fader pushed back up to 0dB. The truncated bits are lost and cannot be recovered.

In the Pro Tools 48-bit mixer, however, this is not the case. The DSPs use a 56-bit register for performing 48-bit calculations, with eight additional bits provided for overflow to avoid rounding errors. There is enough headroom to sum 128 full-code tracks at +12 without internally clipping, as well as enough low level resolution to pull channel faders down to –90dB without losing any of their original bits, as shown in Figure 7.19.

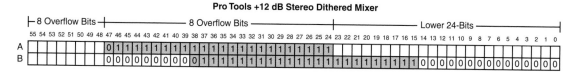

Figure 7.19
24-bit full code signal as placed in the 56-bit register in the Pro Tools mixer.

Dithered Versus Non-Dithered Mixers (Pro Tools|HD Hardware Only)

Whether or not dither is applied at the final output stage of the Pro Tools HD mixer is determined by which mixer plug-in is currently active.

The following four mixer plug-ins are supplied with Pro Tools HD software:

- Stereo mixer

- Surround mixer

- Stereo dithered mixer

- Surround dithered mixer

Caution: Pro Tools HD PCIe hardware systems only support having one of each set of mixer plug-ins installed at any one time. If both plug-in types from the same set are installed, an error message will occur when launching Pro Tools.

The mixer you wish to use must be placed manually in the Plug–ins folder before launching Pro Tools. The dithered mixer plug-ins use slightly more DSP resources than the non-dithered versions.

To switch mixer plug-ins:

1. Quit Pro Tools.

2. Do one of the following:

    - On Windows systems, open the PLUG-INS (UNUSED) folder (PROGRAM FILES\ COMMONFILES\DIGIDESIGN\DAE).

    - On Macintosh systems, open the PLUG-INS (UNUSED) folder on your Startup drive (LIBRARY/APPLICATION SUPPORT/DIGIDESIGN).

3. Locate the mixer plug-in that you want to use, and drag it to the Plug-ins folder.

4. Open the **PLUG-INS** folder, locate the mixer plug-in version that you no longer want to use, and drag it to the **PLUG-INS (UNUSED)** folder.

5. Launch Pro Tools.

It is important to note that the dithered mixer dithers signals at outputs only, and not internal bus destinations. This means that when submixing tracks using buses, Pro Tools mixers are able to pass full 48-bit words to each other. The dithered mixer also has no effect when audio is routed to/from the HD hardware's DSP chips for DSP plug-in processing. Finally, when using a dithered mixer, you must still insert a dithering plug-in on the Master Fader if down converting from 24 bits to a 16-bit master recording (the dithered mixer in this example only dithers down from 48 bits to 24 bits).

Pro Tools|HDX

HDX architecture allows a plug-in process to operate at 32-bit, 64-bit, or 80-bit floating-point utilizing dual precision. (See Figure 7.20.) Unlike Pro Tools|HD, there is no truncation when passing a signal from the mixer to the plug-in process and back again. The 32-bit floating-point value is shifted to allow the signal to pass into the plug-in without truncation. If a plug-in processes at 64-bit floating-point, the plug-in manufacturer will employ a conversion process on the file before it passes out of the DSP chip and back to the mixer DSP chip.

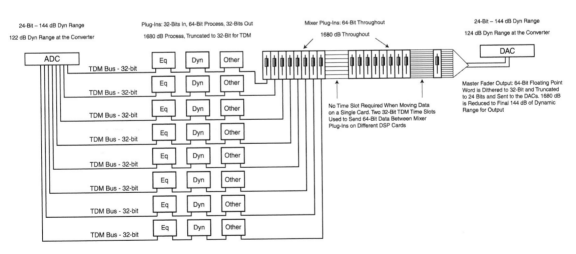

Figure 7.20
Pro Tools|HDX system diagram.

64-Bit Floating-Point Mixing

After analog audio entering an HD-series audio interface is converted to a digital signal, it then enters the mixer at a bit depth matching the session settings (16-, 24-, or 32-bit float). If the bit depth is anything less than 32-bit float, the signal is padded with zeros to fill out the full 32-bit data path of Pro Tools|HDX.

At this stage, the 32-bit streams are summed into a 64-bit mixer. However, HDX differs from Pro Tools|HD in that the data path through the various DSP chips remains at 32-bit (rather than truncating to 24-bit). This allows a file recorded as 32-bit float to pass through the entire mixing and processing path without any truncation or dithering, much like a 24-bit signal on a Pro Tools|HD system. Also different is how the DSPs pass audio between themselves. Unlike Pro Tools|HD, Pro Tools|HDX does not require any timeslots to move data from one DSP to another on the same HDX card—the FPGA chip connects DSPs together. This results in very low latency when stacking multiple plug-in processes on top of each other in the mixer. TDM is still used in multiple HDX card systems to pass signals between cards. Pro Tools|HDX offers 1536 timeslots (at 44.1/48kHz). As already stated, HDX uses floating-point mixing, so headroom is never a factor. With 64-bit summing, resolution is preserved even when applying extreme gain changes and panning with hundreds of tracks in a session. To summarize:

■ HDX uses 32-bit data paths to preserve fidelity and accuracy throughout the mixer.

■ Using floating-point processing allows you to build very large, complex mixers using less DSP.

■ Using an FPGA chip to manage voices allows a single card to have more available voices and frees DSP for other processes.

■ The combination of an FPGA chip managing voices, floating-point mixing, and more powerful DSP results in a four-fold increase in processing power versus previous generation Pro Tools|HD Accel cards.

■ 32-bit floating-point processing prevents internal clipping in plug-ins.

■ 64-bit summing allows for an extraordinarily high number of tracks to sum and not clip the inputs of the HD mixer. For example, 512 audio tracks at full code would still not clip the input of a master bus. However, the master bus fader would need to be lowered to –90dB to avoid clipping the outputs.

Tip: If you plan to do extreme Elastic Audio operations and want maximum fidelity, or plan to print your mixes internally, you should record audio at 32-bit float.

Note: Due to the nature of 64-bit floating-point mixing, a separate dithered mixer is not required.

Master Faders

Master Faders play an important role in gaining the full benefit of the 48-bit mixer or 64-bit mixer, allowing you to adjust the level of any bus or output. Now that you've had an insight into the HD mixer, you will be able to appreciate a different view of exactly what Master Faders are doing. A Master Fader shifts the audio signal up and down within the 48-bit workspace of the mixer with Pro Tools|HD hardware. With floating-point mixers, it is essentially changing the exponent of the 32-bit word to either boost or cut the output. This becomes particularly significant when the signal returns to 24 bits, such as when being bussed or routed to an audio interface output.

With fixed-point processing, you can think of a Master Fader as creating a 24-bit window into the 48-bit mixer. In the case where several signals are being mixed together, creating a signal that spills over into the headroom bits, a Master Fader is used to manually scale the signal back down into the main 24-bit range. With the floating-point mixer, the Master Fader is adjusting the 32-bit floating-point value in the 64-bit mixer by adjusting the exponent and keeping the mantissa in place. This allows the Master Fader to create a window below the clip that you can then pass on to the interface outputs. You can experience this firsthand, and hear a master fader recover an output from clipping, by working through the exercise at the end of this lesson.

Appropriate Use of Native Plug-ins

On DSP-accelerated systems, you primarily use DSP-based plug-ins to keep the host CPU(s) free for other tasks. However, host-based (or Native) plug-in processing, whether AAX or RTAS, can still play an important role and provides a "best of both worlds" solution.

Native plug-ins are generally used in the following situations:

■ When no DSP version of a plug-in is available. Some plug-ins, most notably the AIR instruments, are available only for the Native format. However, the new AAX plug-in format offers a way for formerly Native only plug-ins to run on DSP chips if the plug-in manufacturer recodes the plug-in for the AAX DSP format.

■ When the DSP chips are maxed out. If a large mix uses up all of the available DSP resources (primarily for mixing), you can add additional plug-ins by using Native versions. With Pro Tools|HDX, these plug-ins are seamless.

■ When moving a session to a system with fewer DSP cards. In this situation, the second Pro Tools system may have insufficient DSP resources to load all the plug-ins in the mixer configuration. However, plug-ins that have Native equivalents can be converted.

To convert DSP plug-ins to Native:

1. Open the plug-in window. Whether the plug-in is active or inactive due to insufficient DSP resources, the process is the same.

2. At the top right of the plug-in window, click the word **DSP**. A pop-up menu will appear. Choose **CONVERT TO NATIVE** as shown in Figure 7.21.

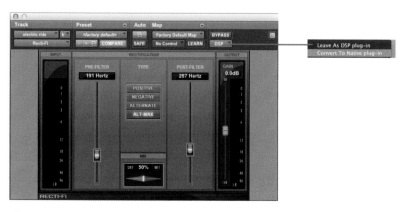

Figure 7.21
Converting a plug-in from DSP to Native.

Native Plug-ins on Aux Input and Master Fader Tracks

When using Native plug-ins on Aux Inputs or Master Faders in DSP-accelerated systems, be aware that voices are required to take the signal from the DSPs to the host processor and back again into the DSP-based mixer. The following sections describe issues around this.

Voice Usage and Total Latency for Native Plug-ins

With Pro Tools|HD or Pro Tools|HDX, inserting a Native plug-in on an audio track does not require additional voices, as long as it is inserted before a DSP plug-in. The Native DSP process is performed on the host before the audio is sent into the DSP-based mixer. However, a Native plug-in inserted on an Aux Input or Master Fader has no way to route the signal from the DSPs to the host CPU without using a voice. The voice allows the signal to leave the DSP mixer and travel along the PCI bus to the host CPU. Another voice is used to return to the mixer.

This means that the initial insert of a Native plug-in will take up two additional voices per channel (one voice for input and one voice for output) and incur latency equal to the buffer amount chosen in the Playback Engine dialog box. The latency from the buffer must be applied for each journey to and from the CPU, so effectively twice the buffer size, plus whatever the delay of the plug-in is. When a Native plug-in is inserted on a track, additional voices are used when the following conditions occur:

■ The Aux Input channel has both inputs and outputs assigned.

■ The track is a Master Fader track.

■ The plug-in is inserted on an Instrument track that does not contain an instrument plug-in. (The track is being used with an external hardware instrument with an input assigned.)

■ The plug-in is inserted after a DSP plug-in on any kind of track.

For example, the initial insert of a Native plug-in on a mono Aux Input track uses two voices (one channel with two voices), while the initial insert of that plug-in on a stereo Aux Input track uses four voices (two channels with two voices each), as shown in Figure 7.22. Again, the latency from the buffer must be applied for each journey to and from the CPU, so effectively twice the buffer size, plus whatever the delay of the plug-in is.

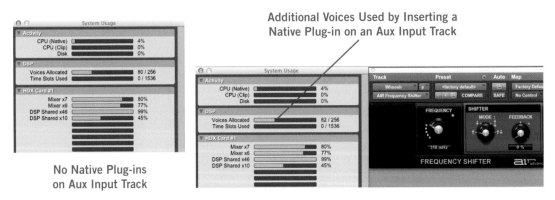

Figure 7.22
Adding a Native plug-in to an Aux Input increases voice count.

Tip: When a track has no input assigned or the input is made inactive, as in the case of an Instrument track or Aux Input that is used for a Native instrument plug-in, only one extra voice is used per channel for the plug-in.

Subsequent Native plug-ins on the same track do not take up additional voices because there is actually no passing back and forth from the host CPU. At this stage, as the audio is being processed by the CPU, it simply continues to process each Native plug-in (much like the Native mixer) and then the voice is used to return the audio to the DSP mixer. However, if passing back and forth between DSP and Native plug-ins, additional voices are used for each trip to and from the CPU. In Figure 7.23, a DSP-based plug-in is inserted between two Native plug-ins, requiring twice the number of voices.

Figure 7.23
Inserting a DSP plug-in between two Native plug-ins doubles the voice requirement.

Caution: As a general rule, avoid inserting DSP plug-ins between Native plug-ins on any kind of track—this causes unnecessary voice usage and may cause additional latency.

Furthermore, one additional voice is used for each occurrence of any of the following conditions when using voices for Native plug-ins on a track:

■ When you use an external side-chain for a Native plug-in on that track

■ When you select multiple outputs for that track (one voice used for each output)

■ When you select an AFL/PFL Path output in the Output tab of the I/O Setup dialog box (one voice used for each channel)

Mixing Native and DSP Plug-ins on an Audio Track

On a DSP-accelerated system, when Native and DSP plug-ins are combined on an audio track, the order in which they are inserted has different results:

- **Native plug-ins grouped before DSP plug-ins:** No additional voices will be used, and no processing latency will occur. This is because Native processing happens before the signal is brought into the DSP mixer. Native plug-ins will be bypassed when either Record or TrackInput monitoring is enabled for that track.

- **DSP plug-ins grouped before Native plug-ins:** Each initial insert of a Native plug-in after a DSP plug-in will cause processing latency and will use extra voices. Native plug-ins will stay active while either Record or TrackInput monitoring is enabled for that track. If Native plug-ins are stacked after each other, no additional voices will be used.

When combining Native and DSP plug-ins on an audio track, choose one of the following two strategies based on your recording needs:

- To ensure that Native plug-ins stay active when you record-enable a track or use TrackInput monitoring, group all DSP plug-ins before Native plug-ins.

- To conserve voices and minimize processing latency, group all Native plug-ins before DSP plug-ins.

- For best results, convert all Native plug-ins to DSP (if DSP equivalents exist) while recording to reduce latency and allow for record enables.

Jitter

An entirely different subject from digital mixing is jitter. Every digital audio system requires a clock that determines when samples occur during digitization (recording) and digital-to-analog conversion (playback). For example, when working at 44.1kHz, the system's frequency clock must make sure all the samples occur exactly one 44,100th of a second apart. Any variation in the time spacing between samples is called jitter.

Recall the sampling diagram in Figure 7.1. The x-axis represents time, and you can see samples equally spaced along this axis. Now, imagine if during recording or playback the sample clock were unstable, causing some samples to occur too late or too early. This inaccuracy would deform the shape of the waveform, distorting the signal at either the recording or playback stage.

The Pro Tools HD frequency clock is derived from the crystal oscillator in either the Loop Sync Master audio interface or the Avid SYNC Peripheral, if present.

Loop Sync connections distribute the clock from the master device. Although the connections are daisy-chained (which removes the need for many clock outputs on the first device), the clock is essentially being delivered directly to each interface from the master. In some studios, you may see an alternate (third-party) clock source being distributed to the interfaces.

Review/Discussion Questions

1. Define the term "quantization error."

2. What is dynamic range? What is the theoretical dynamic range for a 24-bit signal?

3. Which Pro Tools 10 mixers use fixed-point processing? Which Pro Tools 10 mixers use floating-point processing?

4. How is the Pro Tools|HDX mixer different from Native Pro Tools mixers?

5. What is the bit depth used for data pathways on Pro Tools|HD? What is the bit depth on HDX?

6. What are some advantages of the Pro Tools|HDX mixing architecture versus Pro Tools|HD?

7. What happens to voice count when you place Native plug-ins on Aux Inputs, Instrument tracks, or Master Faders on a DSP-accelerated hardware system?

8. How many additional voices would a stereo instance of a Native EQ3 1-band plug-in require if placed on an Aux Input track with the input set to no input? How many voices would be required if the same Native EQ3 plug-in was placed as the only plug-in on a stereo audio track?

Lesson 7 Keyboard Shortcuts

Shortcut	Description
Select the track nameplate and press Option+Shift+D (Mac)/ Select the track nameplate and press Alt+Shift+D (Windows)	Duplicate tracks
Command+Option+M (Mac)/Ctrl+Alt+M (Windows)	Narrow Mix window
Command+move control (Mac)/Ctrl+move control (Windows)	Fine control adjust
Control+Command+Down Arrow (Mac)/ Ctrl+Start+Down Arrow (Windows)	Zoom Edit window tracks to full-screen size

Mixer Experiments

This exercise allows you to experiment with 32-bit float files, the 64-bit Pro Tools mixer, and the different dithering options for Pro Tools.

Media Used:

310M Exercise 7.PTXT (Pro Tools session file)

Duration:

30–45 minutes

GOALS

- Understand gain staging in the HD mixer
- Identify how pan depth settings affect mix levels
- Explore the advantages of 32-bit float files over fixed-bit depth files
- Explore DSP usage in the HD mixer
- Understand dither
- Identify how Native and DSP plug-ins affect voice usage

Getting Started

This exercise contains mixing scenarios to demonstrate headroom availability in the Pro Tools mixer, DSP use with mixers, dithering options, and how the use of Native plug-ins affects voice count. We'll start by exploring how pan laws and gain staging affect clipping in Pro Tools and what steps you can take to prevent the clips. We'll then move on to explore how different mixer configurations affect DSP usage. We'll also review dithering options for Pro Tools and how dither affects sound. We'll end the exercise by examining how Native plug-ins affect voice count when used on Aux Input tracks, Instrument tracks, or Master Faders, as well as ramifications when mixing Native and DSP plug-ins on the same track.

Note: Before starting this exercise, if you are using previous-generation Pro Tools|HD DSP-accelerated hardware, you must switch the playback engine from HD TDM to an alternate Native playback engine option that you are able to monitor sound through.

To open the 310M Exercise 7 session:

1. Open the **310M Exercise 07.PTXT** session file, located on the book's DVD (or other location specified by the course instructor).

2. In the **Save New Session As** dialog box, name the session as desired, saving into an appropriate location on a valid storage drive.

The session includes several tracks and a signal generator to demonstrate clipping and mixing headroom in Pro Tools.

Gain Staging and Mixing

To demonstrate the tremendous amount of headroom in the Pro Tools mixer, we will be using the Signal Generator plug-in on a single Aux Input track that in turn will feed other Aux Input tracks to simulate a full mix. In Figure Ex7.1, you'll notice the Signal Generator plug-in is located on a source Aux Input track (called Sine), which in turn is feeding another mono Aux Input track (Aux 1) through an internal mix bus (Bus 1). The second Aux Input track is feeding a stereo Aux Input Submaster via a stereo internal mix bus (Sub Mix).

Pan Depths

We'll start by reviewing the effect of different Pan Depth settings in the Session Setup window. Understanding the Pan Depth setting is critical when re-creating an exact mix in a different studio or when opening older Pro Tools sessions created on different Pro Tools hardware.

Figure Ex7.1
Signal Generator used as signal source for mixing example.

Caution: Before opening the session, mute your main monitors. During this exercise, use caution when unmuting your monitoring system to hear examples or detect minute clip points. This exercise uses full code audio (extremely loud) for demonstration purposes.

To see the effect of different pan laws:

1. Make sure that **PRE-FADER METERING** is disabled in the **OPTIONS** menu.

2. Check that your monitoring system is muted before beginning. Unmute your Signal Generator plug-in. Notice that the first two Aux Input Submasters are identical in signal level, but the Aux Submaster is lower by –3.0dB as shown in Figure Ex7.2. This is due to the default Pan Depth setting. Move the pan on the Aux 1 track fully left and right and see how the signal is affected. Return the pan pot to 0 or center when done. You can quickly reset the parameter by **OPTION-CLICKING** (Mac) or **ALT-CLICKING** (Windows) on the **PAN** knob.

Figure Ex7.2
Pan Depth effect on sources panned center.

3. To change the pan depth, open the Session Setup window by choosing **SETUP > SESSION** or by pressing **COMMAND+ 2** (Mac) or **CTRL+2** (Windows) on the numeric keypad. Change the **PAN DEPTH** setting to **–2.5**. Notice that the level on the Submaster track rises correspondingly (when the Aux Input track feeding it is panned center). See Figure Ex7.3.

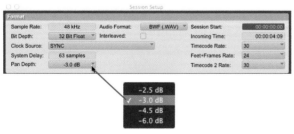

Figure Ex7.3
Changing the Pan Depth setting in Session Setup.

> ## Peak Level Indication
>
> During this exercise, it will be useful to switch the track indicator at the bottom of the track into peak level mode (pk level). This is done by Command-clicking (Mac) or Ctrl-clicking (Windows) until the indicator says "pk x.xx." If you wish to change all tracks to peak level indication, use Option+Command-click (Mac) or Ctrl+Alt-click (Windows).
>
> In this mode, the numeric indicator is on infinite hold. If you wish to reset an individual indicator, simply click it with the mouse. To reset all tracks in pk level mode, use Option-click (Mac) or Alt-click (Windows).

4. Return the **PAN DEPTH** to **–3.0** and close the Session Setup window and the Signal Generator plug-in window.

Gain Staging

When mixing many signals together, it's important to monitor your gain staging. However, the Pro Tools mixer affords tremendous amounts of headroom. With large amounts of headroom, it becomes difficult to clip the input of a mixer, but it remains easy to clip the output. You can resolve the audio clipping in one of three ways:

■ Reduce the gain on the source tracks.

■ Reduce the output gain of the Submaster track.

■ Place a Master Fader inline and assign it to the bus feeding the Submaster track.

Caution: When using the Pro Tools 64-bit mixer, although unlikely, it is theoretically possible to clip the output of a bus and not be able to correct the problem by turning down an Auxiliary Submaster controlling the bus. It is therefore recommended to use a Master Fader inline to scale down the input to the bus in order to correct or recover the clipped signal.

The first solution is simple and a good rule of thumb, but in complex mixes it may become time consuming to change the gain on the source track and rebalance the mix. To complicate matters, the signal reaching the Submaster may be hitting a plug-in source first before going to the output. Changing the source track may affect the sound. In these cases, it may be more appropriate to reduce the input signal feeding the Submaster by placing a Master Fader track inline to reduce the volume.

To see how much headroom the mixer has:

1. Start by selecting the **Aux 1** track and duplicating it once by doing one of the following:

    *   Selecting the track nameplate and choosing **Track > Duplicate**

    *   Right-clicking the track name and choosing **Duplicate** (see Figure Ex7.4)

    *   Selecting the track nameplate and pressing **Option+Shift+D** (Mac) or **Alt+Shift+D** (Windows)

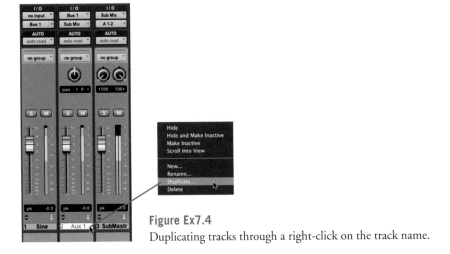

Figure Ex7.4
Duplicating tracks through a right-click on the track name.

2. Click **OK** in the Duplicate Tracks dialog box to make a single duplicate track. Notice that the Submaster track is now clipping. (See Figure Ex7.5.)

Figure Ex7.5
Adding another full code track to the mix bus has clipped the Submaster.

3. To remove the clip, lower the Submaster track fader by **–3.1DB**. This will eliminate the clip, and the audio will sound fine again.

4. With the duplicated Aux Input track still selected (Aux1.DP1), choose the **DUPLICATE** command again and specify **62** duplicates this time. At this point, it may be wise to switch to narrow track view so you can see more tracks at once by pressing **COMMAND+OPTION+M** (Mac) or **CTRL+ALT+M** (Windows).

5. Zoom your window so you can see as many tracks as possible and scroll to the right until you see the Submaster Aux Input track again. Notice how the tracks are clipping the Submaster. Lower the Submaster fader until the clip is removed (about –33.1), as shown in Figure Ex7.6. Carefully lower the volume on your monitoring system and unmute it to hear when the Submaster fader goes from clip to no clip (usually 0.1dB will make the difference). You may need to use Fine control when moving the fader by holding down **COMMAND** (Mac) or **CTRL** (Windows) when moving the fader.

Figure Ex7.6

Lowering the Submaster Aux Input track to remove clipped audio.

At this point you should have 64 tracks (excluding the Sine tone source track) at full code feeding the Submaster track, and you should have had to reduce the fader by only –33.1dB.

6. With the 62 duplicate tracks you created still selected, choose the **DUPLICATE** command again and choose 8 duplicates. Pro Tools will attempt to create 496 additional Aux Input tracks. However, Pro Tools only allows 512 Aux Input tracks total in a session. A dialog box will appear, indicating that you have reached the maximum allowed by Pro Tools, and 510 Aux Input tracks will now be in the session feeding the Submaster track. (See Figure Ex7.7.)

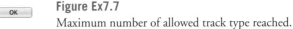

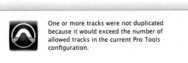

One or more tracks were not duplicated
because it would exceed the number of
allowed tracks in the current Pro Tools
configuration.

OK

Figure Ex7.7
Maximum number of allowed track type reached.

7. Scroll to the far right of the Mix window until you see your Submaster
   Aux Input track. Notice that it is clipping again. Again lower the fader
   until the clip disappears on the Aux Submaster's track meter. This should
   be about −51.2. You now have 510 tracks at full code feeding a single
   stereo bus, and you are still not clipping the input of the bus.

Using a Master Fader to Trim the Bus

Another method for reducing the signal enough to eliminate clipping the Sub Mix
bus is to insert a Master Fader to control, or trim, the bus before reaching the
Submaster Aux Input track, allowing you to leave the Submaster track at unity gain.

To control a bus with a Master Fader:

1. Start by selecting only the last Aux Input track before the Submaster track.
   Create a new stereo Master Fader track.

2. The Master Fader track will be inserted before the Submaster track in the
   Mix window and will default to controlling the Main A 1–2 Outputs. In
   Figure Ex7.8, the Mix window has been restored to normal track width for
   easy viewing.

Figure Ex7.8
Using a Master Fader to trim a bus level before reaching the Submaster Aux Input.

3. Click on the OUTPUT PATH SELECTOR for the Master Fader track and choose BUS > SUB MIX for the output. Notice that it is still clipped. Now lower the Master Fader until the clip is removed on the meter (about –51.2). Return the Submaster track to unity (0.0dB) and notice that the signal is no longer clipped as well.

32-Bit Float Files

Now that we have a simulated session, there may be a time when you bounce a file or receive a file that is recorded so close to clip it is actually clipped. If using 32-bit float files, you can eliminate the clip by using the AudioSuite Gain plug-in to reduce the level to below clip. This is possible only with 32-bit floating-point files; 24-bit fixed-point files do not offer this ability.

Caution: **The Bit Depth setting in the Session Setup window should already be set to 32 Bit Float. If it is not set to 32 Bit Float, change the setting now before continuing with this exercise.**

We'll start by creating a new stereo track in our session and routing to it from our Submaster track. We'll increase the gain on our Master Fader to simulate a +12dB clip and then remove it with the AudioSuite Gain plug-in.

To remove a clip in a 32-bit float file:

1. Select the Submaster track and create a new stereo audio track. Route the output of the Submaster track to Bus 5–6. Route the input of the new stereo track to Bus 5–6. Arm the track for recording. Your setup should look like Figure Ex7.9.

Figure Ex7.9
Routing a track for recording.

2. Raise the Master Fader track to **-39.2DB**. This will now be clipping your record-enabled audio track.

3. Record a five-second pass.

4. In the Session Setup window, switch the **BIT DEPTH** to **24 BIT** and then record another five-second record pass on the same track starting after the first (32-bit float) clip.

5. Switch to the Edit window and scroll to the bottom. Your clipped recordings should be there. Place the cursor on the track and quickly zoom to full screen size by pressing **CONTROL+COMMAND+DOWN ARROW** (Mac) or **CTRL+START+DOWN ARROW** (Windows). (See Figure Ex7.10.)

32-Bit Float Clip   24-Bit Clip

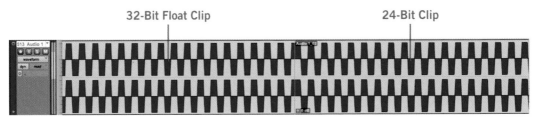

Figure Ex7.10
Recorded 32-bit float and 24-bit clipped files.

6. Zoom in to see the waveforms on the track. Notice how both clips are clipped, as shown in Figure Ex7.11.

Figure Ex7.11
Choose the AudioSuite Gain plug-in.

7. To attempt to remove the clipped signal on both audio clips, select both audio clips and choose **AUDIOSUITE > OTHER > GAIN**.

8. In the Gain plug-in window, use the slider or the **GAIN AMOUNT** field to set the gain to **-12.0DB**. Click **RENDER** in the AudioSuite Gain plug-in. Notice that the sine wave is returned to an unclipped state on only the first (32-bit

float) clip in Figure Ex7.12, but the second (24-bit) clip has not had its clip removed in Figure Ex7.13. The ability to remove audio clips from 32-bit float files is a unique feature that is not shared by fixed-bit audio files.

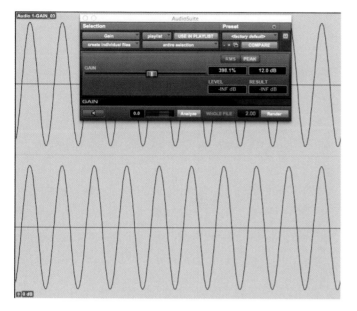

Figure Ex7.12
32-bit float clipping removed by using the AudioSuite Gain plug-in.

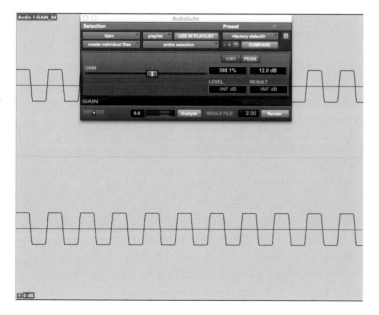

Figure Ex7.13
24-bit clipping can not be removed by using the AudioSuite Gain plug-in.

Caution: Before continuing with the next section of this exercise, if you are using previous-generation Pro Tools|HD DSP-accelerated hardware, you must switch the playback engine of the session to HD TDM (96 voices, 3 DSPs).

Understanding Mixer Creation and Use

As you build larger and larger mixes in Pro Tools, it becomes necessary to understand when new mixers are created and how to monitor resources dedicated for mixing. By understanding the process, you can craft mixers that efficiently use the available DSP in Pro Tools HD systems or understand error messages that state you have run out of DSP processing power.

As you learned previously in the lesson, stereo mixers are created when tracks are summed together into $N \times 2$ mixers. When doing a simple mix, where all tracks are routed to a single pair of outputs, monitoring use is usually not required. But when adding internal mix buses for effects, building discrete output mixes, or mixing in surround, it becomes important to create your mix wisely to utilize DSP chips efficiently.

To monitor how much DSP power is taken by a mixer:

1. If **DELAY COMPENSATION** is enabled, disable it now in the **OPTIONS** menu.

2. Delete all of the tracks from the previous portion of the exercise. Next, create 48 mono audio tracks.

3. The tracks will automatically be routed to outputs 1–2. To see how much DSP is used for 48 channels to a stereo output bus (48×2), open the System Usage window under **WINDOW > SYSTEM USAGE**. Figure Ex7.14 shows the System Usage window using Pro Tools|HDX hardware.

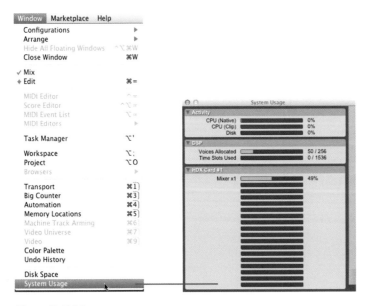

Figure Ex7.14

Opening the System Usage window using Pro Tools|HDX hardware.

4. Create a stereo Aux Input track and route all 48 tracks into the stereo Aux Input using the Sub Mix internal bus you created earlier in the exercise. Notice that the mixer usage may increase slightly because you have created a 48 × 2 × 2 mixer. This is a common configuration when "mixing in the box."

5. If we now split the 48 tracks into four mix output groups and route each of the groups individually to an external summing system, we will use more DSP resources. To see the difference, start by routing tracks 1–12 to Outputs 1–2. Next, route tracks 13–24 to Outputs 3–4, tracks 25–36 to Outputs 5–6, and tracks 37–48 to Outputs 7–8. We have effectively built a 48 × 4 × 4 mixer. On Pro Tools|HDX systems, you can see what mixes a DSP is servicing by hovering the mouse over the DSP gauge as shown in Figure Ex7.15.

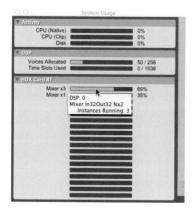

Figure Ex7.15
Hovering the mouse over the DSP usage gauge shows how many Nx mixers are used.

The first three sets of mixers are using the first DSP chip on the card, and the last 12 channels are using the second DSP chip of the card.

6. Create a send across each track to Outputs 9–10. Notice that the DSP Manager allocates and utilizes DSP to be as efficient as possible.

If you then switch the send to an internal mix bus, the send will utilize a different amount of DSP.

Tip: **If using Pro Tools|HD hardware, it may be necessary to choose Purge Cache from within the System Usage window in order for the DSP usage meters to update after a change.**

Dither

As you learned earlier, dither is used when doing bit-depth reductions. How the dither interacts with the audio is an extremely subjective matter that requires auditory experimentation. In this section of the exercise, we examine what dither looks like when amplified to audible levels and the sonic characteristics of each type of dither.

To hear dither:

1. Delete all tracks previously created in this exercise. Create a single mono Aux Input track. Be sure to show all 10 insert positions (A–J).

2. Place the POW-r Dither plug-in on insert A, a Native Maxim plug-in on insert B, and a DigiRack Dither plug-in on insert C. Bypass the Maxim and Avid Dither plug-ins as shown in Figure Ex7.16.

Figure Ex7.16
Inserting POW-r Dither, Maxim, and Dither plug-ins on a track.

3. On insert D, insert a Native **Trim** plug-in. Set the Trim plug-in for **+12dB** mode at the top of the plug-in display and raise the gain **+12dB**. (See Figure Ex7.17.)

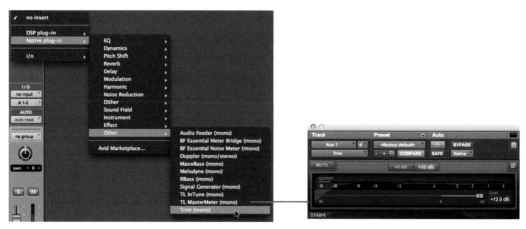

Figure Ex7.17
Adding a Trim plug-in on a track to boost the signal.

4. Copy the plug-in to the next four insert positions (e–h) by **OPTION-DRAGGING** (Mac) or **ALT-DRAGGING** (Windows) on the plug-in nameplate. This will amplify the dither noise, making it sound like pink noise. (See Figure Ex7.18.)

5. Open the POW-r Dither plug-in window and click on the **TYPE** menu. Switch between the dithering algorithms to hear the differences. Which algorithm you choose depends upon the source material being bounced. For full program mixes, Type 2 or Type 3 is recommended. (See Figure Ex7.19.)

Figure Ex7.18
Stacking Trim plug-ins on top of each other to create +60dB of gain.

Figure Ex7.19
Changing POW-r Dither algorithms.

6. Next, bypass the POW-r Dither plug-in and click on the **MAXIM** plug-in to open the window. Un-bypass the Maxim plug-in and enable its built-in **DITHER** option. The Maxim plug-in supports peak limiting and dithering in the same plug-in. (See Figure Ex7.20.)

Figure Ex7.20
Enabling dithering options in Maxim.

Tip: When the Dither On button is unlit, all dithering and noise-shaping options are deactivated. This allows you to use Maxim for peak limiting without dithering or noise shaping. It also allows you to use other dithering algorithms while peak limiting (such as POW-r Dither).

7. Next, bypass the Maxim plug-in and un-bypass the Dither plug-in. Note the difference in sonic characteristics.

This is just a simple experiment to demonstrate how different dithering options have different noise characteristics. Learning how dither interacts with program material takes time and effort beyond the scope of this course. However, if you have time, take a 24- or 32-bit mix you are very familiar with and run through all the dither algorithms as you bounce the files to a 16-bit stereo pair. Burn the results to a CD-R and listen to them in a critical listening environment to see how the different dither algorithms impart a sonic signature on your mix.

Voice Usage with Native Plug-ins and Mixed DSP/Native Plug-in Combinations

Another topic covered in the lesson was the need for voices when adding Native plug-ins to Aux Input, Instrument, and Master Fader tracks on DSP-based Pro Tools|HD and HDX systems. In this section of the exercise you will place Native plug-ins on audio tracks and Aux Input tracks while monitoring voice usage through the System Usage window. You will also combine Native and DSP-based plug-ins on the same track to see how it affects voice usage.

Native Plug-ins on Aux Input Tracks and Voice Count

To see how voices are taken when using Native plug-ins on a track:

1. Delete all tracks previously created in this exercise. Create a mono audio track, a stereo audio track, a mono Aux Input track, and a stereo Aux Input track.

2. Set the mono Aux 1 track to mono input bus 1, and the stereo Aux 2 track to stereo inputs bus 7–8, as shown in Figure Ex7.21.

Figure Ex7.21
Creating mono/stereo Audio and Aux Input tracks.

3. Open the System Usage window by choosing **WINDOW > SYSTEM USAGE**. (See Figure Ex7.22.)

Figure Ex7.22
System Usage window showing the number of active voices.

Ghost Voices

Even though you only have three voices used on the audio tracks (one for the mono track and two for stereo) you may see five or more voices allocated. An extra stereo pair is used for auditioning sounds in the DigiBase browsers as well as import and fade dialog boxes when an audition path has been defined in the I/O Setup dialog box. Also, when using AFL/PFL, two additional voices will be used for the solo bus.

4. Remember that Native plug-ins on audio tracks require no additional voices. To test this, place a Native version of the EQ3 7-Band plug-in on the mono audio track. (See Figure Ex7.23.)

No Voice Increase   Native Version of Plug-in

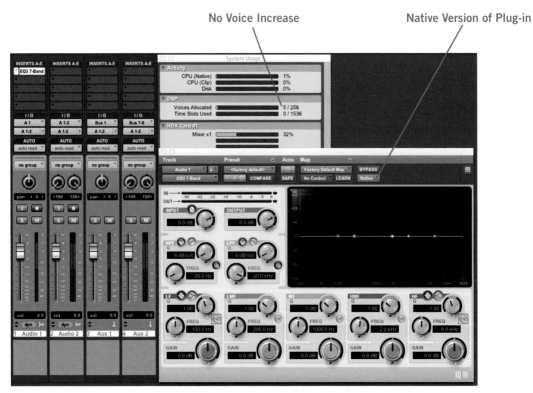

Figure Ex7.23
Only Native plug-ins on audio tracks require no extra voices.

5. Next, move the EQ3 7-Band plug-in to the mono Aux Input track. Notice that the voice usage increases by two voices. (See Figure Ex7.24.)

Plug-in on Aux Track   Voice Count Has Increased   Native Version of Plug-in

Figure Ex7.24
Placing a Native plug-in on a mono Aux Input requires an extra voice.

6. Next, place a Native multichannel version of the Channel Strip plug-in on the stereo Aux Input track. Notice that the voice usage increases by two voices. Adding Native plug-ins to an Aux Input track will always increase the voice count by the channel width of the track (i.e., mono = one voice, stereo = two voices, 5.1 = six voices). (See Figure Ex7.25.)

Stereo EQ3 Native Plug-in on Aux Track   Voice Count Increases by 2

Figure Ex7.25
Adding a multichannel plug-in increases voice count by the channel width.

Mixing Native and DSP Plug-ins on Audio Tracks

As stated previously, placing Native plug-ins on audio tracks typically does not require voices. When the audio is played back in Pro Tools, the audio is processed at the CPU before being passed to the Pro Tools mixer. In essence, the audio arrives pre-processed into the Pro Tools mixer. However, when you insert a Native plug-in after a DSP plug-in on any type of track, the signal must route back to the host, be processed, and return to the DSP mixer channel. This requires double the number of voices.

To see how voices are taken when using Native plug-ins on audio tracks:

1. Remove all plug-ins on the tracks before continuing. Now place a DSP-based version of **EQ3 1-BAND** at insert A on the mono audio track. Next, place a Native Air Frequency Shifter plug-in (under Harmonic). Notice that the voice usage increases by two voices. (See Figure Ex7.26.)

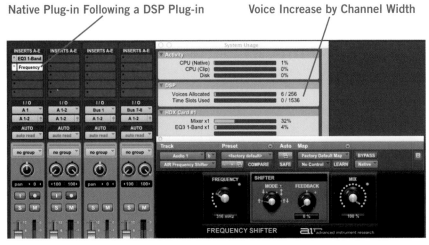

Figure Ex7.26
Placing a Native plug-in after a DSP plug-in increases voice count.

2. Place a DSP-based EQ3 1-band at insert position C. Notice that the voice usage has not increased.

3. Next, add a Native Air Enhancer plug-in (under Harmonic). Notice that the voice count only increases by one. It has not increased by two because it already has a voice to return to the DSP mixer. (See Figure Ex7.27.)

4. Feel free to experiment with the stereo audio track to see how voices are affected there. Essentially, each time a stereo audio signal travels to the host CPU and returns to the DSP mixer, Pro Tools requires two pairs of voices (four voices total).

DSP Plug-in   Native Plug-in Forces More Voices   Increased Voice Count

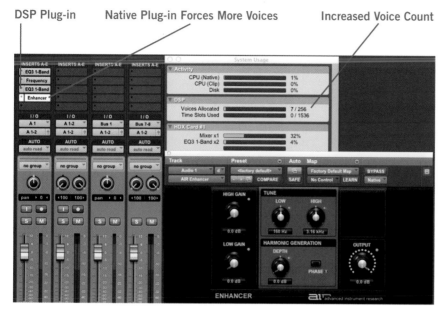

Figure Ex7.27
Inserting DSP plug-ins between Native plug-ins leads to more voice usage.

To see how voices are taken when using Native plug-ins on Aux Input tracks:

1. Remove all plug-ins from the audio tracks. Add a Native Channel Strip plug-in to the mono Aux Input track. Notice that the voice count increases by two.

2. Next add a DSP-based EQ III 1-band on insert B, followed by a Native Air Enhancer on insert C; notice that the voice count has increased.

3. Repeat the process on the stereo Aux Input track and note how many voices are required for this very simple process.

While it may not be readily apparent why voice management is necessary in 44.1/48kHz sessions, it becomes much more apparent when mixing for surround and higher sample rates. With surround mixing, multichannel Aux Input tracks require as many voices as channels for the track. For example, inserting a Native version of a 5.1 compressor on a 5.1 Aux Input Submaster will require 12 voices. If a DSP plug-in is then placed after the 5.1 compressor and followed by a Native plug-in, the Aux Input will require 24 voices to process the audio on the single track.

Advanced Mixing Techniques

This lesson discusses advanced mixing and routing techniques for music production, including Pro Tools advanced automation functionality.

Media Used: PT310M Ch.8.PTXT Pro Tools session

Duration: 75 minutes

GOALS

- Configure advanced mixing preferences in Pro Tools
- Understand advanced delay compensation techniques
- Use advanced mixing and submixing techniques
- Use advanced automation techniques

Introduction

A number of advanced signal routing and automation features in Pro Tools only come to light when faced with real-world challenges. Many less well-known functions in Pro Tools become essential as you become fluent with the process of automating your mix while keeping as many creative options open as possible.

Common Mixing Preferences

Before mixing, Pro Tools provides a number of preference settings that enable you to customize the setup for your mixing environment. Some of the common preference settings that you may want to change include the Solo mode setting, the default send level setting, and various automation preference settings.

Solo Modes

Pro Tools provides various Solo modes that affect how the Solo button works. In the Pro Tools 100- and 200-level books, you used Solo in Place (SIP) exclusively. This is considered a "destructive" Solo mode. In other words, when a track is soloed, the mix is changed, and listeners can only monitor the track or tracks that are soloed. With Pro Tools HD hardware systems, you have two additional "nondestructive" Solo modes, which pass the soloed track out a different output path configured in the Output tab of the I/O Setup window. After Fader Listen (AFL) and Pre Fader Listen (PFL) are useful when you want to solo tracks in the control room without affecting the cue mix going to the live room or, in final mix sessions, when you want to leave the "2-track mix" in place for the producer or artists over the main monitors but solo different sources through headphones to spot check individual tracks or busses.

The currently active Solo mode is specified using the submenu under Options > Solo Mode, as shown in Figure 8.1.

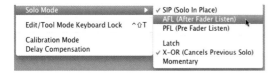

Figure 8.1
Solo mode choices in the Options menu.

The additional Solo modes available with Pro Tools HD hardware systems are as follows:

- **After Fader Listen (AFL)**—In this mode, the Solo button routes the track's post-fader/post-pan signal to a separate AFL/PFL output path (as defined in I/O Setup). This signal will also include any insert processing on the track.

With AFL, the level you hear is dependent on the fader level for that track. Additionally, there is a separate master AFL level that controls the final output level of any tracks soloed while in AFL mode. This level setting is independent of the master PFL level setting.

- **Pre Fader Listen (PFL)**—In this mode, the Solo button routes the track's pre-fader/pre-pan signal to the AFL/PFL output path. However, the signal still includes any insert processing on the track.

  With PFL, the fader level and pan are ignored, and the level you hear is dependent on the signal's recorded level. Additionally, there is a separate master level setting for PFL that affects the output of any tracks you solo in PFL mode. This level setting is independent of the AFL level setting.

These Solo modes are considered "non-destructive" modes. When soloing a track, the mix is left as is, and the soloed signal is sent on a separate solo bus to a different output of the audio interface. The primary application for non-destructive solo is for tracking sessions. However, AFL/PFL solos are also useful during mixing. For example, suppose you have your drums submixed to a stereo Aux Input, and you are using a small amount of reverb on the snare. To hear the submixed drums, you can simply solo the Aux Input through the AFL/PFL bus. Or, if you want to hear just the snare reverb, you can solo the reverb return track. Without AFL/PFL, you would need to solo-safe your Aux Inputs and solo the source tracks. For the reverb, you would have to put the send into pre-fader send first and then solo the reverb return.

Tip: When using an ICON-based mixing system, the XMON monitoring system automatically switches between main Pro Tools outputs and the AFL/PFL bus outputs, so you can hear your solo signal across your main monitors. If you are not using an ICON-based system, you will need to configure which outputs to mute when solo is engaged (known as AFL/PFL mutes) and configure your monitoring system to monitor both busses.

Configuring AFL/PFL Operation

To use either AFL or PFL solo, you must configure an output bus to monitor the output. You configure the bus in the Output tab of I/O Setup.

To configure an AFL/PFL bus:

1. Open **SETUP > I/O** and click on the **OUTPUT** tab.

2. Create a new stereo output path or use an existing stereo path. Name it **AFL/PFL OUT** or something similar so that the path's function is clearly identified.

3. Route the path to a physical output on the audio interface that you want to use for AFL/PFL operation, as shown in Figure 8.2.

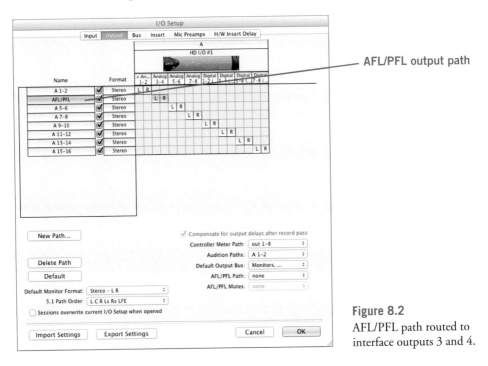

Figure 8.2
AFL/PFL path routed to interface outputs 3 and 4.

4. Physically connect the chosen outputs to your monitoring system. If using an XMON monitoring system, these are inputs 4 and 5 on the **TB/LB/UTIL** connector on the rear of the XMON.

5. Next, click on the **AFL/PFL PATH** drop-down at the bottom of the I/O Setup dialog box, as shown in Figure 8.3. Choose the new output path you just created. This will activate the AFL/PFL bus.

Figure 8.3
AFL/PFL path drop-down menu.

AFL/PFL Mutes

If you are using an XMON monitoring system with an ICON system, you do not need to configure the AFL/PFL mutes. However, if you are not using an ICON, you may need to configure the AFL/PFL mutes.

When you solo a track in AFL/PFL mode, the main mix continues to pass audio out the main outputs while the soloed track uses the AFL/PFL path. If you do not mute the main outputs, you will continue to hear the main mix, thus obscuring the AFL/PFL solos. You can manually mute the main output through your monitoring system or console, or you can have Pro Tools automatically mute the main output.

To mute the main outputs during AFL/PFL operation:

- Click the **AFL/PFL MUTES** drop-down in the I/O Setup dialog box and choose the main output path that you are monitoring your mix through.

How to Change AFL/PFL Solo Bus Level

With AFL, the level you hear is dependent on the fader level for a track. However, with PFL you will be listening to the recorded level as well as any insert processing, which can sometimes be loud. Fortunately, there is a way to set a master solo bus level for AFL and PFL. Once you set a master level in AFL mode, you can set a different master level in PFL mode and vice versa (levels can be set independently for the two modes).

To change the AFL or PFL solo level in the software:

- In **AFL** mode, **COMMAND-CLICK** (Mac) or **CTRL-CLICK** (Windows) and hold on any **SOLO** button on any track. A small fader will appear. Adjust the level as needed. To set the solo level of PFL, switch into PFL mode and repeat the process. See Figure 8.4.

Figure 8.4
Setting the AFL or PFL solo level.

Solo Button Behaviors

In addition to the different destructive/non-destructive Solo modes, you have choices for solo button behaviors, including the following:

- **Latch**—When selected, pressing subsequent solo buttons adds them to the solo mix. This is the default behavior for Pro Tools.

- **X-Or (Cancels Previous Solo)**—This mode causes solo buttons to follow an exclusive-or behavior. When selected, pressing subsequent solo buttons cancels previous solos so that only a single track is soloed at a time. This is useful for line checks or listening to what's on each track quickly when working with an unfamiliar recording or new mix. In this mode, you must hold the **SHIFT** key to add subsequent tracks to the solo mix.

■ **Momentary**—When selected, a track is soloed only while its solo button is held down. When the button is released, the track will immediately un-solo. This is also useful for line checks or listening to particular tracks quickly.

To select a Solo mode:

1. Choose OPTIONS > SOLO MODE and select SIP, AFL, or PFL.

2. If desired, select OPTIONS > SOLO MODE a second time and select LATCH, X-OR, or MOMENTARY to change the solo button behavior.

Understanding Advanced Delay Compensation

As you learned in the Pro Tools 201 book, the Pro Tools software provides ADC (Automatic Delay Compensation) for managing DSP and host-based delays from plug-in inserts, and mixer routing (bussing and sends). With Delay Compensation enabled, Pro Tools maintains phase coherent time alignment between tracks that have plug-ins with differing delays, tracks with different mixing paths, tracks that are split off and recombined within the mixer, and tracks with hardware inserts. This section reviews how delay compensation works with hardware inserts and how to measure additional delays when using outboard processing gear, specifically digital processing gear.

Delay Compensation and Hardware Inserts

The Pro Tools 210M course book explains that using hardware inserts in Pro Tools can introduce signal delay as the signal is sent out of the interface, to an external piece of gear, and back into Pro Tools again. However, when using Avid audio interfaces, the delay is automatically compensated for when delay compensation is engaged in two ways:

■ Latency incurred by passing audio out and back in through an Avid audio interface (whether analog or digital) is automatically compensated for because the amount of delay at the converters (or digital out/ins) is known and automatically compensated for by Pro Tools.

■ Additional compensation time can be entered in the I/O Setup dialog box to compensate for additional delay caused by outboard processing delay (such as digital effect processors). See Figure 8.5.

When using analog gear and Avid audio interfaces, Automatic Delay Compensation in Pro Tools will usually suffice. However, there will be times when you are using hardware inserts for external processing and Automatic Delay Compensation is not enough. This is especially true when using digital effects units as well as third-party

Figure 8.5
I/O Setup: Hardware Insert
Delay Compensation tab.

audio interfaces with Pro Tools|HD that may have different delays with their A/D or D/A converters. In these situations it becomes necessary to measure the delay yourself and manually adjust the compensation time.

Measuring Hardware Insert Latency

Pro Tools|HD has all the tools within it to measure additional hardware delays. This is accomplished by playing a short transient sound out of Pro Tools (typically a sine or square wave), passing it through the insert chain, and recording it back into Pro Tools. You then compare the source and recorded signals and measure the latency between them. See Figure 8.6.

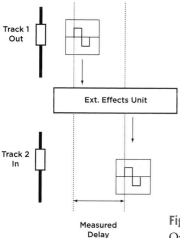

Figure 8.6
Overview of measuring insert latency in Pro Tools.

To measure hardware insert latency:

1. Set the Delay Compensation Engine to **SHORT, LONG,** or **MAXIMUM** in the Playback Engine dialog box.

2. Verify that **AUTOMATIC DELAY COMPENSATION** is enabled by choosing **OPTIONS > DELAY COMPENSATION.**

3. Make sure **COMPENSATE FOR OUTPUT DELAYS** is checked in **SETUP > I/O > OUTPUT** tab, as shown in Figure 8.7, and enable **COMPENSATE FOR INPUT DELAYS** in the Input tab.

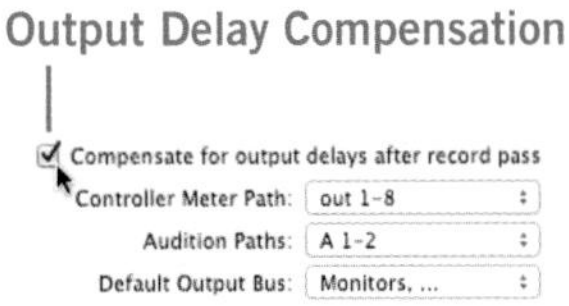

Output Delay Compensation

☑ Compensate for output delays after record pass
Controller Meter Path: out 1–8   ⬍
Audition Paths: A 1–2   ⬍
Default Output Bus: Monitors, ... ⬍

Figure 8.7
Enabling Compensate for Output Delays.

4. Change your session's Main Time Scale to **SAMPLES.**

5. Create two audio tracks. Name them **SOURCE** and **REC.**

6. Route the tracks as follows:

   • Route an insert on **TRACK 1 (SOURCE)** through an audio interface output connected to the device's inputs.

   • Connect the device's output to an audio interface input and route it to the input of **TRACK 2 (REC).**

7. Set the output of both tracks to a null bus (Bus 1 was renamed Null for this example). See Figure 8.8 for routing example.

Figure 8.8
Routing source track output and record track input.

8. Zoom in and make a 1 ms selection on Track 1. Use the SIGNAL GENERATOR AudioSuite plug-in to process a 1kHz square wave on the track.

9. Place the cursor in front of your square wave clip. Record-enable TRACK 2 and then record a brief pass of the audio returning to the track through the external effect unit.

Tip: Calculating hardware insert delay in this manner is only useful when using gain-based processing (such as EQ or compression). If using a multi-effects processor, be sure to disable any pre-delay or other time-based processing.

10. Zoom in very close so you can see the start of the two sections of tone. In order to determine the exact delay amount, use the SELECTOR tool to select the gap between the two sections. See Figure 8.9.

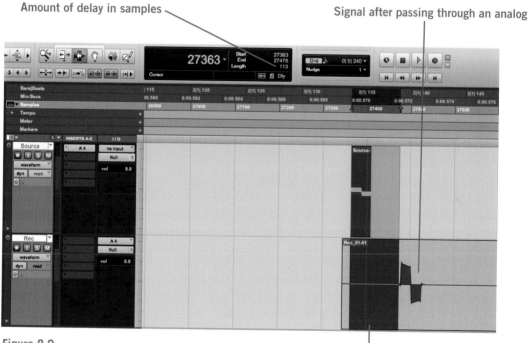

Figure 8.9
Measured delay between source and record tracks.

11. Check the timebase for your session is set to SAMPLES and note the selection length in the EDIT SELECTION LENGTH field in the toolbar. This is the additional delay time required for the signal to return into the mixer.

12. To convert the measured number of samples of delay into ms of delay for use in the I/O Setup window, use this formula:

(samples of delay / sample rate) – 1000 = ms of delay

so, for example:

(113 / 44100) – 1000 = 2.56 ms

13. In I/O Setup, enter this number into the appropriate **H/W INSERT DELAY** field. See Figure 8.10.

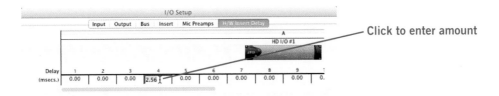

Click to enter amount

Figure 8.10
Entering hardware insert delay time.

Using the Plug-In Preferences

There comes a time in every Pro Tool engineer's life when there are just too many plug-ins to sort through in plug-in drop-down menus. Clicking on EQ or Dynamics can reveal pages of choices. To help you quickly find the right plug-in, Pro Tools provides several different sorting preferences as well as a way to create plug-in favorites.

Plug-In Menu Hierarchy

Plug-in selector lists can be organized in a number of different ways, as chosen in the Display page of the Preferences dialog box, as shown in Figure 8.11.

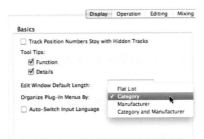

Figure 8.11
Plug-in hierarchy preferences.

Category

By default, plug-ins are organized by category (effect type). Which category the plug-in appears in is up to each plug-in developer. Plug-ins that do not fit into a standard category (such as the DigiRack Signal Generator or third-party plug-ins that have not been defined by their developers) appear in the Other category. Plug-ins may appear in more than one category; for example, ChannelStrip has both EQ and Dynamic processes.

Manufacturer

Another useful sorting method is by manufacturer. In this mode, the plug-in list is sorted into subfolders listed by manufacturer. For example, all McDSP plug-ins will be organized together.

Category and Manufacturer

Choosing the category and manufacturer preference results in two separate lists in the plug-in selection pop-up menu, with plug-ins listed by both category and manufacturer. This is the best of both worlds, enabling you to quickly get to plug-ins by type or, if the type has too many choices, by manufacturer to narrow down the range of possibilities.

Flat List

The Flat List option was the original Pro Tools method for showing plug-ins. In this mode, all subfolders are removed and placed in alphabetical order. This is useful only if looking for plug-ins alphabetically.

Plug-In Favorites

You may also find yourself reaching for the same plug-ins over and over again—a favorite compressor or EQ, perhaps. Pro Tools offers a way to create plug-in "favorites" that place the plug-in at the top of the list, above all Category or Manufacturer folders. See Figure 8.12.

To designate a plug-in as a favorite:

■ COMMAND-CLICK (Mac) or CTRL-CLICK (Windows) on a plug-in Insert button and select the plug-in that you want to designate as a favorite. Release the mouse, and the menu will disappear. Click on the plug-in list again, and your designated favorite will appear above all categories and manufacturers.

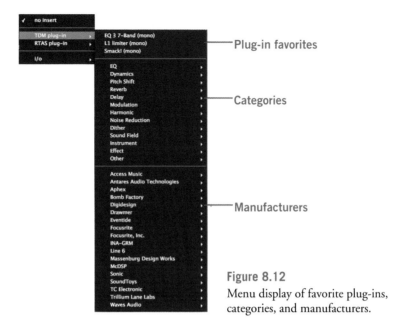

— Plug-in favorites

— Categories

— Manufacturers

Figure 8.12
Menu display of favorite plug-ins,
categories, and manufacturers.

Tip: You need to keep the modifier key (Control or Command) held down until you've selected the plug-in. Creating a plug-in favorite for a Native plug-in does not create a favorite for the DSP equivalent. For example, creating a plug-in favorite for a Native plug-in such as ChannelStrip does not automatically create a plug-in favorite for the DSP version of ChannelStrip. Furthermore, creating a plug-in favorite for a mono plug-in does not create a multichannel equivalent.

To remove a plug-in favorite:

■ COMMAND-CLICK (Mac) or CTRL-CLICK (Windows) on a plug-in Insert button and select the plug-in that you want to remove from the favorites list.

Mixing Techniques

This section discusses a variety of advanced mixing and automation techniques. Some of the material has been discussed in earlier courses, but in this lesson you delve deeper into the advantages of submixing, various automation techniques, VCA automation, and advanced Preview and Capture modes.

Advanced Submixing

You have already encountered the idea of using Aux Input tracks to create submixes several times throughout previous Pro Tools courses. This course expands on this idea and considers how the different floating-point and fixed-point mixing systems deal with submasters and detecting clip points.

Stem Mixing

Working with submixed groups of tracks is sometimes called *stem mixing*. Each of the submixes, or stems, is like a mini-mix of its own, with the main mix being a mix of the stems. There are a number of advantages to working like this:

■ Large mixes are simplified and broken down into manageable sections.

■ It's simple to change the overall balances between, say, drums, vocals, and guitars at any point throughout the project, even after automation has been written.

■ Effects can be applied to sections of the mix as groups. For example, you can apply compression to the drums as a kit instead of individual parts. This can help "gel" a mix together.

■ All the stems can be recorded separately. This makes it easy to rebalance or process the mix at a later time, even on different equipment.

■ It's relatively simple to record different variations of the mix. Often delivery requirements include "vocal up/vocal down" versions, where the vocals are mixed at slightly different levels. It's also common to record a mix without vocals, which can be used for backing track playback in TV performances and other such uses. With stem routing in Pro Tools, you can easily set up these mixes and even record them all with a single pass.

Creating a Mix Bus Stem (Submaster)

An extension of the idea of audio submixing is the technique of putting the entire mix through an Aux Input track before going through the Master Fader. There are two main reasons for taking this step:

■ **Pre-master fader compression**—An Aux Input submaster can be used to add compression (or other inserts) to the whole mix prior to the Master Fader. Inserts on Master Faders are post fader, which is not always an ideal signal flow. For example, if you are using a dynamic processor on the Master Fader, changes to the Master Fader level will alter the threshold of the compression, especially during a fade out.

■ **Routing the mix to internal destinations**—Sometimes you need to route the entire mix to different destinations, including internal record tracks. To do this you will need to use an Aux Input track. You cannot route signals from a Master Fader to multiple destinations.

As you learned in the Pro Tools 110 course, Pro Tools 10 offers an easy way to bus tracks to a new Aux Input submaster in one easy step—the Route to New Track command.

To create an Aux Input submaster:

1. Select all the tracks you want to go to the new Aux submaster.

2. Hold OPTION+SHIFT (Mac) or ALT+SHIFT (Windows) and click on any track's OUTPUT PATH SELECTOR.

3. Choose ROUTE TO NEW TRACK in the pop-up menu.

4. In the subsequent New Track dialog box, notice that Pro Tools has already selected a Stereo Aux Input track. Enter a name in the NAME box. This name will also be used as the bus name, so it can be identified easily in the future.

5. Click OK. A new stereo Aux Input track will be created with all tracks routed to it and the bus named accordingly.

Stem Mixing Example

The mixer pictured in Figure 8.13 shows part of a mix that uses stemming. Only the drum tracks are shown. This example has the following features:

■ The drum tracks have been submixed using a bus called Drums, which routes to an Aux Input track called DrumSb along with another Aux Input track named DrumsSbC (compressed). Both Aux Input tracks are routed to a SubMix bus.

■ A VCA Master track is assigned to the Drum group to enable easy control of the group's overall level before the SubMix Aux and offer easy individual solo versus group solo control.

■ Compression has been applied to the whole drum kit at the DrumsSub Compressed Aux Input track.

■ All Aux Input tracks in the mix are routed to a final Aux Input track named SubMix Master, where final stage limiting/maximizing is applied.

■ The SubMix Master Aux Input track routes the mix to audio interface outputs for monitoring and to an internal bus that is routed to an Audio Track called Mix Print.

To route a track to multiple destinations:

1. Use the OUTPUT PATH SELECTOR to choose the first destination as normal.

2. CONTROL-CLICK (Mac) or START-CLICK (Windows) on the OUTPUT PATH SELECTOR and choose the next destination. A plus symbol will appear in the Output section, indicating that multiple destinations are selected.

Figure 8.13
Example of submixing with Aux Inputs, a VCA Master, a SubMix Master, and a Mix Print Audio record track.

3. Repeat for further output assignments.

Using Bus Master Faders

In Lesson 7 you learned that Pro Tools uses 64-bit summing (48-bit with Pro Tools|HD hardware) to provide extensive headroom when mixing signals and no loss of resolution when making large gain changes to channels. You also learned that Master Faders scale the levels of buses and outputs. In Exercise 7, you performed an experiment with signal generators to see this in action. How do these concepts apply to real mixing practices?

When to Use Master Faders

With 64-bit summing (48-bit with Pro Tools|HD), the input to an internal mixer in Pro Tools is practically impossible to clip. However, the outputs, especially physical outputs, are very easy to clip. With physical outputs, the signal must return to 24-bits no matter what bit depth was used during recording or whether you are using Pro Tools|HDX, Pro Tools|HD, Pro Tools|HD Native, or Pro Tools software only. When you are using the stem mixing technique, you need to be aware that any of your submixes could be clipped at the output of a bus or physical output. Pulling down the output fader will alleviate this condition. But it is also useful to see if the input to a mixer is clipping.

How to See If a Submix Is Clipping

You will be able to see if any of your submix stems are clipping if you work in Pre-Fader Metering mode (enabled in the Options menu). The Aux Input tracks' meters will give you a true reading of the inputs of the channels in this mode. You can also see if a submix is clipping by using the expanded metering view of any source track.

To see the expanded view of a source track:

1. Open the Output window of a track by clicking on the fader icon on the track (see Figure 8.14).

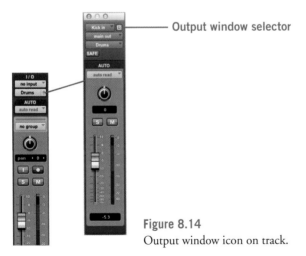

Output window selector

Figure 8.14
Output window icon on track.

2. Once the Output window is open, click on the green zoom button (Mac) or maximize button (Windows) at the top of the window. The Output window will expand to show the meters of the summing bus for the track as dictated by the track's output assignment. This could be an Aux Input bus or an audio interface output. See Figure 8.15.

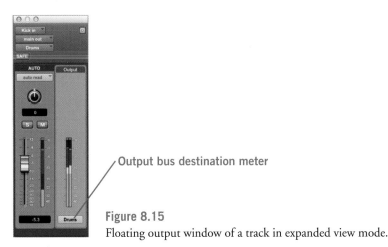

Output bus destination meter

Figure 8.15
Floating output window of a track in expanded view mode.

The meter shows all contributing tracks, not just the one you opened the window on. This meter is identical to the meter of a Master Fader if it were to be routed to control the bus. Using the expanded meter eliminates the need for a Master Fader to show input clips, but a Master Fader may remain a useful tool as described next.

Master Faders as Bus Trims

If a submix is clipping, a Master Fader track can be assigned to the same bus and used to attenuate it and recover the clipped submix. The Master Fader shows the real level of the bus, so it's easy to see clipping. See Figure 8.16.

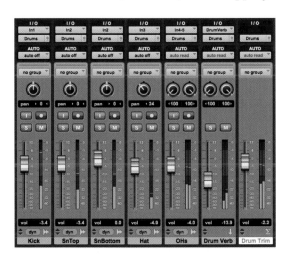

Figure 8.16
Master Fader recovering a signal from clipping on a submix bus.

Using VCA Masters to Adjust Source Tracks

As you learned in Exercise 7, reducing the levels of the tracks that are being summed to a bus has exactly the same result as trimming the bus with a Master Fader. You can therefore also deal with clipping submixes by attenuating all the faders on the tracks feeding the bus. If the source tracks are grouped, a VCA Master track makes this job much easier, especially when the tracks are automated. You will explore the relationship between VCA Masters and automation in the next section.

Should I Use a Master Fader on Every Bus?

Should a Master Fader or VCA Master be used on every submix? In real-world situations, a balance is generally found between practicality and the optimal mixing path. Using Master Faders on all summing points (including reverb sends) or grouping and managing every last section of your mix with VCA Masters would be excessive and unnecessarily complex. A better practice is to record with plenty of headroom, start with all submix faders at unity, and monitor your gain stages as you mix. You can then make up the gain to the desired level at the final mix bus and use a Master Fader to optimize at this stage or a limiter designed to bring up the level of the final mix. If you notice that a bus is clipping earlier in the signal path, use a VCA or Master Fader as necessary.

VCA Master Automation

The Pro Tools 201 book describes how VCA Master tracks can be used to control the members of a mix group. You saw a situation where this can be useful in the previous section. In this section you will learn about the relationship between VCA Masters and automation.

VCA Composite Volume Graphs

Figure 8.18 shows a group of five backing vocal tracks, with a VCA Master assigned to the group. This group has been automated before the VCA Master was created. In this situation, the VCA Master provides an easy way to freely adjust (or trim) the overall level of the group, without interfering with the automation on the tracks or committing to a Trim automation pass.

In Volume view, a second graph is drawn in blue that indicates the VCA Master fader's contribution to the overall level of the track. This composite result is what you are actually hearing as opposed to what the absolute written volume of the track is. This is similar to viewing Trim automation on the track without coalescing Trim. The VCA "trim" automation or volume delta is applied equally across all tracks in the VCA group. See Figure 8.17.

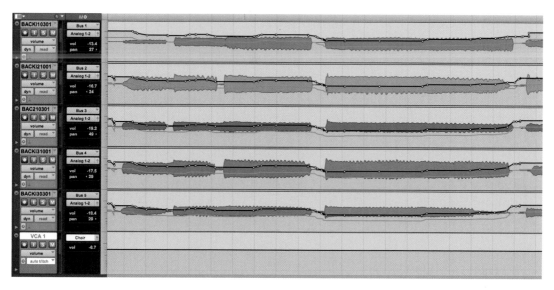

Figure 8.17
Volume automation with composite graph showing VCA contribution.

VCA Automation

VCA Master tracks can also be automated, providing an alternative (or addition) to recording Trim automation on the group members. In Figure 8.18, the VCA Master has been automated to fade out the whole group during one section of the vocal.

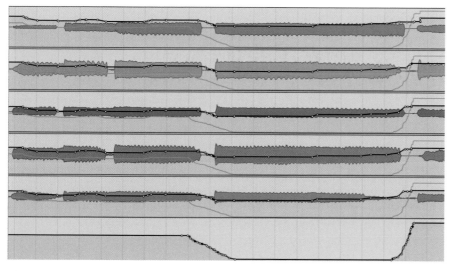

Figure 8.18
Automated VCA Master track.

The blue graphs that show the actual fader paths are no longer simply scaled versions of the original track automation; they are now composites of the track automation and the VCA Master automation.

Coalescing VCA Automation

After writing VCA automation, you lose the ability to make simple level adjustments with the VCA Master, because the fader is now tied to its own automation graph. Subsequent passes must be recorded to this graph, or you can use Trim mode on the VCA Master to adjust the existing automation. At this point, the final fader positions of the group members are the composite of three layers of automation: the original track volume, the VCA Master automation, and the VCA's Trim graph. Often it is more manageable to commit the VCA automation to the tracks. This is called *coalescing*, just as committing Trim automation is called coalescing.

To coalesce VCA Master automation to group members, right-click on the VCA Master's track name and choose Coalesce VCA Master Automation. See Figure 8.19.

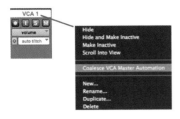

Figure 8.19
Automated VCA Master fader; the Coalesce VCA Master Automation command.

Coalescing writes the composite (blue) graphs to the main volume playlists on the group member tracks and clears volume automation from the VCA Master track.

Overriding VCA Master Automation on a Group Member Track

This is an advanced technique that allows you to protect certain tracks in a group from the effect of a VCA Master automation pass. In the previous example, the VCA Master track was used to pull down the backing vocals over a particular section of the song. Now imagine that you want to pull down all the backing vocals except Track 4. Pro Tools has a special way of managing this situation: When you write automation directly to a group member, it overrides any VCA Master automation affecting the track. In other words, any automation moves you record on a group member's fader are absolute and will play back as you recorded them; they are not relative to any existing VCA Master automation.

In Figure 8.20, the fader for Track 4 has been held still in Touch mode during the dip in the VCA Master's automation. The assumption is that this is how you want the fader automation to play back, so the move needs to appear in the blue composite automation graph. Pro Tools achieves this by adjusting the track's main volume playlist to cancel out the effect of VCA Master automation at this section.

This technique can be used at the same time as you write VCA Master automation, or in a subsequent pass.

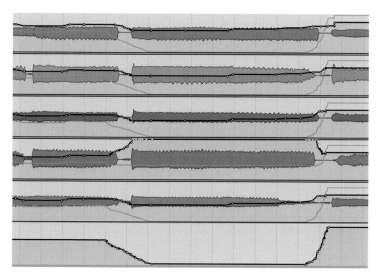

Figure 8.20
Writing automation directly to group members overrides VCA Master automation.

Using Latch Prime

Latch Prime is an important automation preference that enables you to force selected mixer parameters to begin writing from the start of playback, without switching them into Write automation mode. Occasionally, you want to adjust levels or parameter settings while playback is stopped and then have those parameters start writing at those levels once you press Play. Typical examples are pan or plug-in settings. Before Pro Tools 7.2, this was only possible by switching the tracks containing those parameters into Write mode. This, however, would mean that all the parameters on those tracks would start writing unless you managed Write Enables in the Automation window and performed multiple passes. With Latch Prime, only the parameters you have touched or moved while stopped will start writing, with all other parameters continuing in Read mode.

Tip: While writing automation using Latch mode (especially with Latch Prime enabled), when a group member track is under the control of a VCA Master, if a group member track parameter is accidentally touched or bumped, you may end up inadvertently writing or altering existing automation on the group member track, causing it to no longer follow the VCA Master's automation.

Tip: Latch Prime also enables you to activate controls for writing with the Write to All/Start/End/Punch/Next commands while playback is stopped.

Priming Controls

When Latch Prime is enabled, any parameters that you touch or click while playback is stopped are "primed" for automation recording. Any track that has primed controls will display its automation mode in red, and the track's mode indicator will flash on an Avid worksurface. When you begin playback, the parameters that you have touched or clicked will begin writing.

To enable Latch Prime:

1. Choose SETUP > PREFERENCES.

2. Click on the MIXING tab.

3. In the Automation section, check ALLOW LATCH PRIME IN STOP, as shown in Figure 8.21.

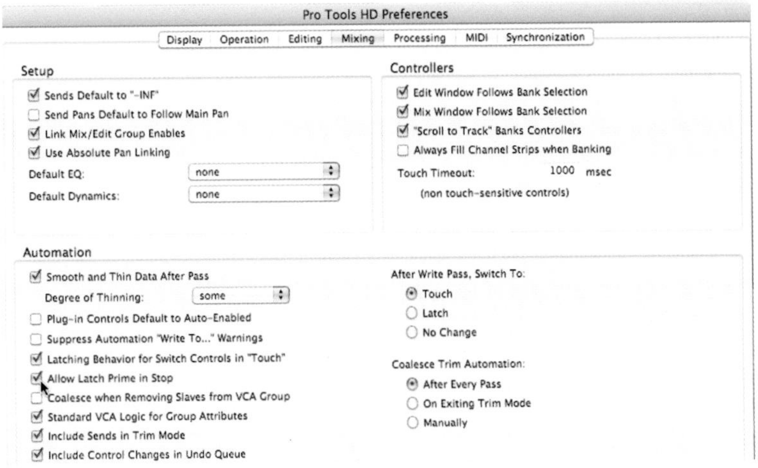

Figure 8.21
Enabling Allow Latch Prime in Stop mode in Preferences.

Unpriming Controls

If you have primed controls, but want to reset them and prevent them from dropping into record when you start playback, you can globally unprime all tracks across the session, or unprime individual tracks:

To unprime all parameters on all tracks:

■ Press the global **AUTOMATCH** button in the Automation window, as shown in Figure 8.22.

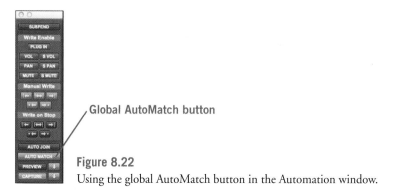

Global AutoMatch button

Figure 8.22
Using the global AutoMatch button in the Automation window.

To unprime all parameters on individual tracks:

■ **COMMAND-CLICK** (Mac) or **CONTROL-CLICK** (Windows) on the automation mode selector on the track, as shown in Figure 8.23.

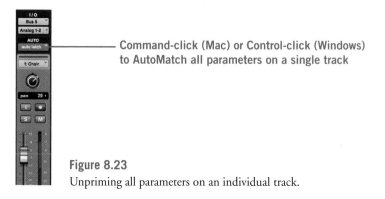

Command-click (Mac) or Control-click (Windows)
to AutoMatch all parameters on a single track

Figure 8.23
Unpriming all parameters on an individual track.

To reset individual parameters across all tracks (volume, pan, and so on):

■ **COMMAND-CLICK** (Mac) or **CONTROL-CLICK** (Windows) on the **AUTOMATION ENABLE** button for the parameter you want to reset. Or, you can simply click the **AUTOMATION ENABLE** button of the parameter you want to reset (such as Pan) and then re-enable the parameter again. See Figure 8.24.

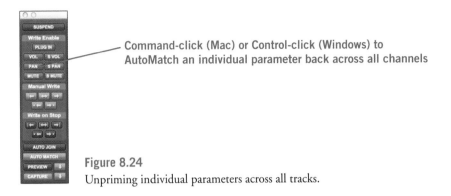

Command-click (Mac) or Control-click (Windows) to AutoMatch an individual parameter back across all channels

Figure 8.24
Unpriming individual parameters across all tracks.

Writing Static Automation Mixer Settings

In addition to writing dynamically changing automation values (such as write, touch, latch, and trim), there are times when you may need to write static (non-changing) automation values.

Writing Static Automation Versus Real-Time Automation

The 100- and 200-level Pro Tools books in the Avid Learning Series describe various ways to record mixer automation in Pro Tools. In many cases you will write dynamic automation, recording real-time adjustments to parameters on the mixer and plug-ins. The Pro Tools 201 book covers techniques for writing static automation using the Write to All/End/Start/Next/Punch commands in the Automation window.

These commands all write flat parameter settings over a range of time, freezing parts of the mixer in a particular configuration throughout a section of the session. This type of static automation is also sometimes referred to as *snapshot* automation, because the settings are unchanging over a specified period of time (like a camera snapshot).

Note: When referring to Pro Tools static automation as "snapshot automation" in this way, it should not be confused with the completely different and somewhat unrelated snapshot capture buffers that are supported on Avid ICON series worksurfaces.

A section of static automation can be as simple as a single plug-in bypass or as complicated as a mixer-wide recall of levels, pans, mutes, sends, and plug-in settings.

There are many music project scenarios where it is appropriate to write static automation in this way, including:

- You need to change an effects preset at different places in the song. For example, you might have the 11 plug-in set to a clean guitar sound at some points but an overdriven sound at others.

- You need to change a virtual instrument's patch during the song.

- You want to set the balance of lead and backing vocals differently during different song sections.

- The song has two distinctly different sections; the entire mix changes between the two sections.

The Two Families of Write Commands

Before looking at some workflows, it's important to understand the distinction between the Write to Start/All/End/Punch/Next commands in the Automation window and the Write to Current and Write to All Enabled commands in the Edit menu (see Figure 8.25). Although they are similarly named and can be used for similar purposes, they are not the same commands and have a number of differences.

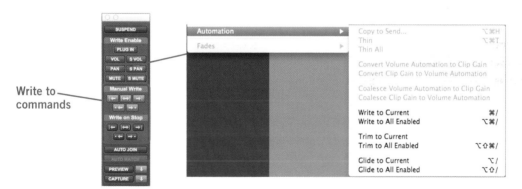

Figure 8.25
The Write commands in the Automation window (left) and the Edit > Automation commands (right).

Write to All/End/Start/Next/Punch Commands

The Write to Start/All/End/Punch/Next commands (in the Automation window) can be used during playback and stop (if using Write, Latch Prime, or Preview and Capture), writing automation to all parameters that are currently writing or (as you'll learn shortly) parameters that are isolated in **PREVIEW** mode.

To recap the material from the Pro Tools 201 book:

- **Write to All**—Writes the current settings of all currently writing mixer/plug-in parameters to the Timeline selection (or the whole session if there's no Timeline selection).

- **Write to End**—Writes the current settings of all currently writing mixer/plug-in parameters from the current time to the end of the Timeline selection (or to the end of the session if there's no Timeline selection).

- **Write to Start**—Writes the current settings of all currently writing mixer/plug-in parameters from the current time to the start of the Timeline selection (or to the beginning of the session if there's no Timeline selection).

- **Write to Next**—Writes the current settings of all currently writing mixer/plug-in parameters from the current time to the next automation breakpoint on each automation playlist.

- **Write to Punch**—Writes the current settings of all currently writing mixer/plug-in parameters from the current time back to the point where they began writing.

Write to Current and Write to All Enabled

Write to Current and Write to All Enabled (and their variants) can be used during stop or playback. These commands only write to parameters on tracks containing an Edit selection and within the current Edit selection's time range. The Write to Current and Write to All Enabled commands are considered automation playlist Edit commands and are unaffected by track automation modes.

- **Write to Current**—Writes the setting(s) of the currently displayed automation playlist(s) within the Edit selection. This means that only one parameter can be written per track. For this reason, it is much more common to use Write to All Enabled.

- **Write to All Enabled**—Writes the current settings of all automation parameters within the current Edit selection except for parameters types that are disabled in the Automation window.

Table 8.1 is a reminder of the keyboard shortcut equivalents of the menu commands.

Table 8.2 lists a summary of the differences between the Write commands.

Table 8.1   Write to Keyboard Shortcuts

Function	Keyboard Shortcut
Write to Current	Command+/ (Mac) or Ctrl+/ (Windows)
Write to All Enabled	Command+Option+/ (Mac) or Ctrl+Alt+/ (Windows)

Table 8.2   Differences Between the Write Commands

Write to All/End/Start/Next/Punch	Write to Current/All Enabled
Located in the Automation window	Located in the Edit > Automation menu
Write to currently writing/isolated parameters	Write to the displayed parameter/all automation enabled parameters
Write within the Timeline selection on all tracks writing automation	Writes within the Edit selection, and only to tracks that contain the Edit selection
Not active if automation is suspended	Can still write when automation is suspended
Will only write to tracks in Write, Latch, Touch, or Touch/Latch modes (with or without Trim enabled)	Will write to track selections even if the track is in Off or Read mode

The following sections of this lesson describe how to use both of these sets of features to write mixer settings to sections of your song and how to determine which method is appropriate in different situations.

Using Preview Mode

When Preview mode is activated in the Automation window, mixer or plug-in automation plays back normally as if in Read mode. However, as soon as you touch or click any control that is write-enabled, that parameter becomes "isolated" from its automation playback graph. The parameter will not follow the automation graph nor write new automation data. The parameter will remain at the new static level or position until you exit Preview mode or "punch" the isolated level in and write the automation.

Preview mode is useful for experimenting with different mixer and plug-in settings while Pro Tools plays back, without having to manage writing, undoing, or managing the automation state of individual tracks. With preview values in place, you can suspend Preview mode allowing you to compare the mix with and without your changes. Once you are ready to commit to the changes you simply "punch" your Preview values and write them by simply playing back or using one of the Manual Write to commands. Furthermore, if you are in Preview mode with preview values in place, you can simply exit Preview mode to undo any changes and return to your prior mix.

Basic Outline for Using Preview Mode

The basic workflow for using Preview mode is similar in all situations:

1. Enable **PREVIEW MODE** in the Automation window (or using an Avid worksurface). See Figure 8.26.

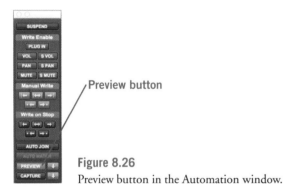
Preview button

Figure 8.26
Preview button in the Automation window.

2. During playback, configure mixer and plug-in settings without disturbing the existing mix or automation.

3. Write the new settings.

Steps 1 and 2 are the same for all examples, whereas Step 3 varies according to the situation and personal preference.

Writing Isolated Parameters

Any changes you make in Preview mode can be discarded by exiting Preview, or you can choose to write your current settings as automation in a number of different ways.

Workflow 1: Using Preview with Write to All

Figure 8.27 shows a keyboard track with a Sci-Fi plug-in. At a particular part of a song (the bridge, breakdown, and so on), you want to create a different sound entirely but don't know exactly what that is yet. In this workflow, you will see an example of how to use Preview mode to disable existing automation and experiment with new mixer and plug-in settings while playing a Timeline selection. After adjusting the mixer and plug-ins controls to the proper settings during playback, the modified automation settings can then be written to the Timeline selection using the Manual Write to All command in the Automation window.

To create new mix settings to the eight-bar section:

1. Recall memory location 69.

2. Put the track into **LATCH** mode.

3. Engage **PREVIEW** mode.

4. Ensure **LOOP PLAYBACK** is enabled.

5. Press **PLAY**. While Pro Tools plays back, adjust all the necessary mixer and plug-in settings to get the sound you need for the section. Notice that no automation jumps back when the audio loops back. When you are happy with how the mix sounds during this section, you are ready to commit it to automation. Notice that the track automation mode indicator is green indicating Preview mode and the isolated parameters in green indicate level/setting differences.

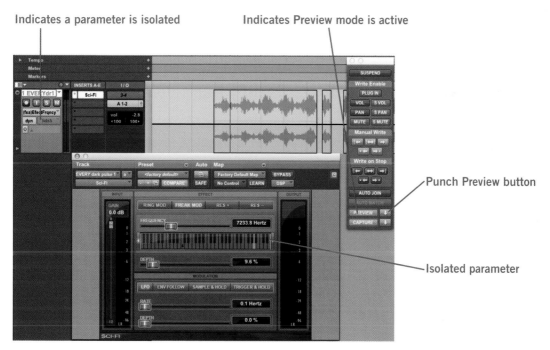

Figure 8.27
Automation Mode selector and plug-in parameters indicating isolated parameters.

6. Check that all the types of automation you have changed (volume, plug-in, send volume, and so forth) are write-enabled in the Automation window.

   At this point stop playback. Next to the Preview button in the Automation window is a Punch button, as seen in Figure 8.27. Click this button to punch the Preview values into the track. The track automation enable button will turn red.

7. Press the **MANUAL WRITE TO ALL** button in the Automation window. Every parameter that you've touched or moved since entering Preview mode will be written at its current level to the Timeline selection. If you've changed parameters on more than one track, automation will be written to the selection on all of the modified tracks. Be aware that if no selection is made, using Write to All will write the new level across the entire session.

8. After punching and writing the new values, you will automatically be exited out of Preview mode. If you want to repeat the process with another parameter you will need to re-enable Preview mode.

You can test that the procedure was successful by playing through the automated sections and watching the mixer/plug-in parameters snap to new positions. See Figure 8.28.

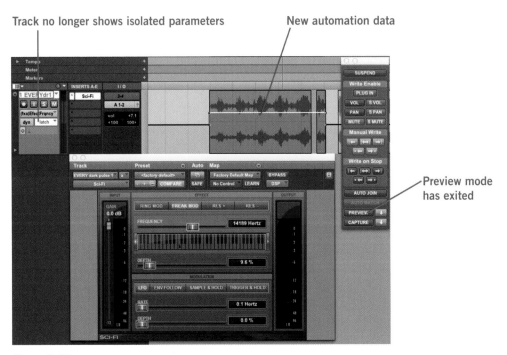

Figure 8.28
Automation graphs indicating the new levels/settings; the automation mode indicator returns to previous state.

Workflow 2: Preview Using Cue Up and Punch

In Workflow 1, you found the settings you wanted for a particular section while in Preview mode and then wrote them across that section. However, once you have a value set in the Preview buffer, for example, a different sound for the chorus, you can use that Preview value over and over again. This is referred to as the Preview buffer.

There are two ways to use Punch Preview (which is the process of punching your changes so you can write them).

Method 1: Punch in During Playback

While you are playing back with Preview enabled, you can immediately commence writing isolated parameters as automation at any time. This enables you to work without setting a precise Timeline or Edit selection and to hear the transition from one section to another as you write. For example, as you listen to a section of your mix, you can switch into Preview mode, adjust some settings, rewind 5 to 10 seconds before the point where the mix changes, and then manually punch in at the desired location.

To write automation on-the-fly with Punch Preview:

1. Enable PREVIEW mode and adjust automation parameters during playback.

2. During playback, click the PUNCH PREVIEW button. Isolated parameters on tracks in TOUCH, LATCH, OR WRITE mode will begin writing. Tracks in TOUCH will be switched to LATCH to facilitate the punch.

Obviously there's little advantage to punching in halfway through the section you're mixing, so usually you would move the play position back to an earlier point. While in Preview, you can freely move the play position without losing the settings of your isolated parameters.

Method 2: Cue Up and Punch

Instead of punching in on-the-fly, you can use Punch Preview while the transport is stopped. Isolated parameters will begin writing when you start playback. This option is often preferable as it enables you to cue up the start point of the automation precisely. So why would you do this instead of just selecting the whole range and using one of the Write commands? This method allows you to write a basic static mix while you make dynamic adjustments at the same time and can work well with linear mixing tasks, such as working through a song riding the levels on vocal tracks, while also writing static automation on several keyboard tracks.

Usage Example of Preview Mode

You are starting a mix of a song that has recorded vocals intermixed with recorded instruments and loops. The loops and instruments need basic volume levels whereas the vocals need to be ridden. This requires a mixture of static balance changes and dynamic fader rides. Playing through the session, you set up a balance that works for the initial verse of the song using typical automation workflows. When you reach the first chorus, you activate Preview mode and try out, or audition, new levels. When you're ready, you park the Pro Tools play position at the start of the first chorus, punch the "preview" values and then start playback. The basic static mix is written as you play back while you continue to make dynamic adjustments on the vocal track. After the chorus, navigate to the next chorus, press Punch Preview, and repeat the process.

To preview and then Punch Preview from a standing start:

1. Start playback.

2. Do one of the following:

   - Enable PREVIEW mode and adjust automation parameters during playback.

   - To preview isolate all currently write-enabled controls, OPTION-CLICK (MAC) or ALT-CLICK (Windows) the PREVIEW button in the Automation window during playback.

   - To preview isolate all currently write-enabled controls on only the selected tracks, OPTION+SHIFT-CLICK (Mac) or ALT+SHIFT-CLICK (Windows) the PREVIEW button in the Automation window during playback.

3. Stop playback.

4. Position the playback position at the point where you want to start writing the PREVIEW settings and do one of the following:

   - To punch in on all currently isolated controls, click the PUNCH PREVIEW button in the Automation window.

   - To punch in on all currently isolated controls on only the selected tracks, OPTION+SHIFT-CLICK (Mac) or ALT+SHIFT-CLICK (Windows) the PREVIEW button in the Automation window.

5. All isolated parameters on tracks in TOUCH, LATCH, TOUCH/LATCH, or WRITE mode will become primed for writing automation. Tracks in TOUCH will be switched to LATCH, to facilitate the punch. Start playback. The isolated parameters will begin writing from the playback position.

Tip: Punching previewed mix settings in Stop is similar to using the Latch Prime in Stop feature described earlier in this lesson. Latch Prime in Stop does not need to be enabled in order for Punch Preview to work while in Stop.

Suspending Preview Mode

While in Preview mode, you can temporarily suspend it, which allows you to toggle and compare between preview values and existing automation.

To suspend Preview mode:

■ COMMAND-CLICK (Mac) or CONTROL-CLICK (Windows) the PREVIEW button in the Automation window or Avid worksurface.

Using Preview Mode with Trim Mode

The Preview and Punch Preview commands work with Trim automation in the same way as regular automation. Using real-time Trim mode with Preview allows you to rebalance your track levels, by first letting you to preview your new track volume offset (delta change), and then writing the new change using Punch Preview.

To use Preview with Trim mode to rebalance audio track levels:

1. In the Automation window, verify that volume is write-enabled.

2. Select the desired audio tracks and enable TRIM with LATCH mode on the selected tracks.

Tip: Although the previous workflow step most often uses Trim with Latch mode, Touch, Touch/Latch, and Write modes with Trim is also supported.

3. Start playback.

4. Do one of the following:

   • Enable PREVIEW mode and adjust the volume automation parameters during playback.

   • To preview isolate all currently write-enabled controls, OPTION-CLICK (Mac) or ALT-CLICK (Windows) the PREVIEW button in the Automation window during playback.

   • To preview isolate all currently write-enabled controls on only the selected tracks, OPTION+SHIFT-CLICK (Mac) or ALT+SHIFT-CLICK (Windows) the PREVIEW button in the Automation window during playback.

5. Stop playback.

6. Position the playback position at the point where you want to start writing the **PREVIEW** settings and do one of the following:

- To punch in on all currently isolated controls, click the **PUNCH PREVIEW** button in the **AUTOMATION** window.

- To punch in on all currently isolated controls on only the selected tracks, **OPTION+SHIFT-CLICK** (Mac) or **ALT+SHIFT-CLICK** (Windows) the **PUNCH PREVIEW** button in the Automation window.

7. All isolated parameters on tracks in **TOUCH, LATCH,** or **WRITE** mode will become primed for writing automation. Tracks in Touch will be switched to **LATCH,** to facilitate the punch. Start playback. The isolated parameters will begin writing from the new trim values you configured from the playback position. Pro Tools saves Trim status when capturing, so if you attempt to Punch Capture Trim values while displaying a non-Trim automation playlist, Pro Tools will automatically apply the values to the corresponding Trim playlist.

Using Capture and Punch Capture Mode

The Capture button, located in the Automation window (shown in Figure 8.29), captures the settings of any parameters that are currently writing automation. It can also be forced to capture selected or all parameters regardless of their write state. Once captured, these settings can then be written to other locations in the session using Punch Capture. When working with long-format music projects (such as live recordings), you can save time by capturing automation from an earlier point in the project and applying it to similar audio at a later point in the project.

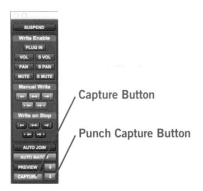

Capture Button

Punch Capture Button

Figure 8.29
Capture and Punch Capture buttons in the Automation window.

Alternatively, you can choose to use Capture All, which uses the static level of all mix parameters at a particular location (current cursor location or start of selection when stopped). For example, you can Capture All in the first song of a live concert with all the pieces of the band playing and then apply the same settings to another song later in the concert with the same musicians performing.

Tip: Capture grabs parameter settings at a single point in your session instead of continuously changing automation data over time. In other words, Capture takes a snapshot of the currently writing settings, Capture Selected takes a snapshot of only the mixer settings for the selected tracks, and Capture All takes a snapshot of the entire mixer, if auto-enabled.

Capture's Basic Operation

To capture settings that are currently writing, press the Capture button in the Automation window. To capture all parameters, regardless of whether they are writing, Option-click (Mac) or Alt-click (Windows) on the Capture button. To punch the captured parameters, press the Punch Capture button in the Automation window.

The following options apply to Punch Capture:

- Activating Punch Capture while the transport is stopped will activate Latch Prime in Stop mode.

- Option-clicking (Mac) or Alt-clicking (Windows) on the Punch Capture button will switch any affected tracks into Latch mode (if they weren't already). If Capture All was used, this will effectively Punch All, although the Automation Enable buttons can be used to write-protect or isolate specific automation parameters.

- Option+Shift-clicking (Mac) or Alt+Shift-clicking (Windows) on the Punch Capture button will only punch controls on the selected tracks.

Capture/Punch Capture Workflow Examples

When using Capture/Punch Capture in a music production workflow, several Capture methods are available:

- **Capturing the actively writing parameters**—Although the basic outline for using Capture is to capture parameters that you are actively writing, this method has rather limited applications. This is due to the fact that you must capture while automation is still writing. If you allow playback to stop and the automation is written, there is nothing to actively capture. However, if you are writing automation, especially with long format material, you may decide during the automation pass that you will need these levels later in the concert. While still writing automation simply click the Capture button. Now you have a Capture buffer that you can repeatedly punch throughout the session.

■ **Capturing in Stop**—If you have Latch Prime mode enabled, any parameters that you touch on tracks in Latch mode are considered to be Writing in Stop and can be captured. This enables you to select (by touch or clicking) a group of parameters to capture at your leisure, rather than just capturing whatever happens to be writing during a playback pass. For example, you have correct levels already set in a song. You need these levels at each repeat in the song. Simply touch the faders enabling Latch Prime in Stop, click Capture, and then navigate to the new section in the Song that requires the same levels. Press the Punch Capture button and begin writing (with normal playback or by making a selection and using a Write to All command).

■ **Capture All**—Taking a snapshot of the whole mixer is often useful, especially when you've finished mixing a particular section of the song that repeats. For example, you have spent hours getting the balance of the guitars correct with different 11 plug-in settings, panning, delay settings, and so on, for the chorus. Simply select the chorus, execute a Capture All, and select the next chorus. Punch the Capture buffer and use a Write to All command. Repeat for each chorus.

Workflow Example 1: Capture and Resume

In this example you are working on a song that features a choir. Automation is needed to balance the choir against the lead singer when both are singing, versus when just the choir is singing. You will need to lower the choir during the chorus and raise the choir when singing alone, such as during the intro and ending.

1. Ride the choir volume during the first chorus of the song. When finished, leave the Transport parked in the first chorus.

2. With **LATCH PRIME** mode enabled and **LATCH** or **TOUCH** mode enabled on all tracks, capture the fader levels of the music that you want to use later (during the second chorus) by touching or clicking all of the faders that you want to copy to the subsequent choruses, and then clicking **CAPTURE**.

3. Next, place the playback cursor at the beginning of the second chorus and then press the **PUNCH CAPTURE** button. The faders that you previously captured will jump to their settings from the Capture point. This will be your starting point for adjusting the music levels during the second chorus. The tracks with the punched fader levels will indicate that they are Writing in Stop by changing their automation mode indicators to red.

4. Resume writing at the captured levels by starting playback. The faders will begin to write automation at their previous levels from the first chorus. You can now adjust the levels using this starting point.

Workflow Example 2: Capture All and Write

For this example, let's assume in a song you've been working with, you have spent hours getting the balance of the guitars correct with different 11 plug-in settings, panning, delay settings, and so on, for the chorus. To then copy all the automation settings to the subsequent choruses, you simply select the chorus, execute a Capture All, and select the next chorus. Punch the Capture buffer and use a Write to All command. This workflow is especially useful for choruses with different audio regions but still requiring similar mix levels.

To capture the vocal delay settings and apply them to the later verses:

1. Select the first chorus of the song and begin rebalancing the guitar mix using TOUCH or LATCH mode.

2. When you are happy with your mix, select the entire chorus.

3. Take a snapshot of the guitar mix by OPTION-CLICKING (Mac) or ALT-CLICKING (Windows) on the CAPTURE button.

4. Select the next chorus of the song.

5. Ensure that the Automation Enable buttons for the values you want to change are enabled (volume, pan, sends, and so on). Punch the captured mixer snapshot by pressing the PUNCH CAPTURE button. All automation parameters in the mixer (including plug-ins) on all tracks that are in either Latch or Touch mode will jump to the captured settings and be primed. At this point, you can simply play back or use the Write to All Command to write the new levels across your selection.

6. Repeat for subsequent choruses.

Tip: Instead of punching to all tracks, you can punch to only the selected tracks by pressing Option+Shift+Punch (Mac) or Alt+Shift+Punch (Windows).

Using Capture and Trim Mode

The Capture and Punch Capture commands work with Trim automation in the same way as regular automation. Pro Tools saves Trim status when capturing, so if you attempt to punch captured Trim values while displaying a non-Trim automation playlist, Pro Tools will automatically apply the values to the corresponding Trim playlist.

Using real-time Trim mode with Capture allows you to rebalance your track levels, by first letting you capture currently writing trim volume offset (delta change), and then writing the new trim value at a different track location using Punch Capture.

To Capture Trim automation and punch in the volume trim values at a different location on audio track:

1. In the AUTOMATION window, verify that volume is write-enabled.

2. Select the desired audio tracks and enable TRIM with LATCH mode on the selected tracks.

Tip: Although this workflow step most often uses Trim with Latch mode, Touch, Touch/Latch, and Write modes with Trim are also supported.

3. Start playback and begin writing new trim automation.

4. Do one of the following:

    • To capture all currently writing trim controls, click the CAPTURE button in the Automation window during playback.

    • To capture all currently writing trim controls on only the selected tracks, OPTION+SHIFT-CLICK (Mac) or ALT+SHIFT-CLICK (Windows) the CAPTURE button in the Automation window during playback.

5. Stop playback.

6. Position the playback position at the point on the track where you want to start writing the PUNCH CAPTURE TRIM settings and do one of the following:

    • To punch in on the currently isolated trim controls, click the PUNCH CAPTURE button in the Automation window.

    • To punch in on the currently isolated trim controls on only the selected tracks, OPTION+SHIFT-CLICK (Mac) or ALT+SHIFT-CLICK (Windows) the PUNCH CAPTURE button in the Automation window.

    All isolated trim controls on tracks in TOUCH, LATCH, or WRITE mode will become primed for writing automation. Tracks in TOUCH will be switched to LATCH, to facilitate the punch.

7. Start playback. The isolated parameters will begin writing from the new trim values you configured from the playback position. Pro Tools saves Trim status when capturing, so if you attempt to Punch Capture Trim values while displaying a non-Trim automation playlist, Pro Tools will automatically apply the values to the corresponding Trim playlist.

Using the Punch Capture and Write to Commands

As mentioned in the "Workflow Example 2" section, after issuing a Punch Capture command, the affected controls will be writing automation (in Latch mode), so any of the automation Write to commands can be used to extend the punched value in the same manner as other automation.

Using Capture and Preview Mode

You can preview and modify captured automation values in Preview mode before punching the values to the automation playlist.

To capture multiple automation values and use them to preview:

1. Make sure the track where you want to preview the value is enabled for automation (**Touch**, **Latch**, or **Touch/Latch**).

2. Make sure the automation type you want to preview is enabled in the Automation window (**Volume**, **Pan**, **Mute**, **Send level**, **Send pan**, **Send mute**, or **Plug-In**).

3. Capture the automation values that you want to preview in another location on the track.

4. Go to a location where you want to preview the captured automation states, and click the **Preview** button in the Automation window.

5. Click the **Punch Capture** button. The affected controls will be isolated and updated to the captured values and the **Punch Preview** button in the Automation window will light to indicate the preview value is available to punch.

6. Start playback and adjust the isolated control to audition the changes.

7. When you are ready to punch the preview value to the automation playlist, click the lit **Punch Preview** button.

When you are in Preview mode, you can capture the values of isolated controls and apply them elsewhere on a track. By capturing Preview values this way, the Preview values can be stored and then recalled at a later point regardless of whether the Preview values were subsequently changed after this Capture, effectively allowing three states of automation to be active at one time—the underlying automation, the previewing automation, and the automation previously captured from Preview.

To capture a preview value:

1. Activate **Preview** mode and isolate a control.

2. Start playback and adjust the isolated control to audition the changes.

3. When you are ready to capture the previewed value, click the CAPTURE button in the Automation window. The PUNCH CAPTURE button in the Automation window will light to indicate a captured value is available to punch.

Using Join and AutoJoin

Latch mode is a common automation mode used for long format mixing. It makes it possible to have several faders writing at once, without needing to keep them held in position. One problem, however, is that if playback is stopped in the middle of a pass, you will be left with sudden jumps in the automation graphs. The Join and AutoJoin functions address this situation.

Using Join

The solution to the situation described previously is to drop all the parameters that were previously writing back into writing during the next pass, before the point where playback was stopped. This could be achieved manually by touching the appropriate faders during the next pass to start them writing again. However, this can be a complex situation to manage manually when working in long format and touching many faders and different parameters during a pass. The Join command gets previously written parameters writing again at the point you want to start.

Note: The Join command is accessed using an Avid compatible worksurface or by Command-clicking (Mac) or Option-clicking (Windows) on the AutoJoin button in the Automation Enable window. For more information about using the Join command using an Avid worksurface, consult the corresponding worksurface guide.

Using AutoJoin

AutoJoin automates the process of resuming automation writing from one pass to the next. With AutoJoin mode enabled, Pro Tools will remember where playback was stopped and which faders were writing in Latch mode. With that information, if the engineer has to stop during an automation pass, Pro Tools will resume writing automation for all previously writing controls at the precise position where the previous pass was stopped. This is useful in situations where you are automating a long format piece and have to stop to check something. As long as you do not move the cursor past the point at which you stopped (the AutoJoin point), Pro Tools will automatically pick up recording the parameters that were last recording. If Pro Tools did not do this, there would be a jump in the automation graph that you would have to manage manually, as seen in Figure 8.30.

When playback is stopped, a red line will appear to show where the AutoJoin will take place, as seen in Figure 8.30.

AutoJoin point

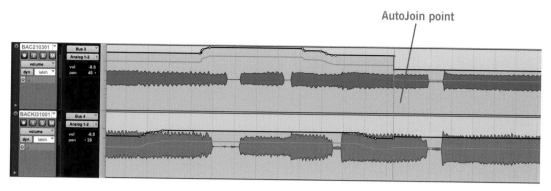

Figure 8.30
A red line indicates where writing in Latch mode last stopped.

Activating AutoJoin Mode

C|24, D-Control, and D-Command have dedicated soft keys for activating AutoJoin mode. In the absence of an Avid worksurface, AutoJoin mode can also be enabled in the Automation window by pressing the AutoJoin button, as shown in Figure 8.31.

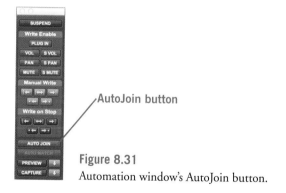

AutoJoin button

Figure 8.31
Automation window's AutoJoin button.

Using AutoJoin

Example of AutoJoin workflow:

1. Enable **AUTOJOIN** from the Automation window or supported Avid work-surface.

2. Start an automation pass with several faders writing in **LATCH** mode.

3. Stop playback and locate the playback cursor to an earlier point. A red line will appear to show where playback was stopped.

4. Touch one of the faders to rewrite automation data. The other faders will drop into **LATCH** record when you reach the point where playback was previously stopped.

Caution: When writing automation using AutoJoin, if you decide to abort an automation pass, do not stop playback until passing the red line. Otherwise, subsequent automation passes will not resume writing of the desired parameters. Instead, automation will resume writing using the last written parameters from the aborted pass.

Understanding the AutoMatch Functions

The AutoMatch Time setting (Setup > Preferences, Mixing tab) is used to specify the rate at which automation values return to their underlying settings when you release a fader or control in Touch automation mode. See Figure 8.32.

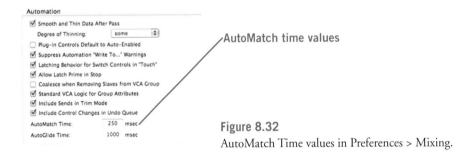

AutoMatch time values

Figure 8.32
AutoMatch Time values in Preferences > Mixing.

Similarly, the AutoMatch control in the Automation window enables the faders (in Latch or Write mode) to glide back to any underlying automation when you activate it. In this section, you will learn how AutoMatch can be used in other automation modes in conjunction with an Avid worksurface. See Figure 8.33.

Figure 8.33
Global AutoMatch button in Automation window.

Using AutoMatch in Latch and Write Modes

With Latch and Write modes, AutoMatch can be invoked manually, instead of by letting go of the fader as you do in Touch mode. This lets you end an automation pass smoothly, instead of by pressing Stop, which usually results in a jump in the volume automation.

Individual Tracks Versus Global AutoMatch

To "AutoMatch-out" of an automation pass on a single track from Latch or Write mode:

1. Start the automation-writing pass.

2. When you want to stop writing automation, do one of the following:

   - COMMAND-CLICK (Mac) or CTRL-CLICK (Windows) on the channel's AUTO button in the Mix or Edit window to AutoMatch-out on that track only.

   - If you're using an Avid worksurface, press the track's individual AUTO switch to AutoMatch-out on that track only.

   - COMMAND-CLICK (Mac) or CTRL-CLICK (Windows) on an AUTOMATION ENABLE button in the Automation window (such as VOL). This will AutoMatch the individual parameter back to previous values on all tracks.

To AutoMatch-out all parameters writing on all tracks:

- Click the global AUTOMATCH button in the Automation window. The automation will glide back to the underlying automation using the AutoMatch time set in the Mixing page of Preferences.

To AutoMatch-out a single parameter writing on all tracks:

- COMMAND-CLICK (Mac) or CTRL-CLICK (Windows) on an AUTOMATION ENABLE button in the Automation window (such as VOL). Doing so will AutoMatch the individual parameter back to previous values on all tracks.

Miscellaneous Automation Techniques

In addition to the advanced automation techniques you have learned in this lesson, some additional automation mute and glide techniques are available.

Resuming Recording of Mute Automation

When working with mute automation, you may need to extend previously created mute automation to capture more of a reverb tail, adjust the timing of a mute in a group of tracks, and so forth. In the following MIDI example (see Figure 8.34), you need to extend the mute, as shown in Figure 8.35.

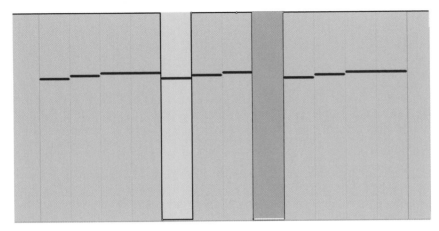

Figure 8.34
Original Mute automation graph.

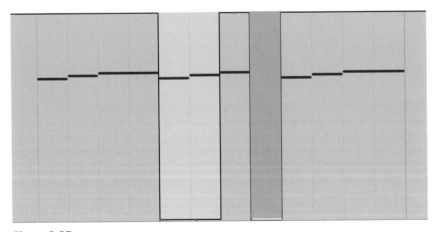

Figure 8.35
Extended Mute automation.

Without editing the mute graph, this would only be possible using Write mode, because the Mute button cannot be held in one state to extend automation. As soon as you press the Mute button, it will toggle to the opposite state.

However, by holding a modifier key, you can extend the mute automation in its present state instead of toggling it. This will work in Touch, Latch, and Touch/Latch modes.

To extend (or overwrite) mute automation:

1. Make sure that **MUTE** automation is write-enabled in the Automation window.

2. Switch to **TOUCH**, **LATCH**, or **TOUCH/LATCH** mode on the tracks you want to update.

3. Begin playback before the point containing the mute automation you want to extend.

4. **COMMAND-CLICK** (Mac) or **CTRL-CLICK** (Windows) on a **MUTE** button. The Mute button will not change its state but instead will begin to write its current state to the automation graph.

Note: In Write, Latch and Touch/Latch modes, the mute automation will continue to be written until you stop playback. In Touch mode, you will need to keep the button or mouse held down to keep overwriting and replacing changes in mute state.

Extending Automation

Sometimes you need to extend an existing area of static automation later in time. Consider a situation in which you have faded a track's volume all the way down during an automation pass and then stopped playback before you reached the end of the audio. See Figure 8.36.

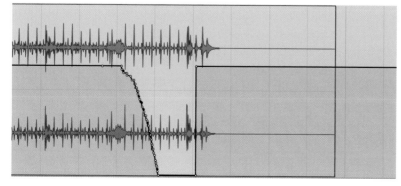

Figure 8.36
Audio clip with incorrect volume automation.

There are a number of ways to resolve this issue, but two quick and precise ways are to use either the Edit > Automation > Write to All Enabled command or the Edit > Automation > Write to Current command (covered earlier in this lesson).

To extend all automation later in time:

1. Use the SELECTOR tool to select from a point near the end of your pass to the point that you want to extend the automation parameter to, as shown in Figure 8.37.

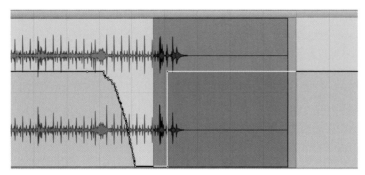

Figure 8.37
Audio clip area selected for extending volume automation.

2. Choose EDIT > AUTOMATION > WRITE TO ALL ENABLED, or press OPTION+ COMMAND+FORWARD SLASH (/) (Mac) or ALT+CTRL+FORWARD SLASH (/) (Windows). Figure 8.38 shows the corrected volume automation.

Caution: Using Edit > Automation > Write to All Enabled will write the current automation values to all enabled automation graphs in the selection, which could overwrite and replace existing automation that you want to keep.

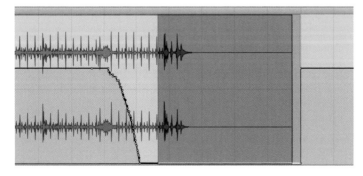

Figure 8.38
Audio clip with corrected volume automation.

This works because automation parks at the beginning of the selection, so these setting are written throughout the selection when you choose the Write to command.

Choosing Which Parameters Are Written

As an alternative to the previous workflow, provided the Allow Latch Prime in Stop Mixing preference is enabled and you are using an Avid worksurface, you can also use the Write to All command to choose exactly which parameters are extended. In the previous example, only the volume automation needed to be extended.

To extend select automation parameters later in time:

1. Use the SELECTOR tool to select from a point near the end of your pass to where you want to extend the automation parameter.

2. Touch the parameters that you want to write (in the example, that would just be the volume fader).

3. Choose WRITE TO ALL in the Automation window or on an Avid worksurface.

Using Glide Automation

The Glide automation commands let you manually create an automation transition (or glide) from an existing automation value to a new one, over a selected area. This is useful in music projects, since it enables controls to glide smoothly (or morph) from one setting to the next, providing smoother and more precise transitions between automated controls (such as plug-ins or volume faders).

Tip: When gliding multiple parameters at the same time, such as with the Surround Panner or plug-ins, use Edit > Automation > Glide Automation > To All Current Parameters with only the desired parameters enabled in the Automation window.

To apply Glide automation to the current automation parameter type:

1. In the Automation window, make sure the automation type is write-enabled.

2. Using the TRACK VIEW SELECTOR, choose the graph you want to automate.

3. With the SELECTOR tool, select the source tracks and area you want to write the Glide automation to.

4. If there is no automation on the track, verify that the track automation is at the correct starting point, and then choose EDIT > AUTOMATION > WRITE TO ALL ENABLED. If there is already automation on the track, you can skip this step.

5. Change the automation parameter to the desired value at the end of the selection. For example, to glide the volume from Unity Gain (0.0dB) to –Infinity, move the Volume fader to –Infinity.

6. Do one of the following:

   • Choose EDIT > AUTOMATION > GLIDE TO CURRENT.

   • Press OPTION+FORWARD SLASH (/) (Mac) or ALT+FORWARD SLASH (/) (Windows).

To apply Glide automation to all current enabled automation parameters:

1. In the Automation window, make sure the automation type is write-enabled.

2. In the Synth track select the Cutoff automation graph with the TRACK VIEW SELECTOR (see Figure 8.39).

3. With the SELECTOR tool, select the first clip on the SYNTH track.

4. If there is no automation on the track, verify that the track automation is at the correct starting point, and then choose EDIT > AUTOMATION > WRITE TO ALL ENABLED. If there is already automation on the track, you can skip this step.

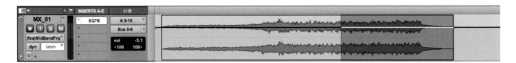

Figure 8.39
Track selection with cutoff graph shown.

5. In each track that you want to automate, change the automation parameter to the desired value at the end of the selection.

6. Do one of the following:

   • Choose EDIT > AUTOMATION > GLIDE TO ALL ENABLED.

   • Press OPTION+SHIFT+FORWARD SLASH (/) (Mac) or ALT+SHIFT+FORWARD SLASH (/) (Windows).

In Figure 8.40, the MidBand Frequency of a 7-Band EQ III has changed. But instead of an instantaneous change, it is a smooth change, or a glide from the previous point.

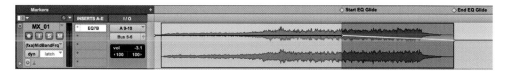

Figure 8.40
Changed cutoff filter setting.

Glide Automation Considerations

When Glide automation is applied to automation data, it behaves as follows:

- When a selection is made, the automation value at the start of the selection is the start point of the Glide automation, and the automation value at the end of the selection is the end point of the Glide automation. The Glide automation that is created between the two is based on the length of the selection and the end value that is selected.

- If a selection is made and automation data exists before the start of the selection, automation breakpoints are written at the start and end points of the Glide automation.

- If automation breakpoints follow the selection, they are not changed, but the value selected for the end of the selection is written from the end point to the next breakpoint.

- If no automation breakpoints follow the selection, the value selected for the end of the selection is written to the end of the track.

- If no selection is made, a breakpoint is written to the current location, and the value selected for the Glide automation is written to the next breakpoint.

Tip: As an alternative to using the Edit > Automation > Glide commands, you can create static snapshots of your preferred starting and ending settings, and then use the Edit > Cut Special Automation commands to smooth the transitions.

Using Trim Automation

Pro Tools lets you use trim automation values as snapshots and apply the relative changes (delta values) to the selected automation by using the Trim Automation command. This works in much the same way as the Write Automation command, except that it writes delta values instead of absolute values to automation data.

You can use trim values in writing snapshot automation to any automatable parameter, such as trimming a pan setting in order to move pan automation more toward the left or right speaker, scaling a reverb decay graph higher or lower to change room size, or even scale an EQ gain graph higher or lower to make an EQ brighter or duller sounding near the center frequency. You can also apply the Trim to automation to more standard automation graphs such as volume and send level, to rebalance track or send levels without the need to completely replace the existing automation.

To create a snapshot of relative changes in automation data:

1. If you're using TRIM TO ALL ENABLED, in the Automation window, make sure that the automation parameters you want to edit are write-enabled. Deselect any automation parameters you want to preserve.

2. Select the area of the track you want to edit. All automated controls update to reflect the automation at the beginning of the selection.

3. Move the controls for the parameter by the amount you want to change the data.

4. Choose EDIT > AUTOMATION and do one of the following:

    • To write the current delta value to only the currently selected automation graphs, choose TRIM TO CURRENT, COMMAND+SHIFT+FORWARD SLASH (/) (Mac) or CTRL+SHIFT+FORWARD SLASH (/) (Windows).

    • To write the current delta value for all automation parameters enabled in the Automation window, choose TRIM TO ALL ENABLED, OPTION+ COMMAND+SHIFT+FORWARD SLASH (/) (Mac) or CTRL+ALT+SHIFT+ FORWARD SLASH (/) (Windows).

Review/Discussion Questions

1. What must you configure first before using AFL/PFL solos?

2. Describe how you would calculate and correct for a Hardware Insert delay.

3. How do you configure a plug-in as a favorite?

4. Describe the differences between Master Faders, Aux Input submasters, and VCA Master tracks.

5. Why is a VCA Master useful when used in combination with an Auxiliary submaster?

6. Briefly explain when or why it is useful to coalesce VCA automation.

7. What are the two families of Write commands?

8. What is the purpose of the mixing preference called Allow Latch Prime in Stop?

9. What is AutoJoin, and how is it useful for mixing?

10. What is AutoMatch, and how is it useful for mixing?

11. Describe the difference between Capture and punching versus Preview and punching.

12. Provide an example of how Glide automation is used to morph effects.

Advanced Mixing and Routing

This exercise allows you to experiment with the advanced submixing and automation techniques you learned about in this lesson.

Media Used:
310M Exercise 8.PTXT (Pro Tools session template)

Duration:
45–60 minutes

Getting Started

Open the 310M Exercise 8 session. This session is a continuation of the same session you have used previously in the course. With Exercise 8, you have all of the original tracks in the session at your disposal to produce a finished mix of the song. You should rely on what you have learned in this course with regard to advanced mixing topics, as well as other Avid learning courses, to finish the mix.

Submixing

Submixing (or stem mixing) allows you to manage large sessions quickly and efficiently. With the addition of VCA Master faders, you can rebalance a mix by moving Mix groups with a single VCA fader while retaining individual fader control. This allows you to quickly rebalance a Mix group or rebalance the whole mix without having to keep track of what groups are enabled/disabled or having to remember to clutch a fader out of group control to fine-tune a mix. VCA-based workflows, when combined with X-OR Solo mode, also allow you to focus in on the sound of individual tracks or groups as well as return to a full mix quickly and efficiently.

In this section you will:

- Group like tracks together

- Route tracks into Aux submasters

- Create VCA Master fader for your groups

Some shortcut keys to remember:

- Route selected tracks: hold Option+Shift (Mac) or Alt+Shift (Windows).

- Route selected tracks into a new or existing track: Hold Option+Shift (Mac) or Alt+Shift (Windows) and click on a selected track's output selector. Then, select track > *track name*, as shown in Figure Ex8.1.

Figure Ex8.1
Using the Route to Existing Track option.

Your first task is to group like tracks together into Mix groups (drums, guitars, and so forth). The drum tracks have already been grouped (into a group called Drums). Follow Table Ex8.1 to group the remaining tracks.

Your next task will be to route the tracks into their appropriate submaster using the appropriate bus. For example, the drum tracks have been bussed to the Drum Sub track using the internal mix bus called Drums, as shown in Figure Ex8.2.

Figure Ex8.2
Drum tracks routed to the Drum Sub submaster track.

Refer to Table Ex8.1 for the remaining group names and routing instructions.

Note: This table relies on track numbers being shown. If track numbers do not appear near track names, choose View > Track Number.

Table Ex8.1	Tracks to Submaster Assignments			
Track	**Track #s**	**Group Name**	**Bus Name**	**Submaster Aux**
Drums	1–19	Drums	Drums	DrumSub and DrumCompressed
Basses	22–23	Basses	Basses	Bass Sub
Acoustic Guitars	25–26	AC Guitars	ACGuits	ACGuits Sub
Heavy Guitars	28–29	Heavy Guitars	Heavy Guitar Sub	Heavy Guitar Sub
Electric Guitars	31–36	Elec Guitars	Guitar Sub	Guitar Sub
Keyboards	40–46	Keys	Keys Sub	Keys Sub
Background Vox	48–60	Bkgd Vox	Ladies Sub	Ladies Sub

Before moving on, make sure the Aux Input tracks are solo-safe enabled and X-Or Solo mode is enabled.

Creating VCA Master Tracks

Now that you have your submixes established, it's time to make VCA Master tracks. VCA Master tracks use group assignments and automation to control individual contributing, or slave, tracks.

To put grouped tracks under VCA control:

1. Create seven **VCA MASTERS** tracks.

2. Name and assign a **MIX** group to each track, as shown in Table Ex8.2.

Table Ex8.2   VCA Assignments

VCA Track Name	Group Assignment
vDrums	Drums
vBasses	Basses
vAC Guit	AC Guitars
vHvy Guitar	Heavy Guitars
vElec Guit	Elec Guitars
vKeys	Keys
vBckGround Vox	Bkgd Vox

Tip: To assign all your VCA Masters quickly, with the tracks still highlighted, use the cascade assignments modifier combination: Option+Command+Shift (Mac) or Ctrl+Alt+Shift (Windows). This will assign all VCAs in order of the group assignments.

Play the session and use just the VCA Masters to solo individual groups of tracks.

Tip: A quick way to see all the VCAs in the session easily is to choose Show Only > VCA Masters in the Tracks List pop-up menu in the Mix or Edit window. In this mode, you can mix the entire song using just the VCA Master tracks once the relative level in each group is set.

Also experiment with soloing individual tracks under VCA control and then use solo on the VCA. Remember:

- Soloing an individual track under VCA control just solos the individual track.

- Soloing the VCA Master track clears any underlying solos (individual track solos) and solos the entire group.

- Clearing the solo on the VCA Master tracks returns you to the full mix.

Tip: Remember, mutes work slightly differently. Muting an individual track will keep the track muted (explicit mute) even if you solo and then unsolo the VCA Master track. The only way to clear individual mutes with the VCA Master involves muting all members with Option+Mute (Mac) or Alt+Mute (Windows) from the VCA Master and then unmuting all members with the same modifier.

Once you feel comfortable with how VCA Masters and member tracks work together, move on to the next section to use the VCA Masters to rebalance the whole mix.

Rebalance the Mix Using VCAs

Once you have set the relative levels of each track to achieve a good group mix, use just the VCAs to rebalance the whole mix.

Note: Remember, a VCA is not a summing point; it's a fader that controls just the level of its contributing members. When raising or lowering a VCA Master fader, you are effectively applying a trim level to the underlying member tracks. In fact, if the underlying VCA members have automation, the VCA Master will just raise or lower the overall level of the track while the track continues to vary its volume with its own automation graph.

You can leave a VCA Master fader at any level all the way through production, but at some point you should coalesce, or write, VCA levels back to their underlying tracks. This will write the trim value of the VCA Master to the main volume graph of each track and return the VCA Master track to its unity position.

Coalescing VCA Master Trims

Now that you have a good balance, you will coalesce the VCA Master automation levels into the contributing slave tracks.

You can coalesce the VCA trim amount into the contributing tracks using any of the following methods:

■ Right-click the **VCA MASTER FADER** name and choose **COALESCE VCA MASTER AUTOMATION**, as shown in Figure Ex8.3.

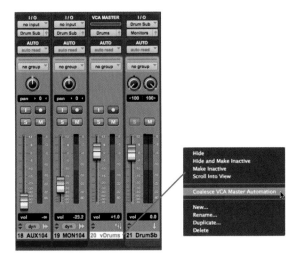

Figure Ex8.3
Right-clicking a track name to coalesce VCA Master automation.

■ Select the VCA Master fader track and choose **TRACK > COALESCE VCA MASTER AUTOMATION**. If you want to do more than one track at a time, select multiple tracks.

Latch Prime Review

Before getting into the more advanced automation modes and workflows, it helps to review Latch Prime.

Latch Prime allows you to set a fader (or any other armed control) to a new value before playback begins. Once playback begins, the new automation level is written until you press Stop, issue an automation write command, such as Write to Punch, Write to End, or Write to All, or AutoMatch the track back. Before attempting to use Latch Prime, you should check to see it is enabled.

To enable Latch Prime mode:

■ Open **PRO TOOLS PREFERENCES > MIXING** and select **ALLOW LATCH PRIME IN STOP**, as shown in Figure Ex8.4.

Figure Ex8.4
Enabling Latch Prime in Preferences > Mixing.

To demonstrate Latch Prime, you will write a new starting fader level for the GtrTheme1 track at the beginning of the session:

1. During the intro of the song, the **GtrTheme1** track has the melody and should be prominent in the mix. Enable **Latch mode** on the track. Ensure that **Volume** is enabled in the Automation window.

2. Before pressing **Play**, raise the fader to a level where it's prominent in the mix. The **Automation Mode** selector on the track will turn red to indicate the track is primed for automation, as shown in Figure Ex8.5.

3. Press **Play**. When the whole band comes in at Bar 11, **AutoMatch** the **GtrTheme1** track back to its original level by **Command-clicking** (Mac) or **Ctrl-clicking** (Windows) on the **Automation Mode** selector, as shown in Figure Ex8.5.

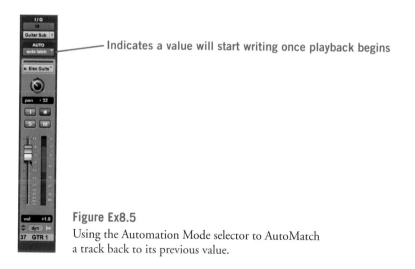

Indicates a value will start writing once playback begins

Figure Ex8.5
Using the Automation Mode selector to AutoMatch
a track back to its previous value.

4. Press **Stop**. Return and listen to the introduction to hear your changes.

5. At Bar 90, the Gtr1 and Gtr2 tracks are the solo guitar. Navigate to this spot and raise the faders so the parts punch. These parts should remain high for the remainder of the song. Use the **MANUAL WRITE TO END** button in the Automation window—by choosing **COMMAND+[4]** (Mac) or **CTRL+[4]** (Windows)—to write the change to the end of the song.

6. Experiment more with **LATCH PRIME** before moving on with other tracks. Latch Prime works with any auto write-enabled parameter (pan, send level, and so on). To review which parameters are enabled, open the Automation Write Enable window.

Preview Mode

Latch Prime is useful when you know what you want to write before pressing Play. But as you may have just experienced, you may not know where the right level is before pressing Play. Preview mode allows you to audition a change without committing or writing in the change. This means you can loop a section of audio over and over, trying new levels and settings without writing any data or having to write and then undo. You'll use Preview mode to set levels of the background vocals, write those values, and then use Punch Preview repeatedly to write the same levels to the different sections of the song.

To enable Preview mode:

1. Start by opening the Automation window if you haven't already done so by choosing **WINDOW > AUTOMATION** or **COMMAND+[4]** (Mac) or **CTRL+[4]** (Windows) on the numeric keypad.

2. Click on the **PREVIEW** button so that it turns green, as shown in Figure Ex8.6.

Figure Ex8.6
Enabling Preview mode in the Automation window.

3. Select **BARS 11–19**. Using the Bkg Vox VCA, solo just the background singers.

4. Enable LATCH MODE on the Bkg Vox tracks and the Bkg Vox VCA track.

5. Using Track#66 (LadiesVc), set all the other background tracks to match the balance of this stereo recording of the choir. As you move faders or adjust pans, the Automation Mode selector will turn green, as shown in Figure Ex8.7. If you're unsure, open the Automation window and ensure Pan is enabled for automation.

Figure Ex8.7
Tracks with isolated parameters will have a green Automation Mode selector.

6. To compare your changes to the original, COMMAND-CLICK (Mac) or CTRL-CLICK (Windows) on the PREVIEW button in the Automation window to suspend Preview mode. The PREVIEW button will turn opaque, indicating Preview mode is suspended, as shown in Figure Ex8.8.

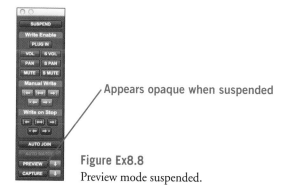

Appears opaque when suspended

Figure Ex8.8
Preview mode suspended.

7. To exit the Preview Suspend, **COMMAND-CLICK** (Mac) or **CTRL-CLICK**
    (Windows) on the **PREVIEW** button again to return to your Preview values.
    If you want to clear the preview values and start again, simply click the
    PREVIEW button to empty the preview buffer.

Punch Preview

Once you are happy with the balance, you'll need to write in the changes (that is,
Punch Preview them).

To punch and write the Preview values:

1. While still in **PREVIEW** mode, switch to the Edit window and show the
    VOLUME AUTOMATION playlists for the tracks.

2. While playing back, press the **PUNCH PREVIEW** button located next to the
    Preview Mode button in the Automation window.

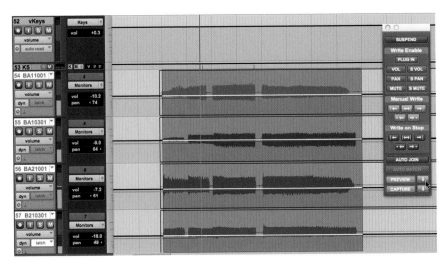

Figure Ex8.9
Punch Preview button in the Automation window.

3. The **AUTOMATION MODE** selectors on the tracks that have Preview values
    will turn from green to red, indicating that automation is writing, as
    shown in Figure Ex8.10.

4. Press **STOP**. You will see where you wrote in the automation. But the
    automation display will have a jump where you pressed the **PUNCH**
    PREVIEW button, as shown in Figure Ex8.11.

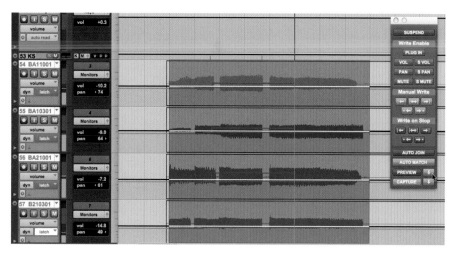

Figure Ex8.10
Punched values written to tracks.

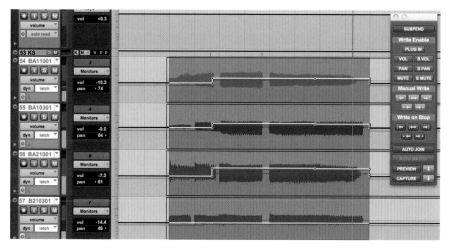

Figure Ex8.11
Automation jumps when the Punch button is pressed.

5. With **BARS 11–19** still selected, press the **PUNCH PREVIEW** button again while stopped. This will set the faders back to the preview values, and the tracks will be ready to write.

6. Instead of pressing Play, use the **MANUAL WRITE AUTOMATION TO SELECTION** button in the Automation window. Notice that the level is written for the whole selection, as shown in Figure Ex8.12.

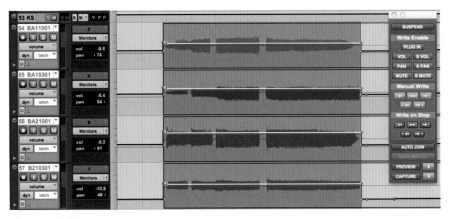

Figure Ex8.12
Writing punched values while stopped.

7. Now that you have solid levels and balance for the whole choir, you can select each choir entrance and punch the mix values and then use the **MANUAL WRITE TO SELECTION** button to write in the changed levels, as shown in Figure Ex8.13.

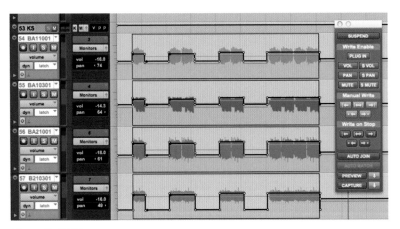

Figure Ex8.13
Writing punched values across all choir entrances.

Again, the workflow is this:

1. Make a selection.

2. Click the **PUNCH PREVIEW** button.

3. Write the change by either pressing **PLAY** or using a **MANUAL WRITE TO** button.

You can use this same workflow to take a mix of the guitars, keyboards, and so forth and punch the levels into the mix for each time the same group of tracks repeats itself.

Using Glide Automation

One of the more advanced automation modes you learned about was Glide automation. Glide automation is a static mixer automation workflow as opposed to the real-time automation workflow you were just working with. With music production, Glide automation is often used for morphing effects such as going from one reverb setting to another over a specified amount of time. You'll use this workflow to add a creative element to the end of the song using the cutoff filter and drive settings of the AIR Fuzz-Wah plug-in.

To use Glide automation to morph a sound:

1. Navigate to the **EVERY DARK PULSE 1.1** track and solo the track. Navigate to Bar 133 and press **PLAY** to hear the current sound.

2. Insert a multichannel Harmonic plug-in named **AIR FUZZ-WAH** on the track. See Figure Ex8.14.

Figure Ex8.14
Stereo AIR Fuzz-Wah plug-in.

3. Enable the **PEDAL MIN FREQ** and **FUZZ DRIVE** parameters for automation by holding **CONTROL+OPTION+COMMAND** (Mac) or **CTRL+START+ALT** (Windows) while clicking on each parameter control, as shown in Figure Ex8.15. The indicator for the parameter will turn green, indicating the plug-in parameter is enabled for automation (it will turn red if the track is enabled for Write/Latch/Touch mode).

Figure Ex8.15
Automation enable shortcut for plug-in parameters.

4. With the cursor at **BAR 133** on the **EVERY** DARK PULSE track, choose **EDIT > AUTOMATION > WRITE TO ALL ENABLED**.

5. Next, move the cursor to **BAR 138**. Adjust the **DRIVE** to 40dB and the **PEDAL MIN FREQ** to 4.00kHz.

6. Choose **EDIT > AUTOMATION > GLIDE TO ALL ENABLED**.

7. Return the cursor to **BAR 133** and press **PLAY**. If you want to see the automation graphs you just wrote, hold down **CONTROL+COMMAND** (Mac) or **CTRL+START** (Windows) and click on the **DRIVE** or **PEDAL MIN** control to see the corresponding automation graph, as shown in Figure Ex8.16. You can also click the **SHOW/HIDE AUTOMATION LANES** triangle at the head of the track to display multiple automation graphs simultaneously.

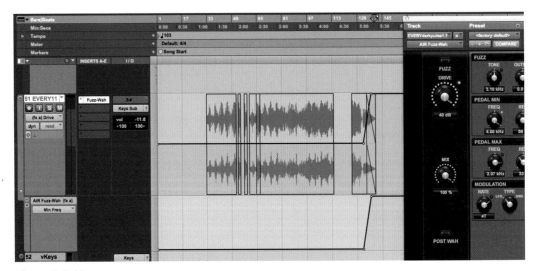

Figure Ex8.16
Multiple automation graphs showing Glide automation.

8. Experiment with other parameters and other plug-ins to create sonically interesting effects.

Creating the Final Mix

Now is your opportunity to use all the mixing and automation techniques you have learned in this course, as well as other Avid Learning Series courses to complete a mix of the song. Reverbs and delays should be added to fill out the mix. Compression and EQ could be used to further sculpt the sound. As a Pro Tools Expert, you should feel comfortable using and explaining all the submixing and automation techniques discussed in these courses. Once you have finished the mix, save your project so you can use it with Exercise 9 to deliver your final mixes to the final stage of production.

Music Delivery

This lesson looks at the different methods for exporting, delivering, transferring, and archiving your finished Pro Tools session.

Media Used: None

Duration: 45 minutes

GOALS

- Export MIDI
- Send to Sibelius
- Export as OMF/AAF/MXF
- Archive and transfer sessions

Introduction

Bouncing your mix to disk is just one of many ways to output your Pro Tools project. Pro Tools can export all the MIDI tracks from the session, either to be worked on in a different software package or to create scores. Pro Tools can also generate online media files such as MP3, with all the necessary metadata embedded. Support is also available for exporting to standard interchange formats such as AAF, allowing the project to be shared with many other professional audio and video editing systems. In addition to looking at these export options, this lesson discusses the points you need to consider when moving a Pro Tools session to another Pro Tools–based studio.

Exporting MIDI

Exporting MIDI tracks from a session is necessary only when moving to another application. All MIDI data is stored within the Pro Tools session file, so if you want to transfer MIDI to another Pro Tools system, you can simply transfer the session file and import the tracks.

Tip: You can also transfer a specific section of MIDI to another Pro Tools system by turning it into a clip group and then exporting the clip group.

Exporting to Another MIDI Application

If you need to transfer MIDI files to another audio package, or even to a hardware device, you can export all the MIDI tracks in the session as a Standard MIDI File (SMF). Pro Tools can export MIDI as both Type 0 (combined) and Type 1 (multitrack) SMFs.

To export a Pro Tools MIDI file into a separate MIDI application:

1. In Pro Tools, choose FILE > EXPORT > MIDI. See Figure 9.1.

Figure 9.1
Export MIDI command in the File menu.

2. In the Export MIDI Settings dialog box, choose a MIDI file format option and indicate whether the sequence starts at the song start marker or the session start. See Figure 9.2.

Figure 9.2
Export MIDI Settings dialog box.

3. Choose whether the MIDI tracks should have their real-time properties (if any) applied.

4. Click **OK**. A Save dialog box will appear.

5. Name the file, and choose where it will be saved.

6. Click **SAVE**.

The MIDI file can now be imported into another program (see Figure 9.3). If you chose a Type 1 export (recommended), the third-party application will be able to bring in all the separate tracks with the correct track names. See Figure 9.4.

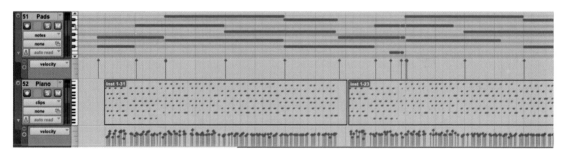

Figure 9.3
The MIDI tracks in a Pro Tools session.

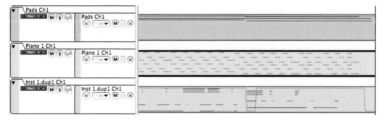

Figure 9.4
The same tracks imported into Reason; controller data and track names are included.

Exporting to Sibelius

Pro Tools 8 introduced notation functionality to Pro Tools, along with improved project interchange features with the dedicated scoring package Sibelius. You can now create native Sibelius project files (.SIB files) from Pro Tools, or you can send the currently open session directly to Sibelius if you have it installed on the same machine.

Tip: To export or send a project to Sibelius, it helps to set up the score in Pro Tools before exporting (that is, Title, composer, key, and so on). Also note that the Export and Send to Sibelius options are available only when the Score Editor window is open and focused.

To export notated MIDI tracks from Pro Tools to a Sibelius .SIB file:

1. Open the **SCORE EDITOR WINDOW** in Pro Tools, shown in Figure 9.5.

2. Use the track list to choose which MIDI tracks are displayed.

3. Define the **NOTATION TRACK DISPLAY SETTINGS** for each part.

4. Configure the **GENERAL DISPLAY SETTINGS** for the project with the Score Setup window.

Figure 9.5
Score Editor window in Pro Tools.

5. Choose FILE > EXPORT > SIBELIUS, as shown in Figure 9.6.

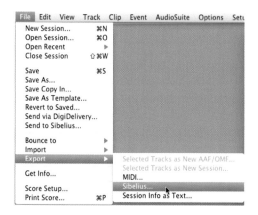

Figure 9.6
Export MIDI tracks to a Sibelius .SIB file.

To send notated MIDI tracks directly to a new score in Sibelius:

1. Complete steps 1–4 from the previous section.

2. Choose FILE > SEND TO SIBELIUS (see Figure 9.7). If Sibelius is installed on your computer, it will launch automatically (if it's not already running), and a new score will be created with the same name as the Pro Tools session.

Figure 9.7
Send to Sibelius command in the File menu.

Viewing Other Parts in Sibelius

When you send a session to Sibelius, or open an exported .SIB file, you will see an almost exact copy of the view you set up in the Score Editor in Pro Tools. Only the tracks that were visible in the Score Editor will be displayed in Sibelius. However, all MIDI and Instrument tracks are included in the export, and the hidden parts can also be viewed and edited in Sibelius.

To view hidden parts in Sibelius, do one of the following:

- Choose VIEW > FOCUS ON STAVES (this will deselect this option, which is on by default in any project sent or exported from Pro Tools).

- Click the FOCUS ON STAVES button in the Sibelius toolbar (see Figure 9.8).

All of the MIDI/Instrument parts from the original Pro Tools session will be displayed.

Figure 9.8
The Focus on Staves button in the toolbar (to view any hidden parts).

Reviewing AAF and OMF Export

The AAF and OMF file interchange formats are discussed in detail in Lesson 4, "Importing and Recording Audio."

Since the AAF standard is a newer, more feature-rich industry standard, it is recommended over the OMF export option. When exporting as AAF, clip names, timeline positions, and volume, mute, and pan automation data are retained. As you learned earlier, AAF sequences do not support information about plug-in assignments or parameters, routing, multichannel tracks, or grouping. Also, AAF/OMF exports are on a track-by-track basis; only tracks that are selected will be included in the export.

Note: Volume and pan automation is removed from AAF/OMF exports when either Enforce Avid Compatibility or Quantize Edits to Frame Boundaries is enabled. If exporting to a platform that fully supports AAF, you should not choose these options on export unless the project is returning to an Avid-editing product.

OMF should be used only for exports to systems that do not support AAF. When exporting OMF files, only timecode addresses, clip names, and clip definitions are retained. Volume, Mute, and Pan information is exported as well if Avid Compatibility and Quantize to Frame Boundaries is turned off.

The following is an outline for performing an AAF/OMF export. The options are discussed further afterward.

To export one or more selected audio tracks as AAF/OMF sequences:

1. In the Edit or Mix window, select the tracks that you want to export.

2. Choose FILE > EXPORT > SELECTED TRACKS AS NEW AAF/OMF. The Export to OMF/AAF dialog box will appear, as shown in Figure 9.9.

Figure 9.9
Export to OMF/AAF dialog box.

3. Select **AAF** or **OMF** from the EXPORT AS pop-up menu.

4. At this point you could choose whether you want to apply SAMPLE RATE CONVERSION. This is often necessary when you're sending a project to a video-editing platform that defaults to 48kHz sample rates. For music-only projects, it's best to retain the original sample rate.

5. Choose an audio file format from the FORMAT pop-up menu. Again, if you're going to another music platform, there is no need to change the audio format unless otherwise specified. See Figure 9.10.

Figure 9.10
OMF/AAF export file type options.

6. Choose a bit depth (16 or 24) for the exported media. Pro Tools will apply the AudioSuite dithering algorithm without noise shaping when reducing bit depth from 24-bit to 16-bit.

7. In the **COPY OPTION** pop-up menu, choose one of the options shown in Figure 9.11.

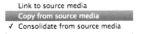

Figure 9.11
OMF/AAF file reference options.

8. After configuring the AAF/OMF export settings as desired, click **OK**. The Publishing Options dialog box will appear, as shown in Figure 9.12.

9. Enter Pro Tools comments (if desired) and a sequence name and click **OK**.

Figure 9.12
Publishing options dialog box for OMF/AAF Export.

10. Name the AAF/OMF sequence file, choose a location, and click **SAVE**. Pro Tools will append the proper AAF or OMF file extension automatically.

    After you save the AAF/OMF file, if you did not choose **EMBEDDED MEDIA**, another dialog box will prompt you to choose a folder for the media files. This should be the same folder as the one with the OMF/AAF folder or an immediate subdirectory. This will facilitate successful relinking on the target system.

Understanding the AAF/OMF Export Options

The following sections explain the options in the AAF/OMF export dialog box.

Quantize Edits to Frame Boundaries

Most video editing programs, such as Media Composer, only support frame-accurate editing. In these programs, you can edit sounds only on whole frame boundaries, limiting your precision. The Quantize Edits to Frame Boundaries setting creates one-frame-long audio clips that force all edits to align to the frame grid (shown in Figure 9.13).

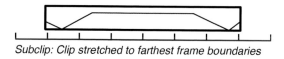

Subclip: Clip stretched to farthest frame boundaries

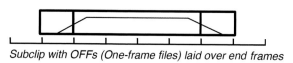

Subclip with OFFs (One-frame files) laid over end frames

Figure 9.13
Quantize Edits to Frame Boundaries media examples.

Sample Rate Conversion Options

These settings allow you to convert the sample rate of your Pro Tools session during export to AAF/OMF by sample-rate converting each sound file. You may want to change the sample rate of a session if you are exporting to a system that requires a different sample rate.

- **Source Sample Rate**—This setting allows you to specify the sample rate of the material you are working with in Pro Tools.

- **Destination Sample Rate**—This setting allows you to specify the sample rate for audio files after the AAF/OMF translation.

Tip: As discussed in the Pro Tools 201 course, you should never perform a sample rate conversion while doing a bit-depth reduction as this would introduce dither noise into the sample rate conversion. If you need to change the sample rate and bit depth, perform a Save Copy In and change the sample rate, and then perform a bit-depth reduction with the AAF/OMF export.

Audio Formats

The available format options include the following:

- **BWF (.WAV) or AIFF**—Creates audio files in these formats.

- **MXF**—See the next section for information about MXF export.

- **Embedded**—If you choose this option, the entire project is packed into a single embedded AAF or OMF file containing all edit data and audio media.

Tip: The Embedded option can be useful, as it ensures that no media can be lost when transferring the project. When exporting as AAF/OMF, Pro Tools limits the file size of any individual media file to 2GB.

Copy Option

This pop-up menu determines how the audio files are treated during the export.

- **Link to source media**—This setting instructs Pro Tools to create an AAF/OMF sequence file that refers to the original media files where possible. This is a good option if you will transport the project on the same drive on which the export was created. Although this option saves drive space, there is a risk you will not transport all the media with the project.

- **Copy from source media**—Use this setting to copy audio to a new drive or folder. You can also sample-rate convert the audio during this translation.

- **Consolidate from source media**—Using this setting when exporting audio files from Pro Tools sessions will copy only the parts of the files that are actually used by the session. This option is similar to the Compact Selected command available in Pro Tools, including the option to specify handle lengths. You can also sample-rate convert the audio during this translation.

Understanding MXF Audio Export

MXF audio files are becoming increasingly popular in many post-production work-flows because they are supported by AAF and on many different editing systems.

You can export MXF audio files using the following commands:

- Export Selected Tracks as New AAF/OMF (AAF only)
- Export Clips as Files
- Bounce to Disk

Exporting Tracks as AAF with MXF Audio Files

To export selected audio tracks from Pro Tools as an AAF sequence referring to MXF audio files:

1. Follow the steps for creating an AAF as described in the previous section.

2. Under OMF/AAF options of the Export to OMF/AAF dialog box, choose **AAF** from the EXPORT AS pop-up menu and enable ENFORCE AVID COMPATIBILITY.

3. Under the Audio Media Options section, select **MXF** from the FORMAT pop-up menu. Continue with the usual steps.

Exporting Clips as MXF Audio Files

You can export clips as MXF audio files with the Export Clips as Files command. Use this command if you intend to use a clip in other sessions or other audio applications without using its parent source file. This command also provides a way to convert clips to a different sample rate or bit depth.

To export clips as new MXF files:

1. In the CLIPS LIST, select the clips you want to export.

2. From the CLIPS LIST pop-up menu, choose EXPORT CLIPS AS FILES or RIGHT-CLICK on a clip in the Clips List and choose EXPORT CLIPS AS FILES.

Tip: The Embedded option can be useful, as it ensures that no media can be lost when transferring the project. However, when exporting as AAF/OMF, Pro Tools limits the file size of any individual media file to 2GB.

3. In the Export Selected dialog box, enable ENFORCE AVID COMPATIBILITY.

4. Select MXF from the FILE TYPE pop-up menu.

5. Click EXPORT to export the new audio files.

Exporting MXF Audio Files Using Bounce to Disk

Use the Bounce to Disk command to create pre-mixed MXF audio files of the current Pro Tools session. This does not export all of the individual files on the timeline, but it does guarantee that the mix you hear in another application will be identical to the mix you hear in Pro Tools, including all panning, effects, and automation.

To export to MXF using Bounce to Disk:

1. After you have finished recording and mixing a session in Pro Tools, highlight the length of the session in the Timeline ruler (or on a track), plus an additional amount of time to avoid cutting off any reverb tails that might continue past the end of the session.

2. Choose FILE > BOUNCE TO > DISK.

3. In the Bounce dialog box, choose your bounce source (usually outputs 1–2).

4. Select ENFORCE AVID COMPATIBILITY.

5. Choose MXF for the file type.

6. Choose a sample rate and bit depth.

Tip: Remember, if you're reducing bit depth while performing a Bounce to Disk, dither will automatically be applied. This is especially troublesome when you're choosing a different sample rate on export.

7. Click **Bounce**.

8. Provide comments and a clip name in the Publishing Options dialog box and click **OK**.

9. In the Save Bounce As dialog box, choose the drive where you want to save the files.

10. Click **Save**. Pro Tools will begin bouncing to disk.

Archiving and Transferring Sessions

As Pro Tools is such a widely used system, it is common for projects to be delivered or transferred to another studio as a complete Pro Tools session, without any need to export to another format. You, or your clients, may also want to archive the project as a Pro Tools session (as opposed to just the final mix or stems) so that it can be reworked in the future.

Manually creating a copy of your session is impractical, as the audio files may be spread out across several drives. Instead, Pro Tools offers a built-in function for creating a copy of your session and all the files that it references.

Using Save Copy In

You encountered the Save Copy In command (accessed from the File menu) in Lesson 1, "Pro Tools HD Hardware Configuration," as well as in the Pro Tools 101 course. This command allows you to save a copy of your session using various format changes, such as changing the session file format for different versions of Pro Tools. It is also used for transferring and archiving sessions because it has the capability of gathering all the files used by the session and placing them in one folder.

To archive or transfer a session using Save Copy In:

1. Open the session you want to copy.

2. Choose **File > Save Copy In**. The Save Session Copy dialog box will open. See Figure 9.14.

3. Choose the session format. You can use this option to create a session file that is compatible with earlier versions of Pro Tools. You will be warned about any changes that may occur to your session if you do this.

4. In the **Items to Copy** section, check the **All Audio Files** option.

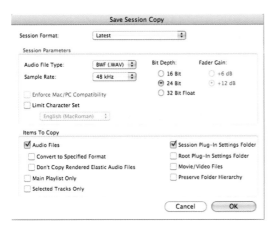

Figure 9.14
Save Session Copy dialog box.

5. You may also choose to include a copy of the SESSION PLUG-IN settings folder and the ROOT PLUG-IN settings folder. These may be useful if you have saved some plug-in settings that might be used at a later time in the project. You do not need to save these folders to maintain the current settings used in the session.

6. Click OK. A Save dialog box will open. Choose where you want to save the copy. This location will need enough free space to contain a new copy of all the media files in use by the session. This includes all audio in the Clips List that is not used in a track.

Exporting Selected Tracks as a New Session

When you're working in collaboration with other studios or engineers, it becomes necessary to pass parts of a session back and forth. For example, you may be working on a session where the drums are tracked at another studio. They will need the guide tracks from you and when done, you'll want to import the new drum tracks back into your session. Pro Tools allows you to select tracks and export them as a new session. Your collaborator can then open the new session and add to it—in this case the drum tracks. When your collaborator is done, you can import the tracks into your original session using Import Session Data.

To export selected tracks as a new session:

1. Select the tracks you want to export as a new session.

2. Select FILE > EXPORT > SELECTED TRACKS AS NEW SESSION. The Save Session Copy dialog box opens, as shown in Figure 9.15.

Tip: You can also open the Save Session Copy dialog box by selecting File Save Copy In.

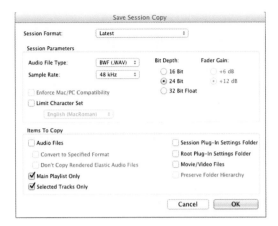

Figure 9.15
Saving tracks as a new session.

3. In the Save Session Copy dialog box, configure the **SESSION FORMAT** and **SESSION PARAMETERS** settings and options as desired.

4. Verify that the **SELECTED TRACKS ONLY** option is enabled, as shown in Figure 9.15.

5. Configure the Items to Copy settings and options as desired.

6. You can also enable the **MAIN PLAYLISTS ONLY** option if you don't want to include any of the alternate playlists associated with any of the selected tracks in the new session.

7. Click **OK**.

8. In the Save dialog box, name the session and navigate to where you want to save the session. Click **SAVE**.

Review/Discussion Questions

1. What is the difference between a MIDI Type 0 file and Type 1 file?

2. Name the two ways to export MIDI tracks to Sibelius.

3. Which options should be disabled when exporting an OMF/AAF in order to retain volume and pan automation?

4. Which types of tracks are exported with OMF/AAF?

5. What does Quantize Edits to Frame Boundaries do?

6. Explain the difference between Link to Source Media, Copy from Source Media, and Consolidate from Source Media.

7. Explain two ways to export audio as MXF files.

8. Explain the steps involved in saving a new Pro Tools session with all associated media.

9. Explain how to export several tracks as a new session.

Exporting Multitrack Sessions

This exercise walks you through saving a Pro Tools session to previous formats as well as exporting a multitrack version as an AAF/OMF Sequence file.

Media Used:
310M Exercise 9.PTXT (Pro Tools session file)

Duration:
15–20 minutes

Getting Started

In today's modern music production world, there will be times you'll need to collaborate with other studios and platforms. These other studios may or may not have Pro Tools systems.

This exercise will walk you through saving an entire Pro Tools session to an earlier format as well as saving parts of a session as a new Pro Tools session file. The exercise will also walk you through exporting the session as an AAF/OMF for collaboration with other digital audio workstations (DAWs) and video-editing platforms.

Exporting to Earlier Versions of Pro Tools

The most common way to transfer a session to another engineer is by using the Save Copy In command. Although a simple Mac Finder or Windows Explorer drag-and-drop copy of the Session Folder is easier, you may set yourself up for failure by leaving behind audio that is not located in your Audio Files folder. For example, you may have imported a file from your boot drive (like an iTunes track) and referenced it in its original location rather than copying it to your Audio Files folder.

By using the Save Copy In command to move a session, you ensure that all the audio in your session is copied from any drives used by the session.

Saving a Whole Session to a New Destination

Start by opening your saved version of PT310M Exercise 8.PTX, or if you'd rather use a prepared session, open 310M Exercise 9.PTXT.

To export a complete Pro Tools session with all media to an earlier version:

1. Choose FILE > SAVE COPY IN, as shown in Figure Ex9.1.

Figure Ex9.1
Save Copy In command in File menu.

2. The Save Session Copy dialog box opens, as shown in Figure Ex9.2. As you can see, **LATEST** is the default session format when using the **SAVE COPY IN** command.

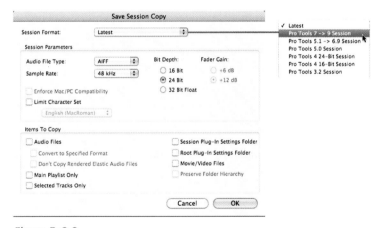

Figure Ex9.2
Save Session Copy dialog box.

3. Click on the **SESSION FORMAT** drop-down menu and choose **PRO TOOLS 7 - > 9**. See Figure Ex9.3.

Figure Ex9.3
Session Format drop-down menu.

4. Once you have chosen a session format, you must enable the **AUDIO FILES** option under **ITEMS TO COPY** as shown in Figure Ex9.4. You can include other items if you want.

Note: If you choose Pro Tools 7–9 or an earlier session format, you will not be able to choose Selected Tracks or Main Playlist Only under Items to Copy.

Figure Ex9.4
Enabling Items to Copy.

5. Click **OK**. A dialog box appears, asking where to save the session. Enter **Ex9 Copy** for a name and choose a destination that has enough disk space. When done, click **Save**. The session file will be saved in the new folder you created, along with an Audio Files folder inside with all your audio from the session.

Saving Selected Tracks as a New Session File

Pro Tools 10 added a new feature to the Save Session Copy dialog box that allows you to save selected tracks to a new session. This has also been added as a menu choice under the File menu (File > Export > Selected Tracks as New Session). This feature speeds up the time it takes to send just a portion of your session to another engineer/musician, such as just the drums for drum tuning or Beat Detective/ Elastic Audio work.

To save just the drum tracks to a new session:

1. Highlight all the drum tracks as well as the stereo loop tracks.

2. Choose **File > Export > Selected Tracks as New Session**.

3. The same Save Copy In dialog box will appear with **Selected Tracks** already selected, as shown in Figure Ex9.5.

Figure Ex9.5
Saving just selected files and associated audio.

4. Next, select **Audio Files** in the **Items to Copy** area, as shown in Figure Ex9.5.

Caution: If you skip this step, no audio will be exported with the session file.

5. Name your session and click **Save**.

Exporting AAF/OMF and MXF Files

There may come a time when you must export your Pro Tools session to another digital audio workstation or video editor in multitrack format. Exporting a multitrack AAF/OMF sequence is very similar to exporting Selected Tracks as a New Session in the previous section. However, exporting AAF/OMF comes with additional options that may affect the final export.

Exporting a Session as AAF/OMF

As you learned in the previous lesson, AAF is a newer format than OMF and should be used when the destination platform can support it. However, not all platforms work with AAF; therefore, you must use OMF when working with certain platforms. In the previous lesson you learned that you have three choices when exporting an AAF/OMF with regard to how audio media is handled: Link to Source Media, Copy All Source Media, or Consolidate Source Media. In this part of the exercise, you'll explore the first two options, which are common in music production.

Exporting AAF/OMF Files Referencing Existing Media
To export a session to AAF/OMF referencing existing media:

1. Select the tracks you want to export.

Tip: You can use Option (Mac) or Alt (Windows) to select all tracks in the session quickly. Only audio tracks and their associated metadata will be exported with the AAF/OMF file.

2. Choose FILE > EXPORT > SELECTED TRACKS AS NEW AAF/OMF. See Figure Ex9.6.

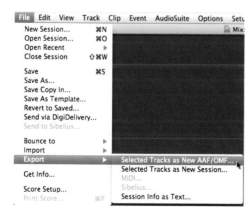

Figure Ex9.6

Export Selected Tracks as New AAF/OMF in the File menu.

3. The Export to OMF/AAF dialog box will open, as shown in Figure Ex9.7.

Figure Ex9.7
Export to OMF/AAF dialog box with defaults enabled.

4. The window defaults to AAF with settings normally reserved for video-editing platforms. With multitrack audio sessions, you will typically enable/disable options as shown in Figure Ex9.8 and the associated list.

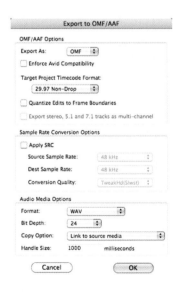

Figure Ex9.8
Export to OMF/AAF dialog box set for multitrack audio platform export.

Under OMF/AAF Options:

- **Export As**—OMF or AAF. However, if the other platform supports AAF, AAF is the preferred format.

- **Enforce Avid Compatibility**—Uncheck. This is normally reserved for video editors that require frame accuracy, not sample accuracy.

- **Quantize Edits to Frame Boundaries**—Uncheck. As stated in the lesson, this choice ensures that all audio edits are to frame edges, which is required for video editing platforms. When exporting to another audio platform, you do not want your automation or clip boundaries to change on Export. Also note, that when this option is checked, no Volume, Mute, or Pan information is included in the export.

Under Audio Media Options:

- **Copy Option**—Choose Link to Source Media (if you simply want to give the other engineer your Audio Files folder) or choose Copy from Source Media (if you want Pro Tools to make copies of all audio files no matter where the files are located on your various drives—similar to Save Copy In). For this exercise, use Link to Source Media.

5. After setting your export options, click **OK**. A Publishing Options dialog box will appear. This is your chance to add more detail about the project. Pay careful attention to the sequence name. This is used by other applications, especially video-editing platforms, for naming purposes (bins, clips, and so on). The more clarity in naming, the better the chance no problems will arise. For this exercise, use the information shown in Figure Ex9.9.

Figure Ex9.9
Publishing Options dialog box when exporting an AAF/OMF sequence file.

6. Click **OK**. A Save As dialog box will appear. The Save As operation will use the sequence name you just entered in the previous step as a default. Navigate to an appropriate place on your drive and click **SAVE**. Your final AAF/OMF sequence file will look similar to Figure Ex9.10 (the file icon will be slightly different on Windows computers).

Everything multi-track v.1.4.omf

Figure Ex9.10

Final exported AAF/OMF file.

Exporting AAF/OMF Files Copying All Media

To export a session to AAF/OMF copying all media:

1. Repeat the previous process by choosing FILE > EXPORT > SELECTED
   TRACKS AS NEW AAF/OMF. This time, select Copy from Source Media
   in the Export to OMF/AAF dialog box. See Figure Ex9.11.

Figure Ex9.11

Exporting AAF/OMF with copied audio.

2. After typing comments and naming the sequence, click **OK**. Navigate to
   the same place you saved your previous AAF/OMF sequence file and click
   SAVE.

3. An Open dialog box will appear, asking where to save the media files.
   The dialog box will default to where you just saved your AAF/OMF
   sequence file. At this point, it is best to create a new folder (call it Media
   Files). Otherwise, Pro Tools just places all files in the same directory as the
   sequence file. With large sessions with thousands of audio files, the sequence
   file can be hard to find.

4. Click **OPEN** to save the files. When you're done, your file hierarchy should
   resemble Figure Ex9.12.

Everyting-mult-track v.1.4.omf	139 KB	Open Media Framework File
Media Files	--	Folder
Everyting-mcycxHFFRrpcsMRVW.wav	37 KB	Waveform audio
Everyting-mfpmxPSCRqpcsMRVW.wav	11 MB	Waveform audio
Everyting-mymbzTFFRrpcsMRVW.wav	1.3 MB	Waveform audio
Everyting-mgrxpRRFRspcsMRVW.wav	13.8 MB	Waveform audio
Everyting-mpbpzPHFRrpcsMRVW.wav	11 MB	Waveform audio
Everyting-mqxgmFQFRspcsMRVW.wav	37 KB	Waveform audio
Everyting-mrsdrVQFRspcsMRVW.wav	1.3 MB	Waveform audio
Everyting-mgsyqXWFRspcsMRVW.wav	13.8 MB	Waveform audio
Everyting-mrrmgYCHRvpcsMRVW.wav	17.3 MB	Waveform audio
Everyting-mcfpbZZHRwpcsMRVW.wav	13.1 MB	Waveform audio
Everyting-mdxcgXRJRxpcsMRVW.wav	17.3 MB	Waveform audio
Everyting-mxrzdPBMRypcsMRVW.wav	13.1 MB	Waveform audio
msmFMID.pmr	4 KB	Document

Figure Ex9.12

Final exported AAF/OMF sequence
and supporting media files.

Pro Tools HD-Series Audio Interface Calibration

This appendix provides calibration instructions for HD-series audio interfaces, including the HD I/O and 192 I/O systems with mixed HD-series audio interfaces.

Calibrating an HD I/O or 192 I/O

The following procedure describes a method for calibrating both outputs and inputs to the same reference level using either an HD I/O or 192 I/O interface. You will need a VU or dBu meter to perform this procedure, or you can use a multimeter (+4dBu = 1.23Vrms). These steps describe calibrating one channel. Repeat the process to calibrate additional channels.

To calibrate an HD I/O or 192 I/O interface:

1. In Pro Tools, create a new session by choosing FILE > NEW SESSION.

2. Choose SETUP > PREFERENCES and click OPERATIONS.

3. Enter the desired Calibration Reference Level value in dB. A level of either –18dBFS or –20dBFS referencing +4dBu nominal is typical for post-production. (It isn't necessary to type a minus sign here.)

Note: Entering a Calibration Reference Level value in the Preferences dialog box only sets the calibration reference mark for calibration mode, and does not set the reference level of the system.

4. Click DONE.

5. Create a new mono Aux Input track, set its input to NO INPUT, and route its output to the first channel you want to calibrate. This must be a single mono output assignment, because stereo and multi-channel output assignments are attenuated when panned to the center based on the session's current Pan Depth setting.

Tip: For more information about the Pan Depth setting in Pro Tools, see the *PT 201 Pro Tools Production II* book.

6. Mute the audio monitoring to your speakers before continuing.

7. Insert the Signal Generator DSP plug-in on the track.

8. Set the Signal Generator's output level. This should be the same value you entered for the Calibration Reference level (for example, –20).

9. Set the Signal Generator's frequency to 1000Hz.

10. Set the Signal Generator's signal waveform to SINE.

11. Connect an external VU or dBu meter to the analog output.

12. Adjust the I/O output level trim pot with a small, flathead screwdriver (preferably with a shrouded tip) to align the output to read "0 VU" on the external VU meter.

13. Now connect the output to the first input you want to calibrate.

14. Create another Aux Input track, and set its input to the first channel you want to calibrate. Mute it, so that feedback doesn't occur.

15. Choose **OPTIONS > CALIBRATION MODE**. The names of all the tracks will begin to flash. In addition, the track volume indicator of the Auxiliary Input track receiving an external input signal will now display the reference level coming from the calibrated output.

16. Adjust the input level trim pot with the same small flathead screwdriver. It is best to calibrate the inputs with the rear of the audio interface facing you and the Pro Tools screen well in sight, or get somebody else to watch the screen. When matched to the calibration level set in preferences, the track name will stop flashing and the peak volume indicator will indicate your headroom value. The AutoMatch indicator arrows on each track show the direction of adjustment required for alignment:

    • When the incoming level is higher than the reference level, the down arrow will appear lit (blue). In this case, trim the I/O input level down.

    • When the incoming level is lower than the reference level, the up arrow will appear lit (yellow). In this case, trim the I/O input level up.

    • When you have properly aligned the incoming peak signal levels to match the calibration reference level, both AutoMatch indicator arrows will light: the up arrow will be yellow and the down arrow will be blue.

    • Below the fader in the Mix window is a peak volume indicator. This indicator will show the dB level above and below your chosen reference level If the peak indicator is showing –21.1, you are –1.1dB below a reference level of –20dB. If the display is showing –16.5, you are +3.5dB above a reference level of –20dB.

Note: Although the HD OMNI interface supports output level calibration, it does not support reference level calibration. The output calibration controls of an HD Omni interface include a combination of Analog Output level and Analog Output Trim functions. These controls are intended for surround sound speaker-level calibration (such as calibration to match Dolby loudness specifications) and not reference level calibration.

Note: An HD I/O can be calibrated just like a 192 I/O. However, the HD I/O has only a single set of trim pots, whereas the 192 I/O interface has two sets of calibration trim pots (labeled A and B) that can be used to switch between two different calibration reference levels (such as –20dBFS and –18dbFS).

Calibrating a System with Mixed HD-Series Audio Interfaces

The 96 I/O is factory set at –14dBFS reference level, and its inputs and outputs are not adjustable. In systems using one or more HD I/O, 192 I/O, or HD OMNI interfaces combined with one or more 96 I/Os, it may make sense to calibrate all I/Os for –14dBFS. This helps ensure that incoming signals will have the same relative levels in Pro Tools regardless of which interface they are connected to.

Caution: When reducing the input and output calibration settings of either an HD I/O or 192 I/O interface in order to match the fixed 14dB headroom of a 96 I/O interface, you are also lowering the available headroom value of the interface. This might pose a problem for professional post-production facilities, as the standard maximum signal level for many professional video/audio devices could overload the inputs of the interfaces.

Exercise Answer Keys

This appendix contains the answer keys to select exercises.

Exercise 1 Answer Key

Tip: Since hardware configurations can vary, the answers provided here are not
the only correct answers.

Pro Tools|HDX System for Music Production

Apple Computer Hardware and Peripherals
- Apple MacPro (Quad-Core, 8-core, or 12-core) with Mac OS X (v.10.7 or later), 8GB RAM and three 1-TB Internal SATA hard drives

Avid Pro Tools Hardware and Peripherals
- SYNC HD I/O—with DigiSerial cable connected to the 1st HDX card
- Two Avid Pro Tools|HDX PCIe cards with Pro Tools HD 10.1x software
- Six Avid HD I/O audio interface 16×16 Analog or equivalent—with mini-DigiLink Y adapters and mini-DigiLink interface cables
- Four Avid PRE remote-control mic-pres with MIDI connections to a MIDI Interface
- Avid D-Control ES or Euphonix System 5 Hybrid connected via Ethernet to the computer (Ethernet switch will be required for D-Control ES)

Avid Pro Tools Software Options
- Avid Pro Tools Machine Control
- Avid Pro Tools Satellite Link Option

Figure B.1 shows an example of the completed schematic diagram.

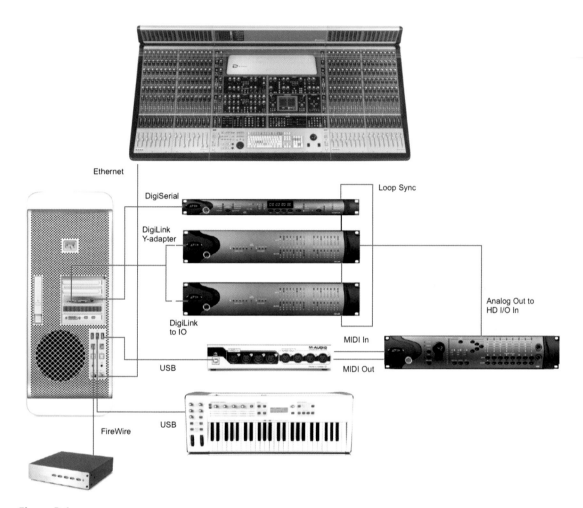

Figure B.1
Completed schematic diagram.

Exercise 2 Answer Key

Tip: There are several Knowledge Base answers for each entry in the table. Be
   aware that answers will vary with each system.

Table B.1   Pro Tools Error Messages

Error	Possible Cause	Solution
Pro Tools failure to launch	Many	More than 20 entries. Depends on PT version.
DAE Error -36	Drive related	Currently two entries, one with nine possible solutions.
DAE Error -9073	Drive related	Currently 21 entries.
DAE Error -909x	Audio clock	Currently 7 entries.

Relinking Offline Media

When opening the session, the following problems will occur:

■ The bass files will not auto-relink properly. The names have been changed,
  so the only way to find the files is to use the Find Candidates button on each
  missing file or to use Find by File ID.

■ The Choir tracks are in fact Heavy Guitar tracks and should be bussed
  accordingly.

■ The acoustic guitars should be bussed into the main guitars bus.

■ The input labels are meaningless.

Exercise 3 Answer Key

Editing Shortcuts:
Commands Keyboard Focus Mode

Table B.2   Editing Shortcuts

Step #	Task Description	Commands Used to Complete Task
1	Recall memory location 2	Press Period+[2]+Period (numeric keypad)
2	Enable Commands Keyboard Focus mode	Command+Option+1 (Mac) or Ctrl+Alt+1 (Windows)
3	Move the cursor with nudge commands to right before audio begins	[+] (plus) key on the numeric keypad
4	Fade the start of the clip	D key
5	Move the Edit cursor down to the GtrTheme1 track	; (semicolon) key
6	Trim the start of the clip	A key
7	Disable Tab to Transients	Command+Option+Tab (Mac) or Ctrl+Alt+Tab (Windows)
8	Navigate to the beginning of the next clip	Tab or ' (single quote) key
9	Re-enable Tab to Transients and navigate to the first hit	Command+Option+Tab (Mac) or Ctrl+Alt+Tab (Windows), Tab
10	Trim the front of the clip to the current cursor location	A key
11	Select the entire clip	Control+Tab (Mac) or Start+Tab (Windows)
12	Trim out the clip start using nudging	Option+[-] (Mac) or Alt+[-] (Windows)

Editing Keyboard Modifiers and Shortcuts

Table B.3   Keyboard Editing Shortcuts

Step #	Task Description	Commands Used to Complete Task
1	Recall memory location 3	Press Period+[3]+Period (numeric keypad)
2	Zoom out to see the entire selection (in one move)	Option+F (Mac) or Alt+F (Windows)
3	Open the Strip Silence window	Command+U (Mac) or Ctrl+U (Windows)
4	Zoom In enough to see the start and end pad edit preview	T key
5	Adjust the start and end pad settings to ensure you have all audio	Mouse only
6	Navigate down the track to the right using key commands to see all the hits	Option+Pg Down (Mac) or Alt+Pg Down (Windows)
7	Zoom to your selection again	Option+F (Mac) or Alt+F (Windows)
8	Click Strip to strip the silent areas from the selection	Mouse only
9	With the resulting clips still selected, apply batch fades with a length of 10ms	Command+F (Mac) or Ctrl+F (Windows)
10	Using the appropriate modifier, show all tracks quickly from the Track List	Option-click track Show/Hide in the Track List
11	Place the cursor across all tracks quickly	Click in the Timeline ruler
12	Select from Bar 83|1|000 to Bar 99|1|000 using the numeric keypad	/ key (numeric keypad) and enter values
13	Open the Time Operations window	Option+[1] (Mac) or Alt+[1] (Windows) on the numeric keypad
14	Apply the Cut Time operation	Command+Up/Down Arrow (Mac) or Ctrl+Up/Down Arrow (Windows) to navigate to Cut Time; Return or Enter to apply the change and close the window

Mixing Keyboard Modifiers and Shortcuts

Table B.4   Commands and Modifiers: Mixing

Step #	Task Description	Commands Used to Complete Task
1	Recall memory location 4	Press Period+[4]+Period (numeric keypad)
2	Bypass the compressor on the LdVc track without opening the plug-in	Command-click (Mac) or Ctrl-click (Windows) on the plug-in window
3	Bypass all dynamics on Insert position A throughout the mixer	Option+Command-click (Mac) or Ctrl+Alt-click (Windows) on the insert position
4	Select all the Drum tracks quickly	Click to the left of group name in the Group List or click on Kick and Shift-click on Room-R in the Track List
5	Record-safe all selected tracks	Command-click (Mac) or Ctrl-click (Windows) on each Record Enable button or Option+Command+ Shift-click (Mac) or Ctrl+Alt+Shift-click (Windows) on any Record Enable button
6	Clear all clips (if any)	Option+C (Mac) or Alt+C (Windows)
7	Select both drum auxiliary submasters	Shift-click
8	Reset drum auxiliary faders to unity	Option-click (Mac) or Alt-click (Windows) on each fader or Option+Shift-click (Mac) or Alt+Shift-click (Windows) on either fader
9	Navigate to the Keys tracks. Disable both tracks with a single click.	Shift-click to select, Control+Option+Command+ Shift-click (Mac) or Ctrl+Start+Alt+Shift-click (Windows) on track icon to deactivate
10	Deactivate all plug-ins at Insert position A	Command+Option+Control-click (Mac) or Ctrl+Start+Alt-click (Windows) on any Insert A

INDEX

License Agreement/Notice of Limited Warranty